# Addressing Xenophobia in South Africa

# Addressing Xenophobia in South Africa: Drivers, Responses and Lessons from the Durban Untold Stories

BY

## BETHUEL SIBONGISENI NGCAMU
*Nelson Mandela University, South Africa*

AND

## EVANGELOS MANTZARIS
*Mangosuthu University of Technology, South Africa*

United Kingdom – North America – Japan – India – Malaysia – China

Emerald Publishing Limited
Howard House, Wagon Lane, Bingley BD16 1WA, UK

First edition 2022

**British Library Cataloguing in Publication Data**
A catalogue record for this book is available from the British Library

ISBN: 978-1-80262-480-9 (Print)
ISBN: 978-1-80262-479-3 (Online)
ISBN: 978-1-80262-481-6 (Epub)

Printed and bound by CPI Group (UK) Ltd, Croydon, CR0 4YY

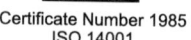

ISOQAR certified
Management System,
awarded to Emerald
for adherence to
Environmental
standard
ISO 14001:2004.

Certificate Number 1985
ISO 14001

INVESTOR IN PEOPLE

# Contents

# List of Abbreviations

| | |
|---|---|
| ANC | African National Congress |
| NGOs | Non-Governmental Organisations |
| NATJOINTS | National Joint Operational and Intelligence Structure |
| PROVJOINTS | Provincial Joint Operational and Intelligence Structure |
| ACCORD | African Centre for the Constructive Resolution of Disputes |
| IDASA | Institute for Democracy in South Africa |
| CSVR | Centre for the Study of Violence and Reconciliation |
| SWOP | Society Work and Development Institute |
| CPF | Community Police Forum |
| RDP | Reconstruction and Development Programme |
| SANCO | South African National Civil Organisation |
| SASCO | South African Students Congress |
| SAMP | Southern African Migration Programme |
| ACC | African Centre for Cities |
| GCRO | Gauteng City-Region Observatory |
| IDRC | International Development Research Centre. |
| SAPS | South African Police |
| WHO | World Health Organization |
| UNHRC | United Nations Human Rights Commission |
| UNOCHA | United Nations Office for the Coordination of Humanitarian Affairs |
| SADTU | South African Democratic Teachers Union |
| MEC | Member of Executive Council |
| IFP | Inkatha Freedom Party |
| DMC | Disaster Management Centre |
| KZN | KwaZulu-Natal |

| SRG | Special Reference Group |
| GoTG | Gift of the Givers |
| MSF | Médecins Sans Frontières |
| CAR | Central African Republic |
| COGTA | Cooperative Governance and Traditional Affairs |
| UCT | University of Cape Town |
| SANDF | South African National Defence Force |
| CCGs | Clinical Commissioning Group |
| CBOs | Community Based Organisations |
| POP | Public Order Policing |
| NAP | National Action Plan |
| OECD | Organisation for Economic Co-operation and Development |

# About the Authors

**Bethuel Sibongiseni Ngcamu** holds two PhDs in Education and Public Management. He started his career as a Geography Teacher in a secondary school and joined the eThekwini Municipality as a Consultant to the City Manager on Research and a Management Advisor where he managed a myriad of projects and conducted change management interventions. He has a vast experience in universities as a manager, consultant and an academic where he has taught and published a number of empirical studies in different disciplines. His specializations include knowledge management, service delivery, performance management, disaster management, organizational development in universities and xenophobia. He has published peer-reviewed journal articles, three book chapters and seven peer-reviewed conference papers. He has won various best researcher awards at different universities.

**Evangelos Mantzaris**, Professor, completed an Honours in Political Science, Economics and Sociology with distinction at Panteios University, Athens. He completed a Masters in Sociology and a PhD at the University of Cape Town, in South Africa. At present, he is a Retired Professor at the Mangosuthu University of Technology. Since 2012, he is a Senior Researcher and Extraordinary Professor at the Anti-Corruption Centre for Education and Research at the University of Stellenbosch. Before 2012, he was a Research Professor at Mangosuthu University of Technology (MUT), a Director of Social Policy Programme at the University of Durban-Westville (UDW) and then the University of KwaZulu-Natal (UKZN), and a Researcher in the Sociology Department at UDW.

He has published eight full scale books in English and Greek, 30 peer-reviewed chapters in books (with four in press), over 80 journal articles, 12 peer-reviewed International Conference Proceedings, and has presented papers in over 70 national and international conferences.

He has completed 14 National Research Foundation, Human Science Research Council and university funded research reports, and over 30 technical reports for Provincial Government Departments, municipalities and NGOs.

He is a National Research Foundation Rated Researcher.

He has done research and completed reports on stokvels and banking, asset allocation in the stockbroker industry, interest rates and repercussion on the British pound, general and specialized funds, international fund allocation and unit trusts, liquidation and estates in the private sector.

# Introduction

## Chapter One: Localizing and Locating the Hidden Causes of Xenophobia and its Ramifications

This foundational chapter details the underlying causes of xenophobia and the xenophobic violence in South Africa by unraveling a myriad of triggers. For instance, the book chapter provides a background on how the media reporters in local newspapers drive a particular narrative which is anti-immigrants. The inadequate and less active government's contingency plans available to deal pro-actively in preventing, mitigating the impacts, and responding proactively to the xenophobic violence are cemented in this chapter. The economic competition which is mostly linked to the causes of the attacks against the foreign nationals is questioned in this chapter and further provides the empirically proven causes which are multidimensional. For instance, the role of the patriarchal mindset where there is a competition involving the local women as they prefer the foreign nationals as compared to the locals. Furthermore, the spontaneous occurrence of xenophobia is overlooked by scholars who have published books in this mul-tidisciplinary field of study. The chapter concludes by providing the conflicting statistics on the presence of the undocumented immigrants in the country.

## Chapter Two: Associating Xenophobia with Criminality: Is it a Fallacy?

A paucity of empirical data on the government's and media reporters' percep-tions and their viewpoints regarding the media's falsified, negative and biased reports on xenophobia in Durban is a major theme in this chapter. Moreover, xenophobic populism by politicians and traditional leaders is explored. In addi-tion, factors and dimensions that have been overlooked by the media feature in this chapter. Several interviewees who have been directly involved before, during and after the xenophobic attacks, including government officials, media reporters and civil society groups, have been interviewed using open-ended questions. Fur-thermore, print and electronic media articles are analyzed, in order for the tone of reporting to be determined. The extent to which the rhetoric, inflammatory and negative tone of reporting by media platforms – considered to have contributed to the xenophobic attacks – is articulated in this chapter study.

Addressing Xenophobia in South Africa:
Drivers, Responses and Lessons from the Durban Untold Stories, 1–4
Copyright © 2022 by Bethuel Sibongiseni Ngcamu and Evangelos Mantzaris
Published under exclusive licence by Emerald Publishing Limited
doi:10.1108/978-1-80262-479-320211001

## Chapter Three: Xenophobia, Media and the "Forgotten Dimensions"

The truth of the existence of the "third force" narrative and material conditions that influence xenophobic attacks against migrants is extensively examined. We examine the understanding underpinning xenophobia and the government's apparatus aimed at detecting and responding to it. Furthermore, informal but crucial businesses in the townships and informal settlements are investigated. The country's porous borders are a serious consideration and a contributing factor to many undocumented and illegal immigrants, which is also examined in this chapter.

## Chapter Four: Media Reporting of the 2015 Xenophobic Attacks in Durban

This book chapter touches on the untouched and hidden dimensions of xenophobia at a local level and examines sections of the print media, the role this plays in social cohesion programs and the resultant impacts. It also provides insight into government agencies and their role and impact on local neighborhoods before, during and in the aftermath of xenophobia. A void in the literature will be filled by the rationale of why xenophobic attacks occur mostly during elections. We also conduct an investigation into the security cluster, and journalists' contribution and impact on the catastrophe.

## Chapter Five: Biased and Falsified Reporting: The Government's Perspectives

A plethora of viewpoints are assessed, mostly in relation to security agencies, and print and electronic media's inaccurate and inciteful reporting and misrepresentation of the facts by certain media houses and platforms. Furthermore, the falsified information and omissions concerning the conditions in the shelters for displaced migrants will be reported on by a host of stakeholders. The security personnel's perceptions of hostile and unethical reporting – influenced by bribery, corruption and careerism – are shared in this book chapter. Finally, we consider how media houses overlook accurate government communications and how journalists exclude this from their reporting.

## Chapter Six: Inter- and Intra-Governmental Response: Unreported Government Response Capabilities

This chapter will focus on the toxic climate that was experienced in the townships that were regarded as hotspots of xenophobia and the militarization of both the locals and the foreign nationals. The processes including screening and acceptance of the victims of xenophobia in the displaced shelters will be analyzed, and challenges and solutions exposed. Different sectors and governments and other professional collaborators' roles and responsibilities will be identified and analyzed in conjunction with other contributions and impacts in the shelters for the displaced migrants. The intergovernmental relationship challenges will be espoused in this chapter together with the negative impacts in the shelter coordination. The SAPS strategies and responses during and in the aftermath of the shelters will be explored. The intelligence-gathering processes, local communities' involvement and migrants' leadership consultation on the possible reintegration will be further analyzed. Humanitarian initiatives at a local level by the municipality, NGOs and CBOs, as well as community involvement in the fight against xenophobia will be assessed. Open-ended interviews will be conducted with the government officials in different spheres and sectors, SAPS, NGOs, CBOs and migrants' organizations.

## Chapter Seven: A Multi-Stakeholder Response on the 2015 Xenophobic Attacks: The Hidden Government Perspectives

This book chapter sought to determine the effectiveness of security agencies' overt and covert strategies in fighting the xenophobic attacks against migrants from African countries. Given the multiplicity of agencies and security apparatus involved in different aspects of actions before, during and after the attacks, this is a very crucial research issue. It was inevitable that different agencies would follow their own courses of action, which could lead to new problems and challenges. There were overt and covert practices undertaken in a number of fronts, including at police stations, in informal settlements ("squatter camps"), townships and shelters for foreigners and during the course of repatriation processes and outcomes.

## Chapter Eight: Managing Shelters for the Displaced

This chapter focuses on the toxic climate that was experienced in the townships regarded as the hotspots of xenophobia and the militarization of both locals and foreign nationals. The processes included analyzing the screening and acceptance of victims of xenophobia into shelters for the displaced, during which challenges and solutions were identified. Different sectors, governments and other professional collaborators' roles and responsibilities are identified and analyzed in conjunction with other contributions and impacts in the shelters for displaced migrants. The intergovernmental relationship challenges are analyzed in this chapter together with the negative impacts experienced in terms of the management and operations of the shelters. We explore the strategies and responses of the South African Police Service (SAPS) during and after the attacks. We further analyze intelligence-gathering processes, local communities' involvement, and consultations with migrants' representatives in terms of possible reintegration with the communities. We assess humanitarian initiatives at a local, municipal level, Non-Governmental Organisations (NGOs) and Community Based Organisations (CBOs), as well as community involvement in the fight against xenophobia. Open-ended interviews were conducted with a number of government officials in different spheres and sectors, SAPS, NGOs, CBOs and professionals representing migrants' and refugees' organizations.

## Chapter Nine: Social Cohesion and Social Justice: Can They Solve Xenophobic Attacks?

Government's systems, processes and structures in the shelters for the displaced are extensively covered in this chapter, in addition to the functions, challenges and solutions of government agencies and civil society. Representatives from civil society, NGOs and CBOs have been interviewed as they are perceived as playing a pivotal role in disaster response and recovery. Civil society groups are considered to be competent and advanced as compared to other key stakeholders in responding to xenophobic attacks in South Africa. These groups' strategies, processes and systems in shelter management and coordination are succinctly presented. Their relationship with government departments and agencies, victims' representatives and other interested groups is analyzed. Civil society groups' representative viewpoints and government agencies' perceptions of the pertinent role played by such groups are gleaned through qualitative in-depth interviews.

Chapter One

# Localizing and Locating the Hidden Causes of Xenophobia and its Ramifications

This scholarly work is aimed at empirically espousing and assessing the hidden root causalities and dimensions of the attacks that were directed at refugees, asylum seekers, legal and illegal immigrants in Durban in 2015. These sporadic attacks against foreign nationals have been popularly termed by scholars, media platforms, civil society groups and foreign governments as "xenophobic attacks." The underlying root causes and actions related to xenophobia are interrogated thoroughly in this book. We examine certain sections of the media and their tone, descriptions and analyses, in addition to considering the influence of journalists' reporting in instigating attacks against immigrants. Furthermore, we assess the effectiveness, efficiencies, responsiveness and pro-activeness of the state's intelligence apparatus in detecting, preventing, responding to and mitigating the effects of xenophobia.

In addition, the contingency plans of the South African Police Service (SAPS) are analyzed in relation to their operations, activities and general attitudes in dealing with the xenophobic attacks in Durban. *Localized Xenophobia in South Africa* further intends to investigate the humanitarian crisis brought about by xenophobia, and the planning and actions of government agencies, civil society and non-governmental organizations (NGOs) in their efforts to avert the situation. The roles, responsibilities and impacts of the leading actors – including the police, the National Joint Operational and Intelligence Structure (NATJOINTS), civil society, NGOs, Community Based Organisations (CBOs) and government departments – are analyzed and dissected. Finally, we extensively assess the financial implications resulting from xenophobic violence.

There is a dire need for this scholarly work to be published as xenophobic attacks in South Africa are caused by a multiplicity of factors which have not been thoroughly and deeply researched through the utilization of empirical and scientific methods. The most common and unhidden causes of xenophobic attacks against immigrants can be categorized according a host of facets. These are mainly socio-economic, political and cultural in nature. The attacks against

Addressing Xenophobia in South Africa:
Drivers, Responses and Lessons from the Durban Untold Stories, 5–25
Copyright © 2022 by Bethuel Sibongiseni Ngcamu and Evangelos Mantzaris
Published under exclusive licence by Emerald Publishing Limited
doi:10.1108/978-1-80262-479-320211002

black foreign nationals cannot be linked solely to economic competition or based on biases and (mostly untested) perceptions that are central to patriarchy. For instance, South African black men tend to believe that they own and are entitled to South African women and that women should not be romantically involved with foreign nationals. Foreign nationals, meanwhile, are perceived to outperform South African men economically. In addition, it is alleged that they have larger sex organs, allegedly making them more attractive to South African women. South African citizens have the belief that foreign nationals use strong traditional medicine (or *muti*) against their spouses which makes women vulnerable to foreign nationals. Another issue is that immigrants use money to entice teenage girls and their spouses to become sexually involved with them, which can result in them becoming involved in prostitution and human trafficking.

Macro and micro businesses, media platforms (both print and digital) and political and cultural leaders have been associated with the scourge of xenophobia in South Africa. Meanwhile, the scholastic writing on xenophobia in South Africa and beyond tends to be dominated by foreign nationals. Their writing can be interpreted as anti-state and biased and leads to South African citizens being labeled as the instigators, while the immigrants are the victims only. The plethora of "scholarly studies" currently published has not pinpointed the core causes of xenophobic attacks and its dimensions; rather, these are speculative writing mostly informed by the media. This has been confirmed by the fact that most of these studies have overlooked reliability and validity testing, although the authors deem them to be empirical. It has been made clear that the Government of South Africa and its agencies have been complicit in the attacks on foreign nationals. The stalemate between these spontaneous warring groups (locals and immigrants) is exacerbated by the porosity of South Africa's borders; the bribery of security agencies and Home Affairs officials; inadequate intelligence apparatus in local communities where attacks are prevalent; corruption; and a lack of enforcement of the country's by-laws.

A common view shared by commentators regarding the 2008 attacks is that they were caused by local business people attacking migrant shopkeepers in Cape Town. The attacks in 2015 in Durban, meanwhile, were allegedly triggered by a labor dispute in one of the supermarkets in Isipingo, south of Durban although it is widely shared that it triggered the Zulu King through his anti-immigrants sentiments.

It has been widely disseminated that the 2019 xenophobic attacks were sparked by the death of a minibus taxi driver in Johannesburg who was allegedly killed by drug dealers who were migrants. However, the Durban 2015 attacks, which led to the looting and vandalizing of a number of foreigners' shops and people being attacked, had the lowest death rate – seven fatalities. Nevertheless, the xenophobia had multiple causalities which scholars, the media, government agencies and interested key stakeholders have failed to point out. In retrospect, the available data are mostly from journal articles and there is no evidence in published books. There are few works (Adam and Moodley, 2013; Akinola, 2018; Crush and Chikanda, 2015; Crush and Tawodzera, 2017; Harris, 2001; Kupe et al., 2008; Nyamnjoh, 2006; Tafira, 2017) that have been published on xenophobia in South Africa and touch on other dimensions.

There is a number books (Adam and Moodley, 2013; Crush and Chikanda, 2015; Crush and Tawodzera, 2017; Harris, 2001; Kupe et al., 2008; Landau, 2012; Nyamnjoh, 2006; Tafira, 2017) that have been published on xenophobia, but they are not scholarly and lack published empirical evidence. The latter recently published books by leading scholars in this discipline have overlooked local areas (mostly townships) which are the hospts to xenophobia and are susceptible to violence. Furthermore, the dimensions that the current work explores remain unexplored by scholars; available data are anecdotal and vague. The host of published data (mostly journal articles) that have been published focus on stories of xenophobia released by the popular media, which qualifies as anecdotal and unscholarly.

The primary data in the public domain lack research designs and methodologies and focus on well-known causes of xenophobia (i.e., economic competition). The current book is unique as it is based on empirical evidence: qualitative interviews conducted with carefully selected and knowledgeable respondents, with results triangulated using documents and media articles. The in-depth interviews targeted the government officials, civil society groups, community activists, victims and the alleged perpetrators.

*Localized Xenophobia in South Africa* sets out to test and develop theories on xenophobia in the attempt to fill the existing gaps of data in the discourse. The work provides evidence-based knowledge regarding the nature and extent of economic competition among foreigners themselves as well between foreigners and local people. Different stakeholders' perceptions are tested to uncover new dimensions, which have not previously been discovered and explored.

The current published literature (Chenzi, 2020; Hendricks and Mati, 2020; Makhado and Tshisikhawe, 2020; Masikane et al., 2020; Tewolde, 2020) has failed to acknowledge that xenophobic attacks occur spontaneously in local areas. The alleged perpetrators' viewpoints have not been heard on the issues, facts and realities. The majority of the published data are dominated by what is reported in the popular media, which is anecdotal, generalized and anti-government, with the success stories of state agencies and government departments going unreported. As a result, this study aims to contribute to the body of knowledge on this subject, to influence policies, to invent new concepts and to upskill managers with proactive strategies to deal with the realities and challenges of xenophobia.

To understand the real historical and social roots of xenophobia across the world is never easy, for many different reasons. It is even more difficult to understand these roots in South Africa because the vast majority of victims of such acts are fellow Africans. One hour in an African township shebeen (tavern) will convince you of this reality because the relations between locals and "amakwerekwere" (a derogatory term referring to foreigners of African descent) are generally strained. This is due to perpetual tensions that are caused by social and ethnic stereotypes, rumors and innuendos, politicians' outbursts, false and manufactured news distributed through printed and social media, and socially and politically created myths.

Listening to the conversations, debates or arguments in social gatherings anywhere in South Africa will convince even the most doubtful person that in most cases "amakwerekwere" is but an ethnic, racial category that is nothing less than a political and social construct. As will be later shown, the xenophobia attacks and their aftermath have resulted in a number of empirical research efforts in South Africa, Africa and elsewhere in the world. Given the social, economic, political, national, continental and international significance of the attacks, it was an urgent necessity for academics, professional researchers, journalists, state and continental authorities and security services to investigate not only the details related to the deaths, injuries, damage and destruction of infrastructure, houses and shops, but also the foundations, main actors, community and state relations as well as the outcomes. Structural persistence of discrimination and xenophobia in South Africa society is severe – the result of implicit and explicit biases which are informed by mostly untested perceptions. The discriminatory and xenophobic attitudes and stereotypes appear to be mentally and physically driven. Society opposes and ill-treats people who look and think differently: this could be race, gender, creed, ethnicity, tribe, sexual orientation or locale. Families and societal structures in South Africa do not have the strategies in place to reduce implicit biases toward others.

Different groups in a society oppose and ill-treat people who look and think differently. Such acts could be based on "race," gender, ethnicity, tribe, sexual orientation or locale. *Families and societal structures in South Africa do not have the strategies in place to reduce implicit biases towards others.*

In undertaking the exercise of establishing the root causes of xenophobia, there could be the possibility of the irrefutable reality being discovered. One possibility is that xenophobia comes about as a result of actions that have been caused by a multiplicity of social, political, financial and economic factors, which this work aims to confirm. Much of the research on xenophobia, but not all, has not been thoroughly undertaken empirically and scientifically. The gaps need to be filled so that new knowledge can be produced and new ideas surface. The filling of the gaps can be instrumental on planning and implementing thorough and systematic action against future attacks.

There cannot be a serious understanding of *Localized Xenophobia in South Africa* without a brief but useful and adequate picture of the demographics of the two groups: the South Africans and the foreigners.

## The Demographics: A Brief Overview

The latest official statistics indicate that South Africa's population in mid-2019 was 58.78 million, with the 18–34 group (17.84 million) making up one third of the population. The provinces of Gauteng and KwaZulu-Natal have the highest populations of youth (28.6% and 19.4%, respectively). Of them, 13% are graduates, with the rural provinces being highly disadvantaged (KwaZulu-Natal). The unemployment among the youth in the country stands at 39.5%, with the members of this group being categorized as illiterate, unemployed and unemployable. A quarter of the youth (28.8%) have tertiary education. In the Living Conditions Survey report of 2014/2015, a total of 33.4% of South Africans were regarded as poor. The previous report revealed that a fifth of those in the youth categories are living below the poverty line of R664 per person (per month). The majority of foreign immigrants are expected to be Africans. The Gauteng province is leading in attracting international migrants (47.5%), followed by the Western Cape at 11.6% (Statistics South Africa, 2019). In 2015, it was recorded that 35.1 million of the adults who are 18 years of age and above were living below the poverty line. In terms of poverty, the leading provinces in South Africa where the poorest of the poor reside are Limpopo and the Eastern Cape at 67%, followed by KwaZulu-Natal and the North West at 60%. The number of women living below the upper boundary of the poverty line is 49.9%, as opposed to 33.0% for men. At this upper boundary line, there is a huge difference between children who have safe and available playing areas (non-poor children at 53.7%) compared to destitute children at 25.7% (Statistics South Africa, 2018). Having briefly examined the grim realities of South Africa's key demographics, let us now provide the realities of foreigners who face the wrath of xenophobia in the country, including Africans and Asians.

Africa Check (2018) has estimated that the number of immigrants to South Africa between 2016 and 2021, would be between 1,643,590 and 493,621. There have been a number of strange, even outrageous calculations regarding the total percentage of illegal immigrants in South Africa. It is these immigrants who have been responsible for an increase in crime, as alleged in 2018 by the country's national police commissioner. He claimed that there were 11,000,000 foreign nationals "who arrived as visitors and never returned to their countries" (Africa Check, 2018).

Since 1998 there have been reports released by the Department of Home Affairs indicating that up to 5 million illegal immigrants are living in the country. This number was widely believed to be the truth, supported strongly by the state-funded Human Sciences Research Council (HSRC) which on occasion claimed the existence of between four and eight million undocumented migrants, academics, researchers and politicians. The HSRC subsequently withdrew its figures (Mwiti, 2015). Following the first xenophobic attacks, *The New York Times* newspaper mentioned the existence of five million migrants, while the leader of an obscure political party in the country calculated their number to be 13 million. When questioned on the numbers provided by the national police commissioner, the SAPS insisted the statement was based on data provided by the country's Department of Home Affairs. There is no such data in existence.

It is understandable that such data do not make real sense when there is an official census in South Africa every five years and its key components – the census and the community survey – include questions for people who were born outside of South Africa. Accordingly, in the country's 2011 Census and the Community Survey 2016, people were asked where they were born and millions (2.2 million) confirmed that they were born outside the borders of South Africa. In the Community Survey 2016, there were 1.6 million who declared their birth to be outside the country. Despite the fact that Statistics South Africa indicated there was a serious investigation of staff and "migration experts" regarding the discrepancy, no results were released. Experts indicated that the calculations of the Department of Home Affairs data might be based "exclusively" on the forms signed by those entering South Africa. One of the country's academic experts at the time wrote that the "likely answer" to the actual number of immigrants living in South Africa lay "between one and three million" (Africa Check, 2018). By 2015, Statistics South Africa had officially estimated that there were 500,000 to 1 million undocumented migrants in the country. This is far less than the total number of 1.6 million (registered and unregistered immigrants) which was recorded by the Forced Migration Studies Programme (Mwiti, 2015). As South Africa and the world reached 2020, the era of the coronavirus, the debate over the facts of legal and undocumented migrants in the country has been relegated to non-existence. There are much more serious questions and debates regarding lockdowns and restrictions from Cape to Cairo and from Madagascar to Morocco. However, as South Africa and the world look forward, no one can forget the realities of yesterday's and today's history, because tomorrow is around the corner, especially after the major challenges following the Covid-19 pandemic. The world and South Africa need to be prepared for better or for worse. Now, given the fact that there has been a debate regarding the genuine number of foreigners in the country from Africa and Asia (potential victims of xenophobic attacks in South Africa), the numbers of foreigners have been confirmed in a report produced by the population division of the United Nations (UN). There is no doubt that statistics which are authentic are very important.

Of course, the numbers seem to be far from the realities of today as the latest statistics that became available in 2019 have conclusively shown. These data show that the crisis which has followed South Africa's efforts to pave the way to a new developmental era has not deterred African and Asian immigrants from continuously arriving in the country, likely due to South Africa's relative stability in comparison to migrants' own countries. In fact, the numbers of those who emigrate to South Africa grow substantially. Such a reality has occurred in the last few years despite the sporadic but devastating xenophobic acts of violence, destruction and death against African and other immigrants and the perpetual fear of reoccurrence. The World Migration Report produced by the International Organisation for Migration (2020), has shown that 2.8% of the population was made up of international migrants, the total figure was 7.2% in 2019. In fact, the highly acclaimed report has highlighted that South Africa is the most significant destination country in Africa for immigrants. The organization has calculated the number of international newcomers in the country as being approximately 4 million. Such a number places South Africa 14th in the world according to the size of its migrant population. The numbers of Zimbabwean migrants estimated to live in South Africa stood at 716,057, followed by 376,668 Mozambicans.

## The Legal Terrain

It is clear that after the 1994 democratic change, South Africa was obligated to reform the depraved system of apartheid and its legal regime – one of the foundations of a non-racial, democratic society. The first legal step relating to immigrants, the Aliens Control Amendment Act, 1995 (Act 76 of 1995) (Republic of South Africa, 1995), was structured in such a way to protect highly qualified and skilled immigrants, which more or less excluded African immigrants. Therefore, as

Crush et al. (2005, p. 11) have shown, in 1995, only 8% of work permits were issued to citizens of the Southern African Development Community (SADC), while 65% went to Europeans. Increased discontent from the majority of the SADC's political leadership regarding the unconstitutionality of various aspects of South Africa's immigration legislation led to a number of amendments of the 1995 Immigration Act, which were adopted in 2002 (Crush and Dodson, 2007, p. 436).

Despite the amendments, the restrictions continued and the "undesirable groups" faced serious isolated and violent attacks in black townships, detention by the police and deportation. As Wa Kabwe-Segatti (2006) has shown, undocumented immigrants suffered serious abuse from the law enforcement agencies during this period before between 1994 and 1996. The debates regarding the Green and White papers (1997 and 1999, respectively) were the next steps and the Green Paper especially indicated the government's determination to further the development and regional integration process within the parameters of the SADC community (Republic of South Africa, 1997; The South African White Paper on International Migration, 1999). The intention was to enhance and increase South Africa's efforts to integrate into the global competitive world; increase job opportunities through macro-economic growth in both the formal and informal sectors, as enshrined in the Growth, Employment and Redistribution (GEAR) policy; and increase people's quality of life (RSA Treasury, 2006).

Interestingly, a number of the progressive points mentioned above were never included in the new legislation, while changes to immigration reform were set aside, at least temporarily. In addition, there was a denouncement of any bilateral agreement for the creation of a free mobility zone between southern African countries (Wa Kabwe-Segatti, 2006, pp. 183–184). The White Paper, on the other hand, was described by the Lawyers for Human Rights (LHR) as an attack on the human rights of non-South Africans as it relates to issues such as xenophobia, border control and the training of immigration officials (LHR, 1999). The categorization of non-nationals as "undesirables" in the White Paper was questioned by the LHR (1999), but received no response.

The Immigration Act, 2002 (Act 13 of 2002), which repealed the Aliens Act, 1991 (Act 96 of 1991) and the Aliens Amendment Act of 1995, substantially increased the complications facing foreigners who aspired to work in South Africa. The Immigration Amendment Act, 2011 (Act 13 of 2011) has terminated employers' access to special exemptions in the recruitment of foreign workers, which was based on ministerial approval. However, it does preserve existing treaties with all governments in southern Africa. The proliferation of undocumented immigrants has been shown to be the result of state inefficiency, immigrants' lack of financial resources and existing legal and regulatory complications (Rasool et al., 2012, p. 405).

The passing of new legislation did not stop the restrictions that led to exploitation and low wages, and clandestine migration increased substantially, especially from Zimbabwe. The Immigration Amendment Act of 2011 brought more restrictions for migrants, such as the "quota work permit" being repealed and the "exceptional skills visa" being amalgamated into the "critical skills visa," a move aimed at limiting foreigners' entrance into the labor market. It has been shown empirically (Eisenberg, 2015) that the Labour Relations Amendment Act, 2014 (Act 6 of 2014) has made formal employment a virtually impossible task for migrant workers. This is because such a position demands a Department of Labour certificate confirming that the prospective employer is unable to find a South African citizen or permanent resident with the experience, qualifications or skills equivalent to those of the applicant (Eisenberg, 2015).

## Legislative Framework

In terms of immigrants in South Africa, the Aliens Control Amendment Act of 1995 was structured in a specific way so as to protect highly qualified and skilled immigrants that more or less excluded potential African immigrants (Crush et al., 2005, p. 11). Such a move created serious discontent within the majority of the SADC's political leadership and this led to a number of amendments of the Immigration Act of 1995, which were adopted in 2002 (Crush and Dodson, 2007, p. 436). The restrictions continued, however, and the African immigrant groups faced serious isolated and violent attacks in black townships, detention by the police and deportation. As Wa Kabwe-Segatti (2006) has shown, undocumented immigrants suffered serious abuse from law enforcement agencies during this period. The Green and White papers (1997 and 1999, respectively) was the next step and the Green Paper especially indicated the government's determination to further the development and regional integration process within the parameters of the SADC and undertake serious progressive developmental steps in the SADC and Africa in general (Department of Home Affairs, 2003, p. 13).

However, as has been shown a number of the progressive points mentioned above were never included in the new legislation while changes to immigration reform were set aside, at least temporarily (Wa Kabwe-Segatti, 2006, pp. 183–184). The categorization of non-nationals as "undesirables" in the White Paper was questioned by the LHR (1999), but received no response. On the other hand, the proliferation of undocumented immigrants has been shown to be the result of state inefficiency, immigrants' lack of financial resources and existing legal and regulatory complications (Rasool et al., 2012, p. 405). The Immigration Amendment Act of 2011 brought more restrictions for migrants such as the "quota work permit" being repealed and the "exceptional skills visa" being amalgamated into the "critical skills visa," a move aimed at limiting foreigners' entrance into the labor market. It has been shown empirically (Eisenberg, 2015) that the Labour Relations Amendment Act, 2014 (Act 6 of 2014) has made formal employment a virtually impossible task for migrant workers.

In terms of refugees, South Africa has a liberal and progressive protection framework and is a signatory and party to both the 1969 Organisation of African Union Refugee Convention and the 1951 UN Convention and its 1967 Protocol.

The country's first Refugees Act, 1998 (Act 130 of 1998) adopted a policy of free movement, allowing refugees and asylum seekers to live alongside citizens and to seek employment as well as having access to social welfare services such as healthcare and education. The Act was amended in 2008 and 2011, and in 2015 another amendment was tabled: The Refugees Amendment Bill. The Bill was signed into law in 2017 and it is believed that the amendments have rolled back the substantial progress made over the years. There have been indications that there is an intention to move away from the human rights, liberal approach (Mfubu, 2017).

The state has over the years introduced a coordination network to monitor, investigate, plan and implement steps and measures that combat xenophobia. The multi-faceted and integrated plan is headed by an Inter-Ministerial Committee (IMC) (the IMC on Migration, the IMC on Social Cohesion and the IMC on Population Policy). In terms of the IMCs' coordination of emergencies, NAT-JOINTS is the government's body that responds to emergencies. It is supported by a technical committee comprising the directors general of all the affected departments. In addition, the Justice, Crime Prevention and Security Cluster (JCPS) is directly involved at both the national and the provincial level, activating the police and the National Prosecuting Authority (NPA) to investigate the acts and develop contingency plans in terms of managing and dealing with all cases of xenophobia efficiently and speedily.

The Department of Justice and Constitutional Development, the police and the NPA have been in charge of dealing and reviewing all cases and active in the reviews of withdrawn and reviewed cases. Community-based campaigns by provincial and local government leaders were in charge of promoting community re-integration of foreigners, promoted the justice system and educated persons about human rights for all. A number of important community events took place in order to support re-integration as a commitment to the protection of human rights, anti-xenophobia and equality. The key state departments have been in charge of the repatriation of immigrants and refugees wishing to return to their countries. The Disaster Management Centre has been basically in charge of researching and deciding for the location of the refugee shelters, while the police are responsible for the safety of their inhabitants (Personal communication with members of the KwaZulu-Natal Disaster Management Centre and NAT-JOINTS, 2019).

A leading member of the PROVJOINTS strategic committee responsible for planning the proactive response to xenophobic attacks mentioned the following:

> Consequently, in the process the UN group became very concerned about how to plan reintegration especially for those in the Isipingo site. This was due to their high numbers and the fact that the majority wanted to return to their home countries, especially those from Burundi and the Democratic Republic of Congo (DRC). More than 80 of them feared for their lives and the UN staff were afraid that the existing circumstances were complicated because these countries were very far. Because of this, the UN advised the displaced to go back to the community, at least temporarily, until they could return to their homelands. In the meantime, specialised teams from the state would play a role in the reintegration process. They would communicate with the communities regarding foreigners and persuade them to stop attacking the immigrants.

For this the state undertook to work together with the UN as an international organisation. Representatives from state institutions were also talking to local business people as part of the dialogue with the community. The members of this sections of the community had promised to refrain from criminal activities and to work with citizens and foreigners.

## Themes of Xenophobia in South African and International Literature

There has been a number of academic theoretical and empirical research on xenophobia in South Africa and the realities and dynamics behind the protests and violence. Most of the work produced in postgraduate theses, academic articles, books and monographs in South Africa, Africa and internationally has attempted to research, examine and analyze the reasons, causes, effects, politics, economy, state security and results of the xenophobic attacks. Within this context and as expected, there have been empirical findings that have been transformed into widely accepted theories. This is despite the fact that the actual research has taken place in townships like Delft, a predominantly colored area in the Western Cape.

In this particular case, the research by Charman and Piper (2012, p. 81) indicated that the attacks targeting foreign nationals were mostly driven by "anti-foreigner sentiments," criminal activities and economic competition between locals and foreigners. There has been research indicating that xenophobia is both a direct and indirect result of the government's failure to control its borders with its neighbors and the economic, social and political crisis in the country, together with poverty, homelessness and unemployment (Crush and Ramachandran, 2014).

Inevitably, within the present context where South Africa and the world are facing new social, political, financial and economic crises, research on xenophobic violence will most likely multiply as the present realities of refugees and illegal immigrants throughout the world go from bad to worse. This is where new substantiated knowledge on past social crises such as xenophobia is needed because specific and significant unknown realities must be exposed to the wider public. Early attacks on immigrants in South Africa have not been in the headlines as much as the massive incidents that occurred in and after 2008. However, the first serious ones took place as early as January 1995, a few months after the first democratic elections in South Africa in April 1994. That month, armed gangs in the Alexandra township in Johannesburg attacked and assaulted Malawians, Zimbabweans and Mozambicans who lived in the area, accusing them of being "illegal" and responsible for crimes and sexual assault against women. The attacks lasted for a few weeks and the police were given ultimatums by the attackers to "clean the township immediately" (Centre for the Study of Violence and Reconciliation, 2008). In September 1998, it was reported in the newspapers that two Senegalese citizens and a Mozambican national were thrown out of a moving train and died. The people responsible were part of a number of groups returning from an anti-immigration rally where foreigners had been blamed for crime, unemployment and the spread of HIV/AIDS (Valji, 2003).

In 2000, it was reported that seven foreigners were killed in the Cape Flats in the Western Cape in attacks that lasted for more than five weeks. The police, after being inactive for a number of weeks, described the deaths as "xenophobic murders" which were "possibly motivated" by the fear that foreigners 'were claiming property' belonging to locals (Independent Online 1, n.d.). Large numbers of residents of Zandspruit, an informal settlement in Johannesburg, gave an ultimatum to Zimbabwean citizens living there – that they were all to leave the area within 10 days. In October 2001, following the foreigners' failure to follow the instruction, attacking groups evicted them forcefully, looting their shacks and burning them to the ground. The attackers claimed that they were angry with the foreigners because they were employed while the local population was not. Foreigners were also accused of being criminals and thieves. There were no victims recorded on this occasion (Independent Online 2, n.d.).

During the last week of 2005 and the first days of 2006, at least four people, including two Zimbabweans, were killed in the Olievenhoutbosch settlement in Pretoria, following accusations that a number of foreigners had killed a South African citizen. Shacks that belonged to foreigners were burnt down and the police were asked by the perpetrators to remove all foreigners from the area. Then, during the last week of August 2006, large numbers of Somalian refugees appealed to the police and government departments for protection following the July killings of 21 Somali traders in Cape Town. Twenty-six more were killed in August of the same year. The immigrants believed that the murders were motivated by xenophobia aimed at driving Somali traders out of the Western Cape in a concerted violent campaign, an assertion that was rejected by police leadership (The New Humanitarian, 2006).

During the last few months of 2007, there were a number of attacks on foreigners, followed by at least 12–15 attacks on foreigners between January and May 2008. On January 8, 2008, two Somali shopkeepers were murdered in East London and Jeffrey's Bay in the Eastern Cape province. Then, in March 2008, seven foreigners were killed, including Pakistanis, Zimbabweans and a Somali national, in the African township of Atteridgeville in Pretoria. Their shacks and shops were ransacked and burnt to the ground (Rank et al., 2009).

On May 12, 2008, a series of riots began in Alexandra township situated in north-eastern Johannesburg, the home of over 600,000 people. Many locals attacked foreigners from Malawi, Mozambique and Zimbabwe, killing 2 and injuring 40. The attackers retreated when over 500 police officers arrived and arrested 15 people. The attacks took place in a fairly planned way as various groups of attackers in different locations met at a specific, predetermined place near the location where large numbers of Zimbabweans and Mozambicans occupy shacks and free government houses. They attacked the houses' occupants, beat them up and looted their homes. There were fears among the police leadership that the attacks would spiral out of control, but they did not at least temporarily (BBC, 2008; Refword, 2008). In the weeks that followed, the violent attacks spread widely, initially in and around the Gauteng province, then to the coastal cities of Cape Town and Durban, finally escalating and spreading to the inland provinces of Mpumalanga, North West and the Free State (Refword, 2008).

Rank et al. (2009) reported a total of 62 people dead (including both foreign nationals and locals), 144 people arrested, 137 convicted, 51 cases withdrawn and 82 investigated further.

Following the attacks, hundreds of foreigners took refuge in police stations and community halls and then moved to temporary camps, with the promise from government that they would be reintegrated into their communities by July (News24, 2008).

In a completely different scenario, between 1,500 and 2,500 farm workers from Zimbabwe were violently evicted from their residences in De Doorns, an informal settlement in the Western Cape. No one was beaten or injured but their homes were looted in the most violent manner. Such evictions were considered to be the greatest displacement since the xenophobic attacks of 2008. The Zimbabweans were moved to a camp for displaced persons and many of them stayed there for a year, until its closure. This occurred during a period of high unemployment for local workers as the predominantly white farmers preferred foreign workers who were paid much less than the minimum wage (Misago, 2009). Following these significant incidents, the ensuing months and years were marked by a number of attacks. Through the country, at least 10 Somali shopkeepers were killed and their shops looted (AllAfrica.com, 2013; World Bulletin, 2013). Then 2015 arrived.

There are serious gaps of knowledge and understanding in the existing literature on xenophobia; this still requires research that is empirically tested, reliable and validated at a local level. Nonetheless, there are very serious social and material dimensions and facts that remain unexplored. Among such realities the role of the state security agencies at all levels of planning, designing and implementing while the specter of an imaginary "third force," as identified and popularized by politicians, still prevails.

The wide variety of scholarly books published over several years have tackled a number of issues such as the phenomenon's historical development (Tafira, 2017) and the relationship between xenophobia, migration and informality, crime and violence. Researchers have focused on foreign nationals' experiences in post-apartheid South Africa (Harris, 2001), xenophobia in southern Africa (Nyamnjoh, 2006) and a comparative study on xenophobia in different countries including South Africa, Germany and Canada (Adam and Moodley, 2013). Furthermore, some authors have dissected the relationship between violence and xenophobia (Kupe et al., 2008; Landau, 2012). There are fascinating books that have recently unearthed regarding foreign nationals' participation in the informal sector in South Africa (Crush and Tawodzera, 2017) and the political economy of xenophobia in Africa (Akinola, 2018).

Within this wide variety and array of research on the phenomenon of xenophobia, it is interesting to note that the Durban 2015 xenophobic attacks led to seven fatalities, a number of foreigners' shops being looted and vandalized, and people attacked and injured . These attacks had the lowest death rate, but had multiple causalities which scholars, the media, government agencies and interested key stakeholders have failed to investigate seriously. There is minimal published data on the 2015 xenophobic violence that took place in Durban. The available data are mostly from journal articles and there is no textbook evidence.

It is indeed a sad situation that a wide range of published literature has failed to acknowledge that xenophobic attacks occur spontaneously in local areas and that the alleged perpetrators' viewpoints have not been heard. The majority of the published data is dominated by what is reported in the popular media, which is anecdotal, less localized and anti-government, with the success stories of state agencies and government departments going unreported.

*Localized Xenophobia in South Africa* aims at empirically espousing and assessing the hidden causes and dimensions of the 2015 xenophobic violence which occurred in the greater Durban area, specifically the causes of the xenophobic violence, and the role of the media and its repercussions. We assess the existing levels of effectiveness, responsiveness and pro-activeness of the state's security services and intelligence apparatus in terms of detecting, preventing, responding to and mitigating the effects of xenophobia. The contingency plans of SAPS are analyzed in relation to their acts, responses and general attitudes in dealing with xenophobia in Durban, while we further investigate the humanitarian crisis brought about by xenophobia. This is supplemented by an analysis of the planning and actions of government agencies, civil society and NGOs in their efforts to remedy the tragedy.

The role and responsibilities, as well as the impact of the leading actors (including the police, NATJOINTS, civil society, NGOs, CBOs and government departments) are analyzed and dissected in this book. Finally, the financial implications resulting from the xenophobic violence are extensively assessed.

This book chapter also covers the research philosophies, design and methodologies which inform this empirical study. The qualitative analysis of the interpretative case study of open-ended, face-to-face interviews is extensively discussed in terms of the role people played in the events that occurred during two months in 2015. These interviews took place with a myriad of stakeholders including government officials; representatives from civil society groups, NGOs and security agencies; community activists and journalists.

As this study is informed by interpretivism and phenomenology (Saunders et al., 2007, p. 103) as an epistemological position, an inductive approach is briefly discussed by focusing on the theory generation of the underlying causes of xenophobia and its adverse effects on society at large. The study utilized qualitative methodology as the appropriate epistemological orientation and was based on the undertaking and thorough content analysis of 17 in-depth interviews. These were based on the judgmental sampling frame and conducted with individuals who were directly or indirectly involved in this historical period through their affiliation with key state institutions, community organizations and civil society groups. Key stakeholders and role players with direct and indirect involvement in and after the attacks were interviewed. This included community leaders and inhabitants, SAPS officials, members of civil society groups and organizations, and municipal and provincial officials. A deductive content analysis was used to categorize, classify and analyze 48 media articles that had been published in local newspapers. The interviews conducted with municipal and provincial government officials took place in the respondents' offices. Furthermore, the civil society groups' representatives were interviewed in their office based in Durban, while the community activists were interviewed in their natural environments near the Durban townships. The researchers sent interview requests to the informants via email prior to the interview, followed by telephonic confirmation explaining the rationale for the interview and its benefits. The appointments were subsequently made.

This study was informed by an inductive approach, where a theory on xenophobia was developed as an outcome of the research (Bryman and Bell, 2015). This included the triggers of the xenophobic attacks, the risk-reduction strategies applied, the financial implications and the overt and covert strategies planned and implemented in order to mitigate its effects. This is due to the fact that the researchers were directly influenced by print and social media platforms, as well as government communication channels rooted in biased, falsified, inflammatory and anti-immigrant sentiments regarding xenophobia. Constructionism as an ontological position on the "social phenomenon" and meaning (xenophobia from a security cluster lens) was continually produced by social actors (in this case, government officials).

This study employed a qualitative research design approach where the researchers attempted to generate a theory from data on the triggers, financial implications and mitigation strategies of the xenophobic attacks of 2015. Qualitative purposive sampling was used in this study as a total number of 13 government officials, mostly from the security cluster, were interviewed. These government officials included a senior provincial policy official, leaders from the Provincial Disaster Management Centre and the eThekwini Municipality Disaster Management Centre, NATJOINTS and PROVPOINTS, senior police and shelter officials. These state officials provided their experiences and viewpoints regarding the discourse on xenophobia. Three community and civil societies activists completed the sample.

The research informants were asked identical open-ended questions (Gall et al., 2003). The respondents were interviewed in their personal capacity and their identities are not revealed in this study as some of the information they provided was considered by them to be classified. The confidentiality of the informants, as well as their anonymity, was maintained throughout.

The open-ended questions permitted the research participants to express their responses in detail (as designed) in order to extract themes. The following questions were posed to the respondents:

- What risk assessment and reduction strategies were in place to mitigate the adverse effects of xenophobia?
- What were the potential triggers of the xenophobic attacks in this province?
- What costs have been associated with the impact of the xenophobic attacks?
- Are the overt and covert strategies applied by the security apparatus able to curb the xenophobic attacks?

The sample size of the in-depth interviews ($N = 15$) was above the limits of phenomenological studies, which ranges between 6 and 10 (Morse, 2000).

The researchers ceased to mine more information from other informants as new information was not discovered during data analysis. Further interviews would have yielded similar findings and can serve to confirm the emerging themes and conclusions (Faulkner and Trotter, 2017a). After a comprehensive examination of the phenomenon (viewpoints on the xenophobic attacks from the security forces), the saturation point was reached (after adequately achieving the aims and objectives of the research study) (Faulkner and Trotter, 2017b). Similar questions were posed to different sampled informants who responded consistently to the questions. The answers yielded common themes including risk-reduction strategies, security agencies' overt and covert strategies and SAPS's contingency plans to minimize the impacts of the xenophobic attacks.

An inductive content analysis, which is an objective method of analysis, was employed in this study. This method was used as no previous research studies have been conducted that focus on the dimensions and the target population explored in this study (security cluster officials' viewpoints on the xenophobic attacks). The Special Reference Group (SRG) Report and the Report to the Security Cluster (2015) were analyzed to buttress the data gleaned from the qualitative in-depth interviews. The SRG Report is an important document on migration and community integration in KwaZulu-Natal, which aims to dissect the causes and socio-economic consequences of the March to May 2015 violent attacks against foreign nationals. This assessment by SRG was mandated by the premier of the KwaZulu-Natal province to also focus on the successes and shortcomings of the past and ongoing initiatives to ensure tensions in communities are minimized. The SRG Report to the Security Cluster (2015) is relevant to this study as the researchers targeted officials from the security cluster who were directly involved and accountable for the initiatives, projects and activities regarding the xenophobic attacks. These reports further played a vital role as a means of triangulation in the form of converging and corroborating the data gleaned from the qualitative in-depth interviews (Bowen, 2009).

The analysis of the selected data was based on a thorough content analysis. This case study research sought to present new knowledge on understanding the root causes and realities of xenophobia at a local level. An external specialist in this field was sourced to study and confirm the data collection and analysis processes as well as the transcripts, with the aim of validating the data. Furthermore, the trustworthiness of the research findings was improved by ensuring that the data gleaned from the informants were submitted to them in order for the authenticity of the transcripts to be confirmed. The researchers conformed to the ethical guidelines as the confidentiality and anonymity of the respondents was guaranteed. A case study research design of more than one individual using qualitative in-depth interviews (Blumberg et al., 2005) as a data collection method was employed to gain an in-depth understanding of the xenophobic violence that occurred in 2015 in the KwaZulu-Natal province. A content analysis was also used where 48 media articles published in local newspapers were analyzed. A content analysis was used in this study and analyzed written media articles published by a popular local newspaper in KwaZulu-Natal (Harwood and Garry, 2003).

The present study seeks to present a new understanding of the realities of xenophobic violence at a local level, and to dissect and challenge the premise and/ or existence of a "third force" as disseminated by the media. It further gauges the public's perceptions of foreigners based on the press framing of the xenophobic violence. The study also explores how the victims and the alleged perpetrators of the xenophobic attacks are portrayed in reports of the incidents.

An inductive content analysis was conducted on a host of media articles, which were analyzed and used to generate a theory, especially as previous researchers' existing data on this phenomenon is fragmented. The current chapter further discusses the ethnographic participant observation which is dominant in this study, focusing on its four core aspects: the long duration; the social relations of a group of people; holism; and the dialectical relationship between intimacy and estrangement (Shah, 2017). A grounded theory is further discussed where it is used to discover and construct a theory on the dimensions of xenophobia in Durban. A thematic analysis is followed, and the data gleaned from the informants, media articles and related documents are analyzed and themes generated. Different non-probability techniques – including purposive and convenience sampling – are discussed in this chapter. The use of qualitative data analysis software (NVIVO version 12) is briefly discussed. This program is used to analyze and categorize data and generate themes. The reliability and validity testing for the qualitative data is briefly discussed as well as the ethical guidelines for the study.

The interpretative case study method was used utilizing an exploratory strategy based on non-standardized interviews. This was done through purposive sampling where government officials in leadership positions were purposefully selected. This included SAPS, the eThekwini Disaster Management Centre and officials directly involved in all operational shelters. The findings were triangulated in respect of the different questions posed in the face-to-face interviews, which were conducted in prearranged venues. The interviews were based on phenomenological tradition and dealt with the everyday experiences of the interviewees, their relationships with the displaced refugees and migrants, and the daily realities of the organizations. A voice recorder was used to record the interviews, which were subsequently transcribed. Version 12 of NVIVO, a qualitative data analytical tool, was used to categorize information that was gleaned from the informants, where themes, patterns and trends emerged (Holloway, 2005). The process implemented to ensure that the findings were trustworthy and valid was maintained and the principles of good practice followed, where the interviewees were given the transcribed scripts to confirm the authenticity of their responses. Furthermore, a qualitative and impartial specialist was employed to evaluate the processes of data collection and analysis. The anonymity and confidentiality of all respondents was guaranteed.

There were nine respondents who were purposively interviewed and those included local activists from places where the violence occurred, NGOs, civil society groups and government officials who were in leadership positions. Furthermore, a qualitative content analysis was used where 48 newspaper articles were analyzed to determine the tone of reporting.

The trustworthiness and authenticity of the qualitative data were assessed and found to be credible, transferable, dependable and confirmable (Bryman and Bell, 2015, p. 44). This study on the 2015 xenophobic attacks was conducted in accordance with the rules of good practice, and its findings can be applied to other provinces in South Africa. An auditing approach to establish research merit in terms of trustworthiness was conducted; the findings were not influenced by the researchers' values and/or theoretical inclinations (Bryman and Bell, 2015). Furthermore, the reliability and validity of the findings were tested through triangulation as more than one method of investigation and source of data were used to cross-check them. In this case, the qualitative content analysis was utilized, where SRG and government reports were analyzed to buttress the findings of the qualitative in-depth interviews. The research participants were fully informed and provided their consent (in their personal capacity) to participate in this study on xenophobia. The aims and objectives of the study were clearly communicated to the research participants and anonymity was maintained at all levels.

The qualitative, non-probability purposive sampling was adopted with a total of 17 informants selected. These included the senior members of the provincial government, representatives of the eThekwini Municipality Disaster Management Center (DMC) and leading civil society groups such as the Refugee Centre. Community activists in a number of hotspots were also selected as sources of information in this seminal study.

## Sampling

A total of 15 informants were sampled as per Dworkin's (2012, p. 1319) number of interviewees from 5 to 50 participants. Forty-eight media articles reporting on xenophobia in the Durban area by major newspapers were analyzed. The local newspapers that are available both in print and digital form include *Isolezwe* (in isiZulu), *Sunday Tribune, Daily News, The New Age* and *The Mercury*. The rationale for this analysis was to determine whether the tone of coverage by media reporters was positive, negative or neutral.

A total number of 48 media articles from popular printed media published in the KwaZulu-Natal province were analyzed. Of these, a total of 19 (35%) articles had a positive tone, 23 (43%) were negative and 12 (22%) were neutral.

Ten in-depth open-ended questions were posed to locally and provincially based government officials, members of civil society, community leaders and activists as well as newspapers, magazines and media reporters concerning the relationship between xenophobia, journalists and the media in general.

Seven questions were posed to state officials:

1. How would you describe the accuracy of local journalists' reporting, analysis, accuracy general position and attitude regarding the xenophobic attacks?
2. How important do you consider the journalistic function to be in the covering of such realities and the role and effects of the dissemination of such information to the public?
3. How would you describe the situation the journalists' attitude and position vis-á-vis the immigrants as it appeared in the media? Would you classify them as positive, negative or neutral? Can you elaborate on the answer?
4. Do you consider that those narratives by media platforms regarding the immigrants as one of the causes of the perpetuating xenophobic violence?

5. Do you have solid evidence which associates crime to the foreign nationals?
6. Do you feel that a xenophobic culture has been created over the years? What do you see as the reasons for this?
7. Are government officials proactive in detecting and preventing the xenophobic attacks and in mitigating its consequences?

A total of 48 newspaper articles were downloaded from media houses' websites to determine the tone of reporting. Keywords were captured in the search engine and all articles published from April 30, 2015 onwards were downloaded, focusing on xenophobic attacks in South Africa.

As indicated, NVIVO software (version 10) was used in this study to organize, analyze and share data from the interviews and media articles where themes, patterns and trends emerged (Elo and Kyngas, 2008, p. 107; Holloway, 2005). The researchers commenced with selecting the unit of analysis (Gurthie et al., 2004) by developing themes (Polit and Beck, 2004) according to the tone of the reporting on the xenophobia that occurred in 2015. A total number of 48 articles published in this period were analyzed and a negative, positive or neutral tone determined. All articles were categorized and classified into three tones: negative, positive and neutral during the xenophobic violence that took place in KwaZulu-Natal.

## References

Adam, H. and Moodley, K. 2013. *Imagined Liberation: Xenophobia, Citizenship and Identity in South Africa, Germany and Canada*, Vol. 4, Cape Town, African Sun Media.

Africa Check. 2018. *11 Million Undocumented Migrants in SA? Police Commissioner's Figure "Doesn't Make Sense"*. Available at: https://africacheck.org/spot-check/11-million-undocumented-migrants-in-sa-police-commissioners-figure-doesnt-make-sense/ [Accessed 18 November 2019].

Akinola, A.O. Ed. 2018. *The Political Economy of Xenophobia in Africa*, New York, NY, Springer International Publishing.

AllAfrica.com. 2013. *South Africa: Shirdon Calls on South Africa to Protect Somali Nationals*. Available at: https://allafrica.com/stories/201306050294.html [Accessed 18 November 2017].

BBC. 2008. South African Mob Kills Migrants, *BBC News*, May 12. Available at: http://news.bbc.co.uk/2/hi/africa/7396868.stm [Accessed 12 March 2018].

Blumberg, B., Donald, R. Cooper, D.R. and Schindler, P.S. 2005. *Business Research Methods*, London: McGraw-Hill Education.

Bowen, G.A. 2009. Document analysis as a qualitative research method, *Qualitative Research Journal*, 9(2), 27–40.

Bryman, A. and Bell, E. 2015. *Business Research Methods*, 4th ed., Oxford, Oxford University Press.

Centre for the Study of Violence and Reconciliation. 2008. *South Africa: Burning the Welcome Mat*. Available at: https://web.archive.org/web/20081215051328/http://www.csvr.org.za/index.php?option=com_content&task=view&id=904&Itemid=21 [Accessed 19 March 2009].

Charman, A. and Piper, L. 2012. Xenophobia, criminality and violent entrepreneurship: violence against Somali shopkeepers in Delft South, Cape Town, South Africa, *South African Review of Sociology*, 43(3), 81–105.

Chenzi, V. 2020. Fake news, social media and xenophobia in South Africa, *African Identities*. doi:10.1080/14725843.2020.1804321

Crush, J. and Chikanda, A. Eds 2015. *Mean Streets: Migration, Xenophobia and Informality in South Africa*, Johannesburg, Southern African Migration Programme (SAMP).

Crush, J. and Dodson, B. 2007. Another lost decade: the failures of South Africa's post-apartheid migration policy, *Tijdschrift Voor Economische En Sociale Geografie*, 98(4), 436–454.

Crush, J. and Ramachandran, S. 2014. *Soft Targets: Xenophobia, Public Violence and Changing Attitudes to Migrants in South Africa after May 2008*. SAMP Migration Policy Series No. 64. Cape Town, South African Migration Policy.

Crush, J. and Tawodzera, G. 2017. *Living with Xenophobia: Zimbabwean Informal Enterprise in South Africa* (No. 77), Cape Town, South African Migration Policy (SAMP).

Crush, J., Williams, V. and Peberdy, S. 2005. *Migration in Southern Africa*. Available at: https://womin.org.za/images/impact-of-extractive-industries/migrancy-and  extractivism/Crush Williams and Peberdy - Migration in Southern Africa.pdf [Accessed 5 February 2020].

Dworkin, S. L. 2012. Sample size policy for qualitative studies using in-depth interviews, *Archives of Sexual Behavior*, 41(6), 1319–1320. doi:10.1007/s10508-012-0016-6

Eisenberg, G. 2015. *South Africa Stripped of Immigration Policy*. Available at: http://www.eisenberg.co.za/single-post/2015/12/01/South-Africa-stripped-of-Immigration-Policy [Accessed 20 February 2020].

Elo, S. and Kyngas, H. 2008. The qualitative content analysis process, *Journal of Advanced Nursing*. doi:10.1111/j.1365-2648.2007.04569 [Accessed 21 June 2017].

Faulkner, S. and Trotter, S.P. 2017a. Data Saturation in *The International Encyclopaedia of Communication Research Methods*, January. Available at: https://www.researchgate.net/publication/320928897_Data_Saturation [Accessed 21 June 2017].

Faulkner, S. and Trotter, S.P. 2017b. Theoretical Saturation in *The International Encyclopaedia of Communication Research Methods*, November 7, Wiley Online Library. doi:10.1002/9781118901731.iecrm0250 [Accessed 21 June 2017].

Gall, M.D., Borg, W.R. and Gall, J.P. 2003. *Educational Research: An Introduction*, 7th ed., New York, NY, Pearson.

Gurthie, J., Petty, R., Yongvanich, K. and Ricceri, F. 2004. Using content analysis as a research method to inquire into intellectual capital reporting. *Journal of Intellectual Capital*, 5(2), 282–293. doi: 10.1108/14691930410533704

Harris, B. 2001. *A Foreign Experience: Violence, Crime and Xenophobia During South Africa's Transition*, Vol. 5, Johannesburg, CSVR.

Harwood, T.G. and Garry, T. 2003. An overview of content analysis, *The Marketing Review*, 3(4), 479–498.

Hendricks, N. and Mati, S. 2020. Counteracting xenophobia in South Africa through popular education, *New Directions for Adult and Continuing Education*, 2020(165), 49–61.

Holloway, I. 2005. *Qualitative Methods in Health Care*, Maidenhead, Open University Press.

Independent Online 1. n.d. *Xenophobic Attacks: Seven Die in One Month*. Available at: https://www.iol.co.za/index.php?click_id=13&set_id=1&art_id=ct20000802102508479X510381 [Accessed 21 June 2016].

Independent Online 2. n.d. *Raging Mob Evicts Zimbabweans, Burns Homes*. Available at: https://www.iol.co.za/index.php?set_id=1&click_id=13&art_id=ct200110212058176Z5321926 [Accessed 28 March 2017].

International Organisation for Migration. 2020. *World Publication Report 2020*. Available at: https://publications.iom.int/system/files/pdf/wmr_2020.pdf [Accessed 27 June 2020].

Kupe, T., Verryn, B.P. and Worby, E. 2008. *Go Home or Die Here: Violence, Xenophobia and the Reinvention of Difference in South Africa*, Johannesburg, Wits University Press.

Landau, L.B. 2012. *Exorcising the Demons Within: Xenophobia, Violence and Statecraft in Contemporary South Africa*, Johannesburg, Wits University Press.

Lawyers for Human Rights (LHR). 1999. *Comments on the White Paper on International Migration*. Available at: http://www.lhr.org.za/submission/comments-white-paper-international-migration [Accessed 23 November 2019].

Makhado, M.P. and Tshisikhawe, T.R. 2020. How apartheid education encouraged and reinforced tribalism and xenophobia in South Africa. In M. A. Mafukata (Eds.), *Impact of immigration and xenophobia on development in Africa*, pp. 131–151, Hershay, IGI Global.

Masikane, C.M., Hewitt, M.L. and Toendepi, J. 2020. Dynamics informing xenophobia and leadership response in South Africa, *Acta Commercii*, 20(1), 1–11.

Mfubu, P. 2017. What Does the 2017 Refugee Amendment Act Mean for Asylum Seekers and Refugees Living in South Africa? *Safe Spaces*, November 2. Available at: https://www.saferspaces.org.za/blog/entry/what-does-the-2017-refugee-amendment-act-mean-for-asylum-seekers-and-refuge [Accessed 24 June 2018].

Misago, J.P. 2009. *Violence, Labour and the Displacement of Zimbabweans in De Doorns, Western Cape*, Forced Migration Studies Program, Migration Policy Brief 2. Available at: http://www.migration.org.za/wp-content/uploads/2017/08/Violence-Labour-and-the-Displacement-of-Zimbabweans-in-De-Doorns-Western-Cape.-Issue-Brief-2.pdf [Accessed 25 March 2016].

Morse, J.M. 2000. Determining sample size, *Qualitative Health Research*, 10(1), 3–5. doi: 10.1177/104973200129118183

Mwiti, L. 2015. Seven of the biggest myths about South Africa and xenophobia – and how they drive attacks, *Mail & Guardian Africa*, April 22. Available at: https://mgafrica.com/article/2015-04-22-six-huge-myths-about-south-africas-xenophobia [Accessed 28 March 2016].

News24. 2008. Camp Conditions Alarm SACC, *News24*, June 26. Available at: https://web.archive.org/web/20080718081359/http://www.news24.com/News24/South_Africa/Xenophobia/0%2C%2C2-7-2382_2346122%2C00.html

Nyamnjoh, F.B. 2006. *Insiders and Outsiders: Citizenship and Xenophobia in Contemporary Southern Africa*, Johannesburg, Zed Books.

Polit, D.F. and Beck, C.T. 2004. Assessing data quality. In *Nursing Research: Principles and Methods*, Eds D.F. Polit and C.T. Beck, 7th ed., pp. 413–444, Philadelphia, PA: Lippincott Williams & Wilkin.

Rank, F., Govender, S. and Nombembe, P. 2009. Recent attacks just the tip of a xenophobic iceberg, *The Times*, January 7. Available at: https://web.archive.org/web/20090107073615/http://www.thetimes.co.za/PrintEdition/News/Article.aspx?id=768363 [Accessed 19 June 2018].

Rasool, F., Botha, C. and Bisschoff, C. 2012. The effectiveness of South Africa's immigration policy for addressing skills shortages, *Managing Global Transitions*, 10(4), 399–418.

Refword. 2008. *South Africa: Burning the Welcoming Mat*, Centre for the Study of Violence and Reconciliation. Available at: https://www.refworld.org/docid/4832c17d11.html.m [Accessed 23 June 2017].

Republic of South Africa. 1995. Aliens Control Amendment Act, 1995. [No. 76 of 1995] – G 16741.

Republic of South Africa. 1997. The DRAFT GREEN PAPER ON INTERNATIONAL M IGRATION. Government Gazette: No 18033.

Republic of South Africa, Department of Home Affairs. 2003. Immigration Act 2002 (Act No. 13 of 2002), Draft Immigration Regulations, Government Gazette, Vol. 453, No. 24587, Pretoria, 14 March 2003.

RSA Treasury. 2006. *Growth Employment and Redistribution: A Macroeconomic Strategy.* Available at: http://www.treasury.gov.za/publications/other/gear/chapters.pdf [Accessed 25 March 2016].

Saunders, M., Lewis, P. and Thornhill, A. 2007. *Research Methods for Business Students*, 4th ed., Edinburgh Gate, Harlow, Financial Times Prentice Hall.

Shah, C. (2017). *Social Information Seeking: Leveraging the Wisdom of the Crowd*, Cham, Springer.

Statistics South Africa. 2018. *Men, Women and Children: Findings of the Living Conditions Survey 2015*, Pretoria, Statistics South Africa.

Statistics South Africa. 2019. *Statistical Release P0302 Mid-year Population Estimates*, Pretoria, Statistics South Africa.

Tafira, H.K. 2017. *Xenophobia in South Africa: A History*, New York, NY, Springer.

Tewolde, A.I. 2020. Reframing xenophobia in South Africa as colour-blind: the limits of the afro phobia thesis, *Migration Letters*, 17(3), 433–444.

The New Humanitarian. 2006. *Fleeing War, Somalis Are Targets of Violence in Adopted Home*, October 10. Available at: https://www.thenewhumanitarian.org/fr/node/ 228119 [Accessed 10 March 2016].

The South African White Paper on International Migration. 1999. Government Gazette (vol. 406, 1 April 1999).

TimesLIVE. 2009. *Xenophobia Cases Must Be Finalised*. Available at: https://www.times-live.co.za/News/Article.aspx/?id=944860 [Accessed 23 June 2018].

United Nations (UN). 2017. *Population Migration Data, South Africa*, UN Population Division, Department of Economic and Social Affairs. Available at: https://www. un.org/en/development/desa/population/migration/data/estimates2/estimates17.asp [Accessed 19 August 2018].

Valji, N. 2003. *Creating the Nation: The Rise of Violent Xenophobia in the New South Africa*, Unpublished Master's Thesis, York University. Available at: https://www. files.ethz.ch/isn/104980/riseofviolent.pdf

Wa Kabwe-Segatti, A. 2006. *Reformulating Immigration Policy in Post-apartheid South Africa*, IFAS Working Paper Series/Les Cahiers de l' IFAS, (8), 171–185.

World Bulletin. 2013. *Two Dead in Xenophobic Attacks in S. Africa*. Available at: https:// www.worldbulletin.net/africa/two-dead-in-xenophobic-attacks-in-s-africa-h138539. html.m [Accessed 23 August 2018].

Chapter Two

# Associating Xenophobia with Criminality: Is it a Fallacy?

While the research-based bibliography on xenophobic attacks in South Africa has provided social, economic, historical, sociological and psychological dimensions, the "whole story" is still in the making for a variety of reasons, some of which will become evident in this work. This truth is based on the fact that "first-hand information" emanating from active participants throughout the xenophobic attack processes, those behind them, the repercussions for all those involved on all sides, has been lacking. Issues that are covered include the poor governance performance and functions of key state departments, the direct and indirect relationship this has with poor service delivery and the poor implementation of existing legislation (which leads to a high crime rate and corrupt practices). This chapter explores other roots, dimensions and foundations of the violence including the realities of competition among foreign business people and their relations with state departments, with local criminal gangs and with South African citizens. The weaknesses of state departments at the municipal and provincial level and their direct and indirect repercussions on existing professional business relations between South Africans and foreigners are examined, together with the daily life circumstances of foreigners in formal townships and squatter camps in the urban areas of South Africa.

The gaps that exist in a wide array of key functions are examined, including prevention, risk reduction and mitigating factors. We also discuss the functions and operations of our municipalities and borders, and the South African Revenue Service (SARS). We tackle these issues in terms of the role they play in corrupt practices and how they relate to foreigners and the regulation, operations and repercussions of informal businesses. It is believed that, in so doing, we will discover the underlying roots and causes of xenophobia.

There needs to be a paradigm shift in understanding the triggers of xenophobia from a macro and micro economic lens to unknown dimensions and scholars have commenced highlighting key empirical factors that have been missed. The xenophobic attacks are collectively considered by scholars to be sporadic and that they do not target and victimize only foreign nationals. Conversely, the perpetrators are not only locals and the reasons are not simply based on economic competition among foreign nationals themselves, which is a narrative shared mostly by the media.

**Addressing Xenophobia in South Africa:**
**Drivers, Responses and Lessons from the Durban Untold Stories, 27–60**
**Copyright © 2022 by Bethuel Sibongiseni Ngcamu and Evangelos Mantzaris**
**Published under exclusive licence by Emerald Publishing Limited**
**doi:10.1108/978-1-80262-479-320211003**

This version of events claims that the warring factions are citizens and foreign nationals. Accordingly, attacks against foreign nationals are regarded as coordinated efforts by people or groups with their own selfish motivations. Such people aspire to cause collective discontent, resentment, hatred and anger toward vulnerable people in communities. This was noticeable in the major violent attacks of 2008 and 2015 which had a similar modus operandi, the symptoms of which were unavoidable socially and politically embedded attitudes. This was observed in Durban when political leaders (including municipal councilors) were involved in instigating and mobilizing local vulnerable groups to attack foreign nationals. In addition, the inflammatory, reprehensive, anti-immigrant and xenophobic rhetoric by influential traditional government, the police, trade union leaders and black entrepreneurs have been reported and widely publicized in the media (Bornman, 2019).

However, there is limited empirical data that unearth the hidden triggers of xenophobia at a local level. This has influenced researchers to investigate the extent of competition among foreign nationals and criminal activities (by organized gangs and government officials) and to consider if this is what was behind the xenophobic attacks in Durban. Furthermore, it is believed that the role of the media platforms, the porosity of our borders and corruption in government departments have contributed to the scourge of attacks against refugees, asylum seekers and illegal immigrants. This has been dissected in society at large with communities divided against the attitudes displayed toward foreign nationals. This is supported by Misago (2019) who opines that different mobilizing techniques such as parochial patronage and haranguing has been applied to entrepreneurs who on occasions have instigated crowds to attack foreign nationals and their businesses. Beetar (2019), meanwhile, acknowledges the discourses of denialism and exceptionalism within South African society which regards locals as being worthy of life and relegates immigrants to zones of figurative and literal death.

In addition, this chapter espouses the root causes of the 2015 xenophobic attacks and unearths the overlooked dimensions of the violence against and among foreign nationals. This study is necessitated by the scarcity of published data in the aftermath of the xenophobic violence that took place in Durban in 2015. Previous research concerned with xenophobic violence and other issues has been largely anecdotal and impressionistic, providing only a reflective analysis of a small and non-scientific sampling of press clippings.

The sporadic and haphazard violence perpetrated against citizens from other African countries and their businesses started at the end of March 2015 in Isipingo (south of Durban). It soon spread to Umlazi, KwaMakhutha, Chatsworth, Clare Estate/Sydenham, Quarry Heights, Verulam, KwaDabeka, Kwamashu, Ntuzuma, Lindelani and the Durban CBD (Mahatma Gandhi Street). Government officials regarded government department and agencies as responding proactively, swiftly and decisively to the generalized violence by establishing multi-disciplinary political and technical committees from a national to a local level. Both administrative and political leaders are said to have activated disaster management systems and procedures nationally and locally and the South African Police (SAPS) joint structures on a national and provincial level, as well as operational centers at a police station level. The security agencies (police, municipal law enforcement agencies and secret service operatives) were commended for their vociferous enforcement of criminal law and immigration law to stabilize the situation and address some of the root causes of the xenophobic attacks against foreign nationals. A multiplicity of projects and strategies were initiated which included implementing a community engagement and communication strategy to reassure local and international communities of the stability of the country, its adherence to democratic values, the application of the rule of law and the mobilization of citizens toward African unity. Furthermore, temporary shelters were provided to persons who were displaced, in line with the UN's Guiding Principles on Internal Displacement, and a reintegration process was initiated in accordance with these guidelines.

In response to the spate of attacks against foreign nationals at the time, the eThekwini (Durban) municipality, together with various government departments, established three shelters: Isipingo with the initial intake of approximately 280 foreign nationals, Chatsworth with 800 to 1,000 and Charon Drive in Greenwood Park with 196. The shelter at Greenwood Park subsequently relocated to Phoenix and the Univale Sports Ground. The objective of establishing these shelters was to safeguard the foreign nationals while repatriating those willing to be repatriated and reintegrating the rest back into their communities. The number of foreigners at the shelters varied; the figures have then escalated. It was noted that figures usually increased when food was made available and when embassy or consulate staff visited the shelters. Infighting among émigrés over access to basic necessities also occurred. Some embassy staff members created expectations relating to repatriation, which was subsequently not always fulfilled. This was particularly the case with the Malawian and Mozambican embassies. One of the shelter managers commented as follows:

> As a consequence of the reintegration programme, the number of persons in the shelters started decreasing rapidly during the latter part of April and the beginning of May 2015, resulting in the closure of the Phoenix Shelter at the end of April 2015 and the Isipingo Shelter at the beginning of May 2015. The residents of [the] Chatsworth shelter were consulted on the intention to officially close the shelter on the 30th of June 2015. However, on the day which was set for the closure, about 143 displaced persons refused to integrate, claiming that they [were] from Burundi and [the] DRC and [did] not want to reintegrate within South Africa but want[ed] the UNHCR to take them to the second country within the World. The shelter was indeed officially closed and all amenities were taken away and there was neither food nor shelter for them. As they illegally stayed [at] the site, the South African Police opened a case of illegal camping.

These violent attacks of March 30, 2015, fondly called "xenophobia" by the media, scholars and opposition parties, were triggered by the employment of foreign nationals and the dismissal of locals in one of the grocery stores in Isiphingo (South of Durban). While these attacks were meant to target immigrants and their businesses, the landlords who had been renting their properties to foreign nationals were also attacked. The perpetrators turned violent, looting businesses and destroying property. South African families who were renting their properties to foreign nationals also became the targets of the xenophobic attacks. The levels of violence increased and the number of casualties rose. The situation was exacerbated by the accidental shooting of a South African woman in Umlazi. The looting that took place in Isipingo was allegedly organized by the Umlazi business owners, grouped as the South African Traders' Association and led by Mvuso Mkhize. The looters were supported by the South African National Civil Organisation (SANCO) eThekwini regional and provincial structures led by Mvuso Hlope and a group of homeless people. In Umlazi G Section, tuck shop owner Qaphelani Jeza was identified as one of the instigators, a number of which were taken into police custody. Of interest was the use of social media for mobilization and incitement. The victims of the attacks were mainly Mozambican, Congolese, Zimbabwean and Malawian. Later, Somali and Ethiopian nationals as well as South Africans were targeted. The immigrants who were not perceived to be competitors – such as Pakistani, Chinese and Bangladeshi nationals – were not targeted.

There is a multiplicity of causes of the xenophobic attacks against foreign nationals of African origin. Government officials have increased competition for various resources including low-cost housing and services, job opportunities and informal businesses. The situation has been exacerbated by the failure of municipal officials to enforce by-laws relating to the registration of spaza shops in townships and the involvement of foreign nationals in criminal activities.

The attacks against immigrants in Durban had adverse effects on South Africa's relationships with other countries in Africa. The implications collectively mentioned by government departments and agencies were the following:

- The violence exposed a culture of lawlessness, with the warring factions disregarding the authority of government agencies in handling the situation.
- There has been reputational damage to South Africa in the international environment.
- The informal economic system that supports poorer communities was disrupted.
- The social cohesion in the affected communities was weakened.
- There was an increase in opportunistic criminal activities.

The above led to the South African interests (embassies and businesses) in some African countries being affected.

Having outlined a number of key issues and challenges that have shaped the foundations of the present research project the theoretical framework is identified and dissected.

## Theoretical Framework

### *Frustration–Aggression Theory*

The most significant theory that is relevant to this study is "frustration–aggression theory, also known as the frustration–aggression hypothesis." This theory has been utilized in psychology, sociology, anthropology, criminology, ethnology and medical research, has its roots in the 1930s and is considered to be one of the leading theories in research on issues associated with both frustration and aggression. Broadly speaking, it began with the hypothesis that aggression is the consequence of frustration and that in most cases frustration is a necessary condition for aggression. The theory and empirical research of Yale University psychologists, which started in 1939 and underwent a number of changes over the years, was based on a combination of behaviorism, psychoanalysis and dialectics. From its inception until the present, frustration–aggression theory has been applied by scholars in different disciplines and sub-disciplines. It is utilized as the instrument of analyzing, dissecting and outlining the empirical evidence of the foundations and processes involved in the link between frustration and aggression (Friedman and Schustack, 2014).

Inevitably, like every other theory, it began with a variety of simplistic analyses of aggressive behavior and frustration, the research of social and group terrains, and environmental realities and characteristics, such as aggressive responses to frustrating events. These connections and relations were essentially deterministic in nature and especially related to an increase in prejudice, depression, impulsivity, a lack of social or group interaction and/or understanding of situations and circumstances. International research has conclusively shown that the sources of frustration are rooted in a wide variety of diversified and on many occasions complex circumstances, leading to both frustration and aggression (Anderson and Bushman, 2002, pp. 32–33).

One of the most researched and proven foundations of aggression, and in particular frustration, is competition between multiple parties or groups. This began with the research of two of the key exponents of the theory, namely Berkowitz (in Breuer and Elson, 2016) and Deutsch (1993). This research is based on different contending groups with conflicting goals competing for limited resources, which leads to frustration and aggression. Of course, the same is true of individuals at all societal levels. Given the existing circumstances facing societies throughout the world, such as social, economic, financial, political and environmental realities, this can lead to a number of different frustrations and aggressions, which inevitably modify the existing theories and their empirical manifestations. This reality led one of the key theorists of the hypothesis to reformulate it, especially as it relates to the etiology of aggression which led to research on the causes and effects of frustration (Berkowitz, 1989, in Breuer and Elson, 2016). As time passed, the significance of social, political and economic conditions in society led to groups' frustrations and subsequent aggression, which on many occasions was also guided by the social dynamics of prejudice and stereotyping, and scapegoating became evident. Such socially created realities led to aggressive behavior and retaliation against the "existing sources of frustration" that became the "target/victim groups." On many occasions the attacking groups tend to be socially disadvantaged; their social condition is instrumental in their own prejudice and violent activities. There is no doubt that the frustration–aggression hypothesis has had a significant influence on social sciences research and literature despite criticism of what has been described as theoretical overgeneralization and rigidity.

At present, it is generally widely accepted that, given the rapid changes in societies throughout the world, the nature of the relationship between existing or hidden frustration and the display of violence in its various forms has become much more complicated at all societal levels. Even the widely acknowledged theoretical and empirical modifications of Leonard Berkowitz's suggestion that frustration is a psychologically based state leading to aggressive behavior has been seriously challenged (Breuer and Elson, 2016, pp. 3–4).

Inevitably, frustrations cause negative effects that often elicit aggressive inclinations, although this is not always the case. The circumstances of social stress, unemployment, poverty, homelessness and poor living conditions could easily be the causal path from frustration to aggression (i.e., xenophobic violence). These are the key elements of a process that is complicated in its simplicity, consisting of a number of steps forward or back and a multiplicity of stages and factors accumulating in the life of an individual or a mob. In this sense, individual frustration leading to aggression is much easier to study, analyze and describe when compared to that of a mob's or a community's. To study and analyze collective aggression and violence within societies, a deep understanding of the social, political and economic realities is fundamental in the analysis of individual or group behavior at all levels, especially violence. These existing realities are fundamental in the refinement of the theoretical and empirical dimensions and the application of frustration–aggression theory in the intellectual attempt to research, analyze and explain an extremely wide range of behaviors and actions of groups, communities and systems through the utilization of psychological, social and sociological analyses. Although there is no doubt that historically and at present, the frustration–aggression framework of analyses has seriously advanced our knowledge and understanding of human behavior and actions, new shifts, discoveries and problems have surfaced in the era of xenophobia. Societal and environmental changes and present and future pandemics present both theory and humanity with massive future challenges (Friedman and Schustack, 2014).

### Scapegoating Theory

Scapegoating denotes a process by which a small or large group or an individual person is unfairly blamed for something they did not do and consequently the real source of the problem is ignored. Scapegoating in practice and in theory (and on occasion, its repercussions) has been the subject of both psychological and sociological theorists and researchers internationally. Inevitably, such a difference lies in the fact that psychologists concentrate on the individual, while sociologists focus on scapegoating among groups and their surroundings in terms of their existing social, political, economic and environmental conditions. It is widely accepted that the terms are rooted in the religious Christian writings of the Book of Leviticus, which speaks about a goat (foreign nationals and the poor) sent into the wilderness to atone for a community's sins. A scapegoat therefore symbolizes any group or person that, although innocent, bears the sins and blame of others. The process of scapegoating has been described by psychologists as a complex individual and social phenomenon. Carl Jung's "darkness of the human psych" was dominated by shortcomings and weaknesses, aggressive and sexual urges and human darkness, but also the seat of human creativity. Jung believed that all these structures, systems, components and elements of society's unconscious, collective experiences were accumulated through history and shared by the whole of humankind. Jung's scapegoating denied the shadow of God and "man" as this shadow could not conform to the idea of the "ego" (Enders, 2018). Scapegoating as "a one-on-one" phenomenon, in which an individual blames another for their actions, has also been a topic of research for sociologists, as is the case with the "one-on-group" trend, where one person accuses a group for a problem they did or did not create such as theft, death, robbery or societal problems (immigrants' experiences in South Africa). Such scapegoating accusations could and have been founded on class, economic, racial, ethnic, religious or anti-immigrant bias. Sometimes scapegoating takes a "group against the individual" form, when a group of people single out and blame one person for a problem. In the South African landscape, it has become almost the norm for a whole community to, for example, blame the mayor or the municipal manager for the malfunctions of local government or the immigrants for the social-ills in communities which leads to the xenophobic attacks.

Sociologists' and most historians' interest concentrates on the "group-on-group" method of scapegoating history, including the challenges, particularities, differences and similarities. This takes place when one group blames another for problems created through actions or inaction, leading to collective experiences that could be environmental, political, economic or generally social. Accordingly, in South Africa the realities or falsehoods associated with the corrupt practices of foreign traders (mainly of African origin) in the market could lead to organized or community-initiated attacks and the looting of businesses of such entrepreneurs. Such types of scapegoating are often based on ethnicity, national origin or religion. Michael Foucault's seminal work, entitled *Madness and Civilization: A History of Insanity in the Age of Reason* (Foucault, 1988), vividly describes the disappearance of the leprosy epidemic, which likely produced the most ostracized group in the European landscape in the Middle Ages. One of his key arguments was that the mentally ill were forced to fill the leper colonies which had been vacated, despite the fact that they lived a mainstream rather than a segregated life. They were the scapegoats of the "normal people."

Scapegoating of one group by another has been historically evident throughout the world for centuries. At present in most cases it is the result of social, political, environmental and economic problems and challenges that lead groups, communities and gangs to harm the scapegoat(s) without realizing that it is they themselves who suffer because of their actions and behavior. The poor have nothing to gain when they attack scapegoats who are equally poor. In today's Africa, South Africa and the "developing" world, the scourges of poverty, homelessness and the unequal distribution of wealth within society are the key foundations upon which scapegoating is built.

The cordial relationship between the South African liberation movements, leaders and people across Africa can be traced back to the dark days of the apartheid regime where freedom fighters sought refuge and resources to fight the system. Post-apartheid South Africa saw a massive movement of immigrants from other countries to South Africa in search of work, business prospects and education opportunities. A number of them were verified as asylum seekers and refugees due to the political and economic turmoil in their home countries. Such a movement of hundreds of thousands over the years has triggered jealous and unhealthy competition between locals and foreign nationals, compounded by xenophobic feelings directed toward immigrants. This has led to sour relationships between African countries, with major economies such as South Africa and Nigeria described as "known rivals" in terms of leadership of the continent. The latter tensions have attracted some researchers such as Adebisi (2017) to analyze the causes of xenophobia in South Africa and to point out ways to eliminate it, which could lead to an improvement in the strained relationships between the countries. This researcher indicated that xenophobia among South Africans can be described as being the result of relative deprivation, extreme poverty-stricken lives and nationalism. A panacea to xenophobia has been suggested by Adebisi (2017) and that is for the government to focus on effective poverty alleviation programs, social orientation and good governance.

Meanwhile, Dauda et al. (2018) depict South Africans as having a parochial mindset due to the belief that immigrants are behind the problems of unemployment, poverty and disease. Citizens have the notion that their socio-economic conditions and employment prospects have been hijacked by immigrants. These researchers have described the attacks against Nigerians as "barbaric," and which have been associated with the existing negative relations with the Nigerian Government. Dauda et al. (2018) research study recommends that African countries promote tolerance, cooperation, peace and development on the continent. Mojisola (2019) has observed hostility toward foreign nationals despite the fact that they supported the South Africans in fighting against apartheid. The displaced hostility mentioned by Mojisola includes the destruction of property and physical attacks, which have led to homelessness, joblessness and people being wounded and killed. This researcher's empirical study, which used frustration–aggression theory to examine the causes of xenophobia, found that the negative effects of apartheid brutality, poor service delivery and competition for scarce economic resources were the causes of the xenophobic attacks.

Rasila and Musitha (2016) attribute the causes of xenophobia in South Africa to the lack of communication between foreign nationals and locals. The authors acknowledge economic competition as being behind xenophobia; however, what they singled out as the trigger of the xenophobic attacks was the lack of effective communication in integrating foreign nationals into local communities. Piper and Charman (2016), meanwhile, argue that attacks against spaza shops owners (immigrants) in the townships occurred as a result of the belief that foreigners have taken over informal businesses in various areas. The authors' survey among 1,000 spaza shop owners revealed a fascinating finding, pinpointing the fact that those with expensive goods experienced less violent attacks than those with cheaper goods. Piper and Charman (2016) concluded that violent attacks have nothing to do with nationalities but are linked to the pricing of the goods. Another interesting study, by Hågensen and De Jager (2016), which examined the underlying triggers of the xenophobic attacks against foreign nationals in De Doorns in 2009, included a number of fascinating findings. These included the threat and fear of the unknown because of the influx of immigrants into the farming community, labor brokers' opportunism and government's inefficiencies, all of which were compounded by a culture of lawlessness and poor labor relations. Mensah and Benedict (2016) attributed the sporadic attacks against foreign nationals since 2008 as being caused by citizens' sense of desperation due to widespread poverty' which have caused them to express this discontent through extreme violence. These authors suggest that this dissatisfaction could be managed through introducing business development and entrepreneurial skills programs within the communities, which would help to upskill the local population and target unskilled people who are poverty-stricken.

The synthesized literature above clearly shows that the scholars who have published on the major xenophobic attacks of 2008 and 2015 solely relied on secondary sources of literature. Primary data are lacking, which makes it difficult to validate their claims regarding the causes of xenophobic attacks. This is a serious gap which has necessitated the researchers of the current work to fill this void by targeting a region and informants who were directly involved in the xenophobic attacks of 2015 in the greater Durban area.

## Xenophobic Violence Triggers

The local people (including the security forces) who were familiar with the developments in the Durban South Coast (Isipingo) area repeatedly confirmed that the trigger of the 2015 xenophobic attacks was related to a labor dispute between locals and the owner of a local supermarket. The SAPS member who is based at the Isipingo Police Station supported this by saying:

> The attacks were mainly against foreign nationals and their spaza shops after it started, following a dispute between the workforce and the owner [of] the KwaJeena Store located [in] Isipingo which is a small town south of Durban. The local staff members in the store and South African part-time staffers started attacking the foreigners and then went on a strike outside, pulling crowds of support from shoppers and bystanders, mainly from Umlazi … [they] started the attacks and loot[ed] the place, the spazas, everything. In the beginning, the attacks were not centrally coordinated, but there were these incidents in the supermarket, the infighting between South African and foreign "scab" workers who were paid peanuts but [had] a job at least; that triggered flare-ups amongst them and then during the first days of the attacks there was an accidental fatal shooting of a[n] SA female [in] Umlazi that further triggered the looting. The Isipingo and Umlazi looting was mainly planned and coordinated by a number of spaza owners who belonged to a township organisation called [the] South African Traders Association so their clients could see that they were

locals and not foreigners. From the first day they had the support of all [the] structures of SANCO, the Umlazi-based eThekwini regional groups and the provincial leadership and structures, and they were also supported by a number of homeless people living in shacks. A number of spaza owners in Umlazi G Section were also involved.

A community leader from Ntuzuma, a predominantly working-class township of more than 120.00 people near Kwamashu and Inanda had this to say on the issue of the attacks on foreign shops in mid-April 2015:

> We were aware of the situation regarding the attacks at shops and all these things because we all have families and these things had already started in KwaMashu and other areas. The newspapers did not cover the situation in (Kwa) Mashu with too much detail but the young ones kept in touch with us telling us all the stories from FACEBOOK and other social media and we knew it was coming to us, because those involved in these attacks do not stop until the job is finished as they say. With us it started late after 10 at night and a few neighbours just got out of the churches and saw the crowd running wildly in the area as the news were also coming that they had started in Lindelani, very near us. We did not follow the crowd that started mobbing towards the shops although some of the young ones were very keen. We kept them because we saw that the attacks would create serious problems because the crowd was very determined when they violently attacked foreign shopkeepers and we knew they would spread fast. We have seen enough of these attacks on TV and we knew more or less what was about to happen. There were small and bigger groups between 5 to 10 people carrying knives, sticks, machetes, and stones, but they knew there was no resistance because the shop owners had double locked their shops. This did not stop the crowd from breaking the locks and the other security devices in the shops. Then they entered and they looted, whatever was available there they ripped the places apart and a number of them grabbed refrigerators and double beds. There were also a small number of skirmishes amongst people fighting for some items. There was also a lot of solidarity amongst the looters as a number of shops were very difficult to unlock and there was a need for some expertise amongst the looters. A small number of them utilised their skills to unlock the shops and claimed more that the other. Before the police came, and they came a little late there was a feeling that a number of the attackers wanted to burn down the shops, so a number of arguments begun, but they stopped after the police arrived. The police was firstly successful in stopping those determined to burn the places, one of which included an ATM. This

was their only achievement for the night, as while they tried to stop the attacks, the actions and aggression of the crowds made them run away. They were pelted with stones while the young ones took out their knives. These crowds were joined by more attackers from kwaNdlanzi and moved from one area to another fast because of the expected "competitions" from the surrounding areas. They moved steadily and fast towards more stores, they removed their roofs and continued to loot. There was a large number of women involved in the situation, they were extremely happy, shouting and laughing, grabbing the groceries, vegetables and cool drinks, and while talking to themselves carried them home. Their priorities were flour, soap maize meal and Coca Colas, together with Oros. A number of them had their young children with them as helpers. The young ones seemed very happy as they grabbed small size cool drinks, chips and sweets. As we entered home after one in the morning we heard on the radio that a 15 year old boy was shot dead in KwaNdlanzi, near us. Three bullets.

A senior police officer had this to say about his experiences in the areas around Kwa Mashu in mid-April 2015:

We were trying to survive the terrible happenings in KwaMashu in April when we received a phone call at around 10 at night from a friend in Lindelani calling us to drive there immediately because a big crown was attacking Somalis and other foreigners' shops and looting them. He said a member of the Ward Committee tried to pacify them but they also attacked him and chased him away. He called the Police to come fast because the situation was really dangerous for the foreign shop keepers, but also for the residents because foreign shop keepers had guns. Seven of us moved fast towards the place. When we arrived and tried to talk to the attackers they begun stoning us from a distance. They did not move against us because we were carrying our guns. I took the microphone and notified them that we were on high alert, we do not condone and will not allow attacks on shops or people, that we have been successful in our efforts in Isipingo and Umlazi against criminals and we have the clear support of the tactical response teams and the Public Order Police National Intervention Unit. We told them that we had arrested many attackers in Umlazi, Chatworth and Ntuzuma and there were at least five deaths of both South Africans and foreigners. We told them to disperse, otherwise we would be forced to do our duty and arrest them. They continued to loot. When we moved at them they started throwing stones at us and started running after us. There was a mass of looters. We were few. We were ordered by the superiors to leave the place, join the colleagues at the station and expect new orders.

There was an outcry from the administrative and political leadership (mostly from the ruling party, the African National Congress [ANC]) who blamed "covert forces" as being behind the violent attacks against the foreign nationals. Such serious allegations were leveled against the opposition political parties, civil society groups, Non-Governmental Organisations (NGOs), church leaders and affluent individual business people who rejected such spurious accusations outright. One of the members of a prominent civil society group that has worked with both victims and alleged perpetrators of violence believed that:

> there is no third force. There are no opportunities but only problems and challenges because many of the attitudes and the ideas of the poor will not change, because they see the foreigners as chancers, criminals, foreigners and all these things. They don't see them as human beings like us; many have resided in our communities for more than 10 years; some possess the work permits and are married to local women. But then there are the realities of life: there is no housing and jobs for young and old people; this is a challenge, the foreigners with money buy these houses.

The above was also confirmed by a social activist who felt that "[in] my experience as an activist in this community and the surrounding areas, the only third force I have observed is the government and its agencies."

The government officials felt that the rights of the immigrants in South Africa had been violated by South African citizens and their leaders. A senior policy specialist in the KwaZulu-Natal provincial government had this to say:

> It is a very complicated problem for many reasons, but on the other hand the whole issue is one associated with human rights in respect of the refugees and the immigrants. On many occasions it has been accepted that things have [got out of] control although they should not have. The reality is that there has been a historical prejudice against refugees and African immigrants in general based on the perceptions that "they steal jobs," "they open shops," "they promote crime," "they bring diseases," all these things. When these real or perceived facts become repetitive over the years they become a part of the culture, they become culture [itself]. It will recur again, no doubt. It is embedded. This culture is basically created because of the nature and processes through which the country's economy has developed since 1994; it is the result of a push–pull factor: creating a culture of intolerance and hatred.

This policy analyst further analyzed the realties, saying:

> This culture embedded in people makes South African see foreigners as "aliens" [and] "runaway competitors." This means that the only way for this culture to change is what has been described for

years as "radical economic transformation" of the economy, [the] redistribution of wealth, massive job creation and growth through redistribution [and] no fiscal discipline on behalf of capital. The Home Affairs Department needs to take urgent steps for the benefit of refugees and immigrants that will start with the closure of Lindela or [the] continuous improvement of the conditions of the people there. It is crucial to have progressive rules and regulations for refugees especially; they must be treated like fellow human beings according to the laws of the country and our Constitution. It is important that economic refugees should be separated from war refugees and the latter must be treated with respect and be accommodated, in accordance with African humanity and international treaties.

The provincial government officials who normally conduct surveys in communities relating to their quality of life noticeably linked such attacks to the socio-economic inequalities in the country. The director of the National Disaster Management Centre held the following view:

I think that in a nutshell this problem is going to keep recurring as long as the deep-rooted socio-economic problem is not addressed adequately. These things are there and people are frustrated by many realities that do not allow people to compete for opportunities and jobs [in] the market. Even the grandmother who has been waiting for an RDP house and wheelchair, while given a double story of promises, knows and understands that selling RDP houses or renting to a foreigner will create tensions amongst the locals.

A young person who was forced to leave university for financial reasons, now a community activist, who studied media and communications some years ago, and keeps notes of what is happening in his community (KwaNdengezi) observed the following concerning the xenophobic attacks in the area:

The majority of the foreign nationals who were targeted at KwaNdengezi and the surrounding informal settlements were Zimbabweans and Mozambicans. They were mostly targeted by the youth made up of 10–15 who were armed with rocks, knives, and baseball bats. It was also clear that almost all the attackers were unemployed youth who do not have any skill or post-secondary education. I have also noticed that the perpetrators were influenced by alcohol and drugs as well as boredom [which] can be linked to their haphazard actions. I have noticed a total of eight attacks against the foreign nationals; the majority of the attacks took place after the service delivery-orientated meetings. When listening [to] the attackers' grievances, it included [the fact] that the foreign nationals were romantically involved with their women and

> stealing their jobs and that they [the immigrants] were involved in criminal activities including [the] stealing of the electric cables. These attacks had criminal elements as the foreign nationals' cellular phones and money were stolen by the perpetrators. What was disturbing was the police's reactive approach ... the whole episode has taken place even though they [impending incidents of violence] have been reported beforehand [regarding] looming attacks against the foreign nationals.

One of the key people behind these attacks according to the interviewee is Paul Mkhize, a "known gangster" "operating" in cable theft, burglaries, car-jacking and other offenses. Mkhize's relationships with young township people are well known and he is able to use and/or abuse existing "skills" and then drop those involved, safeguarding himself. There are many young people in the township who have been involved in relatively small criminal acts who are prepared to work with people like Mkhize, although they are aware that he is wanted by SAPS. Mkhize is allegedly protected by the KwaNdengezi police. A group of between 10 and 12 young people with branches, sticks and knives have at least 3 times attacked Malawian and Zimbabwean drug dealers in the area, leaving them beaten and bleeding after stealing their "merchandise" and everything they had, including their shoes. Some of these groups of young people have been involved with Sbu Papale, one of the most sought-after criminals in KwaNdengezi who has apparently been arrested by the SAPS and is awaiting trial. He has been involved in a series of criminal acts including theft, burglaries, car-jacking, murder and rape. He operates with gangs of between 5 and 12 people at a time, and it has been reported that he has criminal networks with over 30 young people who have helped him in his endeavors. He is known to pick and choose young people who are prepared to commit crime.

A community development practitioner from the eThekwini Municipality touched on a number of issues which can be considered to be the root causes. He said:

> It started in Isipingo and it was a labour dispute between employees and a business owner. The employer expelled South African labourers and replaced them with the foreigners. Communities were not happy with service delivery and there were elements of criminality that attacked, vandalised and stole from the foreigners' shops. There [are] a lot of complaints levelled against these foreigners, including selling drugs, killing for muti (*traditional medicine*) and stealing of girls and jobs. On the other hand, there are township residents who prefer and allow foreigners to rent their tuck shops instead of locals because South Africans do not pay them the rentals. They prefer the foreigners although they know they are stealing business from the locals, but they pay the rent, their prices are low and more affordable, and they sell expired milk, cheese, yoghurt [and] even meat in the fridges.

The community activist in the hotspot areas observed new tactics that were not used in the previous attacks. The activist said that what was really of interest was the fact that the attackers wore balaclavas, something that was never witnessed before. A member of the security agencies, which were active in planning and coordinating their operations, provided an overall picture of the situation and the reasons the perception was created. He said:

> It is too late to start pointing fingers [at who] is responsible, but we must start absorbing the lessons; when it starts somewhere, it spreads, there is no middle road. These attacks are in many ways coordinated in one way or another, if you look at 2008, 2011, 2015, the patterns could be a little bit different, but not much. It starts here, it moves there, there are sparks beginning [which then] start fires, that's how it goes. eThekwini in that period was bad, but for one reason or another there were wrong news and perceptions that the violence really took place in one or two places, and these stories guided and [were] fuelled by the press and the social media. There were a number of different areas within the municipality's boundaries that faced many attacks on a large number of foreign nationals. These attacks were carried out for days and nights and they only came under control and calmed down because of the coordinated effort of the following: local, provincial and national government intervention, the police, COGTA [the Department of Cooperative Governance and Traditional Affairs], Home Affairs, [the] Department of Social Development and the disaster management staff . Then they [the xenophobic attacks] became sporadic in some areas and these incidents left new scars and fears in the lives of foreign nationals, many of who[m] were even prepared to die to save what they had, as they told us.

The eThekwini Municipality coordinator who was in charge of the overall operation at one stage provided a brief description of the attacks in Umlazi as it seemed to be the most affected area. This respondent indicated that:

> it was bad in Umlazi, worse than other areas, for many reasons; one of them was based on the in-fighting between local and foreign spazas. The attacks were mainly in the most affected areas/sections (D, J, G, K, T and W). Most of the attacks and retaliation took place at night so the attackers could use the dark to avoid and escape the police.

The government officials held the view that a research-based analysis, conducted to find ways to uproot the causes of the xenophobic attacks and the basic issues, would be helpful, but it came back empty-hand, it did not reveal much. It was stated by a member of the Provincial Joint Operational and Intelligence Structures (**PROVJOINTS**) that:

this was a key issue that surfaced ... there were a number of things that were said and analysed as this was not the first time that such things happened in KZN and the whole country; they started in 2008 and before, then in 2011 and some other times, they come and go and create serious problems time and again; they make us enemies with [our] African brothers and sisters, all these things. The analysis and questions raised and responses were based on all sorts of sources: national intelligence, police intelligence, community informers, politicians with contacts, NGOs [and] community leaders who know their people and are trusted [and who] came up with new and old ideas, some of which have been known and repeated by different sources over the place for years and they are spread passing as the true situation on the ground . Things however change fast. [The] key issue that came is [a] lack of service delivery, especially in informal settlements where there is sometimes no water, electricity, etc., while the foreigners buy RDP houses from locals [and] rent houses in the townships because they have money. It is a type of resentment, jealousy, competition [over] money, resources, jobs and job opportunities. [There is] business competition between South Africans and foreigners, competition amongst foreigners themselves, for example Pakistani business owners taking each other hostage for ransom ... they attack each other; it is known that foreigners are involved in criminal activities, selling drugs, [trading] and sell[ing] stolen commodities; [they] have their own hit squads and groups. State authorities are also to blame as the municipality has failed to regulate the registration of existing businesses, the same with SARS, but this is not only for foreigners, [it is] also for the local spazas at local government level. When this is tried, on the other hand, the officials are sorted out with bribes and protection money both to foreign gang leaders [and] state organs in authority. The media according to our analysis played a serious role in this behaviour, especially after [it] was thought on our side to be a complete misrepresentation of that speech made by King Goodwill Zwelithini. It was felt that such misrepresentation provided an alibi for the SA attackers to attack and it was in other words exploited by them, [giving them a reason] to attack. There was also [the] spreading of misinformation on social media that incited especially youths to attack.

## Competition Among Foreign Nationals

There are a number of diverse factors which have been linked to the causes of xenophobia by government officials, politicians, scholars, civil society groups and community leaders. This has been clearly articulated by a senior member in the KwaZulu-Natal Provincial Government, who stated that research has shown that the majority of foreigners are not criminals, although a significant minority are.

Community activists and civil society groups that have been active for many years in the hotspots of the attacks held different viewpoints on the causes of the xenophobia. This was explained by a senior member of civil society who has many years of experience of issues directly related to refugees and immigrant services nationally and in KwaZulu-Natal. The respondent said this:

> It is extremely difficult to answer quite a number of deep questions [on] the causes and effects of xenophobia throughout the country, but there is a feeling that there is an agenda amongst state officials to hide their inadequacies behind a number of theories regarding foreigners [but the] theories and facts contradict themselves on most occasions. It is known that there have been internal contradictions amongst state agencies and internal conflict for a number of reasons, such as territory, objectives and modes of operation, amongst others. There are also contradictions and conflicts amongst business people in a number of foreign groups within the same communities. This we have heard here for a number of years, but this is not known; Ethiopians for example are considered successful business people, and they are hard-working and [have their businesses] open 24/7. On many occasions there is in-fighting and competition that lead to fights and attacks as some of them hire some local crooks and small-time gangsters to attack the "competition shops." This turns into [an] opportunity for looting, as happened yesterday in Quarry Heights, an attack that was completely ignored by the newspapers. It lasted between four [and] five hours. Then there is no proper scrutiny of the newcomers who are friends or relatives of the business people who have "connections" in the [Department of] Home Affairs and its various branches and it becomes fairly easy to get documents. Not all of the newcomers are hard-working, honest people and a number of them are used as "security," both amongst Ethiopians and Somalis. Ethiopian and Somali shops mainly are becoming easy targets because they are open 24/7 and on many occasions they become victims because when people in the townships see new people running the shops, they see it as an opportunity to steal or attack. This [is] because a number of foreigners who run shops (both Somalis and Ethiopians) run more than one shop and import young people, relatives, neighbours, friends ... they make them work for very little money until they "find their feet" so to say.

Pointing out a number of other important aspects of life and work that shape sentiments, life, actions and behavior of different social groups the senior civil society activist who has lived the foreign immigrants and refugees day to day challenges painted a bleak picture on the exploitation of illegal immigrants by shop owners throughout Durban. This is what was said:

Many of these young people who work in the shops come as refugees and as they are basically illegal it is easier for the business people to exploit them. When in 2015 the refugees, mainly from Ethiopia and Somalia, tried to establish a refugee community association to protect themselves, there was animosity between the initiators and the local "community leaders" because the refugees were clear that many of them were exploited by the shop owners who ... bribed Home Affairs officials when they brought their wives or relatives to South Africa. The major problem amongst these communities is that on many occasions there are internal power struggles and this became more evident during the 2008 and 2015 attacks when refugees were displaced ... many of them went to the camps to be relocated.

One of the community activists who was interviewed shared similar sentiments indicating that illegal businesses plying their trade in the Durban townships were partly behind the scourge of xenophobic attacks against foreign nationals who have been for years in an array of illegal businesses including the involvement in the theft of electrical cables and water pipes. Such realities, it was said, provided a watertight scenario of the failure of the eThekwini Municipality and SAPS to solve the electricity and water theft by both locals and foreign nationals. The community activist based in the Clermont Township had this to say:

The foreign nationals are said to be very skilful in conducting illegal connections of water and electricity and outsmart the locals, a fact that leads to jealousy. There was competition on the lucrative business which has exacerbated the divisions between the warring factions (foreigners and the locals) and the thugs were paying the protection fees to the police and other municipal officials. The eThekwini Municipality officials who were commissioned to prevent and act on the increase [of] stealing of the municipal property, including the electric cables, were violently attacked by local communities who benefit from the illegal electricity connections. The illegal electricity connections is at the extreme level in the disadvantaged communities and the eThekwini Municipality electricity departments are called [on] daily to install new cables.

## Criminal Ethos of the Xenophobic Attacks

### *Criminal Activities Fueling Xenophobic Violence and the Role of SAPS*

The key member of a civil society group who observed the emergence of the attacks as it is an integral part of her job mentioned that the refugees who witnessed them were adamant that:

when the attacks started, there were crowds that attacked and started destroying tuck shops owned by foreigners. The looting pulled people together and a number of young people participating were very eager to speak to one or two journalists to tell them that all these things happened because immigrants were responsible for the violence and that the people just retaliated.

There were unproven allegations leveled against foreign nationals, leading to the xenophobic attacks of 2015. Some of the allegations, however, were disputed by government officials. As the senior policy member of the provincial government said:

> there are very strong perceptions that crime is mostly perpetrated by refugees and immigrants, but this is not true; crime is perpetrated by both South Africans and the refugee and immigrant groups. Research has shown that the reality is that the majority of foreigners are not criminals, but a significant minority are criminals. This is the result of the lack of legitimate opportunities that exist in the country, the lack of jobs – even menial ones – for them to [do] ... hence they turn to crime to make a living, [as] they have no other alternative. Crime like drugs, prostitution, etc. in many ways prompt South Africans to attack foreigners because they affect them and their communities.

It was clear from the interviews conducted in the present study that the alleged criminals were supported by local communities who were the beneficiaries of such criminal acts. The interviewed community leader clearly indicated that local residents regularly seek the services of the gangs who perform illegal activities in the township for a number of reasons when he said:

> Foreigners live in nearby informal settlements. The main reasons for the conflict have been electricity cuts because of cable theft as well as the real fear of crime which, according to them, is basically committed by foreigners. On the other hand, there is an almost chronic problem of the area's residents. Throughout mid-October 2011, there were attacks on Zimbabwean casual workers doing renovations or extensions to a number of houses in the area ... the attackers were young unemployed people who attacked the workers, accusing them of stealing cables. When you need help [with] electricity, you know it is the foreigners that will offer [to do it] for a price. If you don't need them, they are easy targets for a/crowd.

### *Xenophobic Violence, Criminality and Armed Groups of Youth*

The security agencies had consistently argued that the attacks against the foreign nationals had criminality undertones. Such a position was basically supported by a police operative who was directly involved in the analysis of the planning of the coordinated attacks who had this to say:

> The attacks in KwaMashu started on the 11th April and the attacks throughout eThekwini now were at a vicious cycle because they were committed and led by criminal elements followed by communities after a few hours. Community members waited [for] the attack to start, just in case the foreigners retaliated with guns, but when this did not happen they moved in and looted whatever was available. Criminal elements capitalised on the existing situation and the gaps and opportunities, and what became very worrying for the authorities was that more and younger people got involved in the violence and looting. A good number of them were armed, especially those from the Umlazi hostels. This created more problems for the police because the youngsters were violent and [the] violence expanded. The state analysts in this case believed that these nationals were not seen as real competitors with the locals in terms of resources such as housing and services. The Isipingo case shows that the locals want the jobs now occupied by Zimbabweans and one can say this is the root of the problem. Then those who want to loot get the opportunity to attack together with the criminals. Then they are joined by community members. There have been community members and business people who have said and strongly believe that all these actions have been organised beforehand, but there is no hope that such beliefs and claims can be confirmed

**Access to Basic Services, Corrupt Government Officials and the Xenophobic Attacks.**   There were SAPS officials who were puzzled by the selective nature and extent of the attacks against the foreign nationals, especially because all those targeted were immigrants and refugees from the African continent. This was explained by the member of the police force who was responsible for dealing with crimes related to xenophobia, who said:

> One of the things that stuck in many people's minds was that all the attacks were against African foreigners and on occasions when things became very hot and ugly, South African nationals [were] also targeted, but Pakistanis, Chinese or Bangladeshi nationals were not targeted. Access to resources, housing and services are key issues, because there are many people in the townships who rent spare rooms and spaces to foreigners, while others live in squatter camps. This creates jealousy and divisions amongst people; hence the bomb attacks against fellow South Africans in Umlazi, KwaMashu and elsewhere.

The municipal official dealing with issues revolving around the small business sector (Business Support Unit) and who dealt directly with the key issues have over the years accumulated information unknown to the public. They have a different and interesting angle in relation to a number of possible new causes of xenophobia. It starts with the reality of foreign nationals owning unregistered spaza shops and operating in close proximity to locals' established, registered businesses, creating competition. Within these existing parameters, the inefficient efforts of state and municipal officials to enforce the by-laws for small businesses have been instrumental in exacerbating the turf wars between these business people. The member of the Business Support Unit had this to say:

> The market for spazas and small business[es] in the townships [is] congested; there is no way that the competition between South Africans and foreigners will end. The situation becomes worse because the competition between foreign small business people becomes very violent on occasions and such things involve Pakistanis, Ethiopians, Zimbabweans, Somalis. For the average person to understand these things are difficult, but we see it every single day throughout the city, the townships and the squatter camps because there are many ways these people operate there are hostage takers, attacks and looting of shops, burning them at nights. While all these things take place the situation becomes worse because the government departments do not function according to the laws of the country and they are a state within a state. Home Affairs gives out permanent residences for a price, the departments dealing with licences, registration even the Receiver of Revenue, the municipality and all its sections have become the big beneficiaries of the foreign shops. Things would be very different and better if all the relevant state institutions played their roles according to the rules, regulations and laws of the country. While SAPS does what [it has] to do, following instructions of the leadership and the relevant authority's instructions, Home Affairs, SARS, etc. [the officials] do not do the jobs they ought to [do].

Government officials at the local level have identified a plethora of factors which have perpetuated tensions between South Africans and foreign nationals. What was noteworthy was the fact that government officials (councilors) were directly and indirectly involved in corrupt activities such as selling government-subsidized (Reconstruction and Development Programme [RDP]) houses to foreign nationals, while indigent locals continued living in the shanty towns without basic needs such as electricity, water or sanitation. Furthermore, the foreign nationals were linked to a number of criminal activities including human and drug trafficking and kidnapping, which has increased anger among local people. This was echoed by the community development practitioner of the Durban Metro who mentioned that:

> [the] key issue that came is [a] lack of service delivery, especially in informal settlements where there is sometimes no water, electricity,

etc., while the foreigners buy RDP houses [and] rent houses in the townships because they have money, it's a type of resentment, jealousy, competition [over] money, resources, jobs and job opportunities. All these realities, however are overtaken by the anger of the local people and especially the small spaza shops when they see how the in-fighting amongst foreigners in their areas have a negative effect on their lives. This because these fights amongst foreigners have become very violent on occasions and have a very negative effect on the lives of the locals. It is not fair to label all foreigners as criminals, but the market is small and very competitive. This means that there is a number of both foreigners and South Africans who are involved in all kinds of illegal actions to survive or become rich. They sell counterfeit cigarettes, alcohol, drugs, and stolen furniture. They have money to hire their own hit men.

## Communication Channels and Xenophobia

While the government officials were satisfied with their own tireless efforts, they were despondent at the divisive printed and electronic information – what they described as "unknown anti-immigrant sources." The media liaison officer who was in the middle of disseminating information about the xenophobic attacks commented as follows:

> There were hundreds of thousands of pamphlets sponsored by the KwaZulu-Natal government and the eThekwini Metro leadership with messages such as "Stop the attacks!," "This is not who we are as a nation," "Every effort is being made to prevent this situation recurring," "Attacks on African immigrants will not be tolerated," "Negative perceptions that African immigrants are using resources meant for South Africans are invalid," "We must not forget the hospitality and support we received from fellow Africans" [and] "We all have a role to play to ensure peaceful co-existence in communities." In what seemed to be a well-coordinated effort, there [were] a number of letters in isiZulu demanding migrants to leave the country immediately. These letters emanated from townships such as KwaMashu, Inanda, Ntuzuma, KwaNyuswa, Ntuzuma and ... Dundee. There was an effort from the police to investigate the sources, [but] without success. The general situation in eThekwini seemed calm, but the tension was evident.

The state apparatus had an issue with what was perceived as the media's bias and their reporting that may have instigated xenophobia. This is despite the fact that the media was updated regularly by relevant government departments and agencies on the action plans dealing with the xenophobic attacks. A senior member of the police force who was also a member of NATJOINTS provided this sad background:

One of the saddest situations the state institutions faced during and after the xenophobic attacks was the complete ignorance of their actions and activities [that were] planned and taking place from the first hour of the attacks till the end of the problem. This, despite the fact that the various arms of the committees and action groups that were created were careful in distributing communications to the press, TV and all media through the legitimate channels available. There were open communication channels with all media, newspapers [and] TV stations, who were made aware [of] who was in charge where, which institutions, all their contact details, etc. What was the latest news [was] basically communicated [to] them in detail with the exception of sensitive, intelligence-driven and collected details; these were kept for the state apparatus.

A number of government officials and the state agencies they represented felt that the foreign nationals who were regarded as the victims of the attacks were complicit in the violence. The government departments and security agencies attempted to provide assistance to immigrants in the form of protection from the South African communities. However, the authorities received resistance and unbecoming attitudes from the foreign nationals. This unhealthy relationship between the foreign nationals and state agencies was confirmed by a police commander who had first-hand experience of such conduct: "Otherwise, all other incidents happened in the townships," he said:

The damages have varied in many ways, and it has been very difficult to collect the correct information for many reasons, because foreigners on many occasions do not want to provide information for damages etc.; they do not trust the police or the government departments.

## Xenophobic Violence, Reactive Media and the Reactive Approaches of Government Communications

The government agencies and the police have always complained about the biased reporting emanating from journalists, who were considered to be complicit in the attacks against foreign nationals. The senior police officer who was on occasions responsible for communication provided this viewpoint:

The newspaper and other social media coverage do not even cover the realities of the situation despite the fact that the police and state departments have very strong communication channels so that the people know what's happening. In the 2015 attacks and events a big number of KZN areas were affected by xenophobia, but the journalists were sleeping. The tensions were there, the attacks were there, but the journalists were sleeping. They wrote about Isipingo while half of Durban was under attack. In fact, the 2015 attacks were not only in Isipingo and parts of Umlazi, as the newspapers continued reporting for days, but spread to KwaMakhutha, Chatsworth, Malukazi, Clare Estate/Sydenham, Greenwood Park, KwaMashu and surrounding areas, and elsewhere and continued for a few weeks. For two to two and half weeks and more, attacks and looting took place and hundreds or even thousands of people were affected: refugees, displaced immigrants and local communities.

## The Effects of Action Plans on the Xenophobic Violence

There were clear indications from stakeholders from all walks of life who indicated that the majorities in the communities were against the attacks on foreign nationals. The government officials who were present in communities observed that even in hotspot areas, a number of the householders spoke out against the barbaric behavior and violent acts against the immigrants. The above sentiments were echoed by a disaster management coordinator in the eThekwini Municipality who said:

> There was a Joint Coordinating Committee, a task team of all the MECs, the premier, the eThekwini leadership, all of them … there was mobilisation in the ward committees [that] wanted to help; some ANC branches which were close to the MECs, all government departments, most church leaders (but not all) played a role in the mobilisation of the people for the march. These came from the president, the premier, national ministers, KZN-based MECs, the mayor and all spokespersons. There were over 10,000 people participating in this march, together with politicians, NGOs, political organisations, representatives of migrants [and] personnel from African and other embassies. It was a peaceful march that started at Curries Fountain and was led by the premier, MECs and many religious leaders. A number of DJs and popular artists participated. The march was well attended by local people and migrants and we all believed that this was a powerful message of solidarity and peace … to all, a very important message of unity, peace and tolerance and strong condemnation of xenophobic violent attacks on foreigners.

## Porous Borders and the Illegal Acquisition of SA Citizenship Through Bribery

The government officials from different departments associated the attacks against the foreign nationals with the porosity of South Africa's borders. A member of the senior provincial government posited that

> the contribution is immense because the borders are unguarded and hence the free flow of immigrants and refugees from all borders. The situation will be worsened in the years to come because it seems that these budgets that are slim will become even slimmer.

The civil society leader with deep knowledge of issues of immigration challenges, and refugee problems provided this background regarding the scramble of foreign nationals to get to South Africa. The official declared:

> We know that this foreigner invasion of RSA started in 1995 when there was great hope for big and good things in South Africa. This made thousands of people from Africa and Asia ... arrive, many through legal means, but most without documents, papers, etc. This happened because people thought things will be better in South Africa, and there will be plenty of opportunities, because the RSA borders are wide open; those people who guard them are bribed; thousands come with tourist visas [and] become permanent residents in a few months because they bribe the Home Affairs officials. This is the reality of the situation, from 1995 onwards.

## Refugee Status and Economic Competition

There was an accepted narrative from other stakeholders, including the media, that the xenophobic attacks were triggered by the economic competition between the two warring groups. The community activist who saw the episodes of the attacks unfolding in Cato Crest in early June observed that:

> for those who have lived in Cato Crest for many years, things are clear. There were a large number of foreign immigrants living in Cato Crest, mainly from Zimbabwe, Mozambique and Somalia. The crowds started with 50 people, mainly young, and more and more people joined [of] all ages, and even from surrounding mjondolos [shacks]. This is strange it seems because Cato Crest is one of the only places [where] immigrants are welcome.

The majority of the government officials interviewed blamed the relevant government departments dealing with the illegal immigrants. The members of the PROVJOINT who has over the years dealt with senior official from the provincial government further insinuated that:

> we are dealing with the symptoms; why are we having so many illegal and undocumented visitors, refugees and immigrants in our country? We are having an open system [at] our border. Some of these questions are 'intelligence' questions and I cannot send you to the SAPS to seek ... such classified information; it will compromise them. There is information and in actual fact there is nothing classified I have said.

The civil society leader who has been dealing with immigrants daily said that:

> the response mechanisms are inadequate and contradictory at all levels. The Green Paper on Immigration talks about free movement,

trade permits, student visa[s] and asylum etc. which are basically progressive, but what really happens is completely different. People who should know the laws do not follow them. You need to know the laws to follow them.

The municipal officials who have been involved for years in improving social cohesion in townships shared different perceptions on the relationship between the locals and the foreign nationals in the region. One of the community mobilizers gave the following perspective:

I don't think that locals hate foreigners, as people benefited from the foreigners ... they get cheap stock [but] there is a small group that has triggered this violence. In some areas, shops were closed and local residents called them [the foreign nationals] back as they cannot afford food sold by South African local business owners as their prices [are] exorbitant.

The civil society leader who has over the years worked and studied both the historical and present conditions that exist spelled out the issues as follows:

Most of these foreigners believe that there are better opportunities for them here and many come as asylum refugees because of persecutions in their own countries. Many have settled in SA and [have] acquired refugee status. The Department of Home Affairs has been very busy all these years dealing with all [the] requests for refugee status and other legal status in SA. These things have created many problems: first there is competition amongst local business and foreigners, and [then] there is competition for resources among local communities and foreigners.

## Impacts of Xenophobic Violence

A SAPS official who was tasked with monitoring and evaluating the effects of the xenophobic attacks provided this picture of the situation on the ground:

The situation was bad and violent and as days went [by] it escalated; a lot of properties were petrol-bombed; this was a new thing because initially there was only looting of spazas and homes when the attacks started. There were foreigners who rented places in South African-owned homes and these [people] were attacked, petrol-bombed, etc. As time passed, the levels of violence increased and there were a number of casualties, mainly because foreigners and South Africans were heavily armed and used petrol bombs, firearms and machetes, and a number of foreign nationals had military training, especially [those] from the DRC ... there was a feeling that they were ready to take on SAPS. Initially it was evident that the attacks were not centrally coordinated and it was mainly various separate incidents that triggered flare-ups, starting with the Isipingo looting. There was evidence that a number of Umlazi SA business owners, helped by SANCO's structures and group of homeless people and spaza shop owners, were involved and some instigators were arrested by SAPS.

An executive member of the eThekwini Municipality who was representing the municipality on the provincial and national task teams dealing with the xenophobic attacks held the following view:

> The first [aim] is the continuous efforts of the attackers to destroy the good name of RSA in Africa and the world; and the second, that the attackers through their actions challenge the peaceful people of the country and the state and government ... [and attack] the authority of [the] state which aims at guaranteeing peace, good life and good human relations to all who live in it . These attackers do not like the foreigners and do not respect the government and its institutions, the police, the army, the laws [and] their fellow citizens who are peaceful and loving. These people do not respect us because they think they will not be arrested.

The eThekwini municipality staff member who was in charge of community social and economic development and was a member of the municipal task team responding to the xenophobic attacks commented as follows on the financial impacts of the events:

> There are serious financial and budget implications because of the destructions of homes, shops [and] infrastructure [and] the setting up of the shelters, and new infrastructure through the widespread violence. There is major displacement and [the] disruption of law enforcement and many other services that allow the UN, UNCHR [the United Nations Commission on Human Rights] and UNICEF [the United Nations International Children's Emergency Fund] to interfere directly and indirectly in South Africa's domestic affairs; it's a threat to social cohesion in the communities, [there is an] increase of the influence of opportunist elements and gangsters [which] disrupts the townships' informal economic development. All these are against the poorest of the poor.

Murray's descriptions of groups in Britain that live in the "fringes of society" because of the high rates of unemployment, poverty, degradation and homelessness lead to the belief that criminally based attacks on relatively vulnerable social groups are inevitable Murray (1996, 2001). Murray's description of frustration of both young and middle-aged males who cannot find and "hold on to" a job bears many similarities to the South African conditions. In Murray's analysis of

Britain, there were three interlocking realities of crime, illegitimacy and idleness and the periodization of such social phenomena throughout the years has shown that in periods of social and economic crisis their increases lead to social upheaval and even turmoil. Such situations became very visible in the 1950s and 1960s, and increased dramatically in the late 1970s and after, with thousands of illegitimate children being born in the poorest areas where social problems and challenges multiplied substantially. These problems existed for years among the poorest sectors of the population, with levels of unemployment increasing despite the benefit systems introduced by the Labor government. Poverty and illegitimacy, according to Murray, led to individual and collective violence as well as to an increase in violent behavior of the poor and the marginalized. The absence of fathers has exacerbated the problem and resulted in an increase in the already high levels of frustration that led to aggression and violence at a number of levels, in terms of both self-defence and attack. Such social realities resulted in the prevalence of crime in many areas where poor, unemployed and young people lived, with crime increasing, mainly because the possibility of being arrested was slim (Murray, 1996, 2001).

Inevitably, individuals and groups are concerned with their own needs, which in South Africa take many different forms, especially in the poor urban areas that face communal, economic and social restraints. Existing needs and the repression of impulses could easily frustrate an individual or a group on occasion, leading to hostility and aggression against individuals, groups or communities of people who are seen as the cause of that frustration (Montagu, 1973). In an analysis of the functions and forms of prejudice, Wurzel (1986) wrote that people hold and perpetrate prejudicial attitudes that lead to aggression which seeks to gain certain rewards. At the same time, such people perceive the victims of the aggression to be a threat to their way of life, security and social norms. The aggression, then, targets people who challenge their values and threaten their possibilities and opportunities. On many occasions these are in fact imaginary threats. Such processes are the foundations of scapegoating, which targets people who appear to be a threat and focuses on specific individuals, populations or communities (Wurzel, 1986). All of the above, or most of these aspects, are evident in the findings in terms of the empirical realities and analyses at a number of levels, although there are other truths evident that pinpoint the causes of the actions and behaviors of xenophobic attacks.

There was general agreement that the spark of the widespread attacks began after a labor dispute and strike at an Isipingo shop against foreigners being employed. This continued with the looting of foreign-owned shops in the vicinity and in nearby Umlazi. Despite the fact that there was evidence that at the initial stages the attacks were planned and coordinated, it very soon transformed into a collective action against a group of "others," that is, "foreigners" and "criminals." Throughout this period, the attacking crowds were not a "third force" but groups of people who decided to loot and destroy. These peoples' social situation, a repercussion of the continuing social and economic situation in the country, has led to a condition of intolerance. Every human being aspires to fulfill desires and ambitions, and has goals in life. Nonetheless, on many occasions the dreams associated with these desires are not fulfilled, leading to frustration which can often (but not always) lead to anger. However, as events unfold internationally, even before the devastation of the coronavirus pandemic, the signs of increasing poverty and relative or expanded deprivation in the developing and underdeveloped world became evident. This means that the social and economic "gaps" created because of a lack of improvement and progress of the marginalized and the poor, the expectations of satisfying everyday wants provides impetus to already existing frustrations. This can lead to attacks and violence on vulnerable groups, as Davies (1973, p. 247) has conclusively shown. Deprivation is relative, therefore, to previous gratifications and expectations.

Social and economic inequality has been acknowledged as being one of the causes of xenophobic attacks as they are seen and described as the roots of boredom, alcoholism and drug abuse among most sectors of the population, both in formal urban areas and in informal settlements, especially among the youth. The attacks by youths described in at least one instance have been aggressive and led by well-known criminal elements in the planning and execution. This shows a different angle of aggression and scapegoating, most likely because a good number of the attacks not only target small-time shopkeepers, but also foreign drug dealers who are known to be protected by the local police station personnel. The existence of well-organized criminal gangs and criminal networks (consisting of more than 30 young people in one area alone) is somehow different, because it is directly related to a perpetual capacity for aggression and/or looting and violence. This is true because crowds that are frustrated do not necessarily become violent, unlike "professional" criminals (Gurr, 1970, pp. 36–37). Within this context the recorded and seemingly well-coordinated effort of "unknown persons" or organizations mentioned earlier that distributed penned letters in a wide array of Durban areas such as Inanda, Ntuzuma, KwaNyuswa and even Dundee and demanded the immediate expulsion of migrants from the country as indicated earlier poses a number of serious questions to a number of state organizations and state apparatuses at all levels. This because such initiatives can easily lead to fresh xenophobic attacks in such local areas and surrounding communities as it occurred during the 2015 attack that begun in Isipingo but expanded almost immediately. The mere fact that such propagandist letters were described as being the "people's response" to the tens of thousands of the KwaZulu-Natal Provincial Government and the eThekwini Municipality pamphlets pleading for the immediate halt of the attacks and peaceful co-existence with fellow Africans at all levels pinpoints the challenges ahead for the state institutions.

The fact that there are South African township residents who have close relations with foreigners does not change the picture radically because immigrants pay citizens for their affordable rent and in the end they might even become the victims of the "scapegoat realities." The wearing of balaclavas could possibly signify a new, more systematic criminal aggression and coordination in terms of attacks, as do the continuity of the Durban 2015 incidents, which continued throughout the day in a number of locations until a decisive and planned response from the police. The fact that most attacks continued in Umlazi, a geographically expanded suburb that suffered extensively especially at night, also pinpoints the clear possibility of well-planned aggression. The same pattern was followed in the

KwaMashu attacks that began a few days after the widespread incidents. It was the well-armed gangs that began the onslaught and were subsequently joined by the crowds. A significant number of armed Umlazi hostel residents who led the KwaMashu crowds on their rampage highlighted the role of criminal elements in the processes of destroying and looting.

There are clear empirical truths in this adventurous undertaking that completely negate both the theoretical frames of reference and hypotheses attached to scapegoating and the frustration–aggression landscape. The selective nature and extent of the xenophobic attacks are planned and executed mostly, if not exclusively, against immigrants and refugees from the African continent – mainly traders. This reality must be borne in mind, together with the fact that group- or community-based xenophobic attacks have not taken place against Asian groups such as Chinese, Bangladeshi or Pakistani nationals. This points to two alternative explanations vis-à-vis the hypothesis of the frustration–aggression and the scapegoating theories: the first one is that both these theories are only directed at one targeted group (i.e., Africans). The second is that a new reality, even a theory, can be advanced, but not found in empirical or theoretical literature that is sociological, historical, criminological or psychological in nature. This premise is that scapegoating can be a "selective" action of small, large or community groups irrespective of their economic, political or social circumstances and/or material conditions.

The latter part of the assessment is important because it is been evident that Asian businesses, including the massive Chinese operations throughout the country, including Durban, do not use different "underground" operations from those of their poorer African counterparts in terms of their relations with SARS, the Department of Home Affairs, SAPS and other state institutions. These are everyday, medium- and long-term challenges regarding registration, taxes, by-laws and operations relevant to all businesses, including the informal sector and landscape. The empirical reality of the perpetual conflict among business people belonging to the same or different African groups in this case is also a negation of the theoretical hypotheses set at the beginning of the attacks and the different dimensions of xenophobic attacks. The "business collaboration" between foreign business people and local gangsters is of significance, as is confirmed and corroborated by information from foreign business people and/or their local "mediators." Such people are instrumental in "organizing" a wide array of documents from state institutions such as the Department of Home Affairs. The existence of "local intelligence" – i.e., local people keeping an eye on mainly Somali and Ethiopian shops and their daily operating hours – makes attacks more "calculated" and planned. The existing and widely accepted animosity among locally based foreign immigrant leaders is generally directly related to existing business competition.

Within this context, there is a strong and widespread belief that economic competition between small local businesses and foreign nationals is one of the key causes of the xenophobic attacks. This is highly questionable and the examples provided by the interviewees are real and tangible, but cannot answer the question of why these mass attacks target African-owned shops while the small Asian enterprises are left unscathed. It is true that the competition between South African and African small traders is real, but so is the rivalry with their Asian counterparts. One must bear in mind that most of the time the prices of African traders are cheaper compared to the South African stores, but this is said to be an insufficient reason for the attacks.

Another issue that poses serious questions to the theoretical hypotheses under consideration is the reality of the contradictory relationships associated with cable theft and illegal electricity connections. It is a seriously under-researched issue that has over the years led to a perpetual conflict between local and African perpetrators. A little-known fact is that illegal electricity connections do not exist in only informal settlements, but also in large parts of established suburbs inhabited by working and/or middle-class people. This tends to occur with people who have financial difficulties, a situation which has been exacerbated over the last 12 months. It is a well-known fact that African foreigners are considered more skilful in this art, which creates two groups of people in the operational areas: the competitors and the poor and middle-class families who benefit from the illegal connections. These individuals pay nominal and/or affordable prices to mainly Mozambican and Zimbabwean operators who install the illegal connections. This situation, both in informal settlements and suburban areas, creates social alliances between the poor and the illegal electricity connection masters who are also the enemies of their South African competitors and small-time criminals. There have been enough reported attacks on foreign nationals by individuals or groups both inside and outside informal settlements.

The existing material conditions of the population in the areas where the 2015 attacks took place were described as being instrumental in the creation of frustration–aggression and scapegoating processes and acts. There is evidence of the complete ignorance of mass media as it relates to the actions and activities of the state, despite the fact that there was continuous, hourly communication to all existing media channels. The responses from government were planned and implemented in an effort to stop the attacks and create an environment leading to either peaceful repatriation or well-planned reintegration into communities. The government appeals and efforts were ignored in most cases with the exception of the well-attended, anti-xenophobic march in the Durban CBD, which attracted over 10,000 people. The statement that "they [the journalists] wrote about the attacks and looting in Isipingo while half of Durban was under attack" was not an exaggeration of the prevailing situation. There were recorded attacks and looting taking place in at least eight areas in and around Durban that continued for several weeks, with the resulting displacement of thousands of people in those areas.

There is no doubt that the more empirical research continues to be conducted in response to periods of xenophobic violence in South African urban areas, the more realities and truths will be unveiled. It has been said that history is always written by the victors, but the truth is that in most, if not all, cases throughout the history of humanity there is no victor in war. Alexander the Great and Napoleon were considered the victors of many wars, but no historian would dare claim that their dying was a "final victory."

The more historical and deep research takes place on xenophobia, the more questions and answers will emerge because all elements that make or break a society are present: real and fake humanity; humanism; class- and inter-continental

struggles; existing theories and empirical findings; state and community contradictions and alliances; economic, financial and social dynamics; compromises and
rejections; love, honesty and dishonesty; and building and destroying. The catalogue is as vast and as wide as life and death combined.

The methods used to collect information are always a puzzle, not only for new
researchers but also for well-trained and experienced ones. Even a case as simple
as a death due to a municipal mayor's car tyre bursting could be as complicated as
the municipal mayor's Mercedes Benz being destroyed by a 10-tonne truck along
the semi-rural N2. New dimensions of xenophobia and Afro-phobia are in need
of research because only then can the relevant authorities plan and implement
strategies and tactics that are based on a deep understanding of the foundation,
roots and triggers of xenophobia. This should not only be based on historical,
sociological, psychological, geographical or anthropological angles, but also
from an analysis of the real material conditions of the urban terrains that are
instrumental in shaping behaviors and actions. It is critical to fill the existing gaps
in deep research, analysis, dissection and absorption of the real dimensions of
xenophobia, analyzing the historical role of all key actors. If this doesn't happen,
the possibility of repeated xenophobic violence is likely, just waiting around the
corner the same way wild rabbits wait patiently for the Kentucky Fried Chicken
workers to throw the potato peels into the massive red bins.

Real, hard-core, authentic, empirical factors regarding both the massive and
sporadic xenophobic attacks throughout the country are still missing, but it is
understood that the other problems and challenges facing our country currently
could be regarded as more urgent. Individual foreigners continue to be targeted,
attacked and victimized. And on many occasions they retaliate. Petty and organized criminals throughout the country become perpetrators unless they create
alliances with well-connected politicians, administrators or entrepreneurs and
take advantage of existing tender opportunities. The competition between small
businesses owned by South Africans and by foreign nationals has not ceased and
the same is true of the rivalry among foreigners themselves.

The South African borders are still wide open to migrants, refugees and those
seeking to escape undemocratic regimes. There are differences in opinion regarding the modus operandi, strategies and tactics of the attackers, and the role and
energy, planning and tactics of the state institutions at all levels. Such realities
are in both the center and the peripheries of behavior and activities. Are all
these attacks well-coordinated, strategically planned and executed? Or are they
the result of hatred, resentment, or anger against the state, society at large or
migrants and refugees, even while Chinese shopping centers and Pakistani restaurants continue to operate? And what about the vulnerable South Africans in communities who try to make a living by letting their houses and rooms to foreigners?

There were visible differences and similarities in the well-researched efforts
relating to the violent xenophobic attacks of 2008 and 2015. Our own empirical
work has studied and analyzed most of this research in our published work, with
emphasis on the modus operandi; symptoms; realities on the ground; political
interventions; instigation and mobilization of a wide variety of social groups; and
anti-immigrant and inflammatory rhetoric from various social figures. The present

work seeks to go deeper into untouched areas and realities, including the role of the media and their discourses of falsifications and denialism. We seek to examine the underlying causes and dimensions of the 2015 xenophobic violence in Durban, which is only remembered through essentially anecdotal and impressionistic narrations. Specifically, we aim to explore and analyze the existing causes of the xenophobic atrocities that occurred, through comprehensive interviews with stakeholders who were directly involved before, during and after the attacks.

It is only time, history and the people who are the judges of this effort.

## References

Adebisi, A.P. 2017. Xenophobia: healing a festering sore in Nigerian–South African relations, *Journal of International Relations and Foreign Policy*, 5(1), 83–92.

Anderson, C.A. and Bushman, B.J. 2002. Human aggression, *Annual Review of Psychology*, 53(1), 27–51.

Beetar, M. 2019. A contextualisation of the 2008 and 2015 xenophobic attacks: tracing South African necropolitics, *Current Sociology*, 67(1), 122–140.

Bornman, J. 2019. Alarming surge in xenophobic language, *Mail & Guardian*, August 6. Available at: https://mg.co.za/article/2019-08-06-alarming-surge-in-xenophobic-language [Accessed 17 August 2020].

Breuer, J. and Elson, M. 2016. *The Frustration–Aggression Hypothesis According to Berkowitz (1989)*. doi:10.6084/m9.figshare.4224270.v2

Breuer, J. and Elson, M. 2017. Frustration–aggression theory. In *The Wiley Handbook of Violence and Aggression*, pp. 1–12, New York, American Cancer Society. doi:10.1002/9781119057574.whbva040

Dauda, M., Sakariyau, R.T. and Ameen, A. 2018. Xenophobic violence in South Africa and the Nigerians' victimization: an empirical analysis, *Pertanika Journal of Social Sciences & Humanities*, 26(4), 2677–2700.

Davies, J. 1973. Aggression, violence, revolution, and war. In *Handbook of Political Psychology*, Ed. J.N. Knutson, pp. 234–260, San Francisco, CA, Jossey-Bass.

Deutsch, M. 1993. Educating for a peaceful world, *American Psychologist*, 48(5), 510–517. doi:10.1037/0003-066X.48.5.510 [Accessed 13 March 1997].

Enders, S. 2018. *Scapegoat Theory: Shifting Blame and Displacing Aggression*. Available at: https://cdn.websiteeditor.net/ff826d98c3824defa40776de2b015c4d/files/uploaded/EndersScapegoating.pdf [Accessed 16 August 2020].

Foucault, M. 1988. *Madness and Civilization: A History of Insanity in the Age of Reason*, New York, NY, Random House.

Friedman, H.S. and Schustack, M.W. 2014. *Personality: Classic Theories and Modern Research*, 5th ed., pp. 204–207, Boston, MA, Pearson.

Gurr, T.R. 1970. *Why Men Rebel*, Princeton, NJ, Princeton University Press.

Hågensen, L. and De Jager, N. 2016. Xenophobic attacks in South Africa: the case of De Doorns 2009, *Strategic Review for Southern Africa*, 38(1), 107.

Hendricks, N. and Mati, S. 2020. Counteracting Xenophobia in South Africa through popular education, *New Directions for Adult and Continuing Education*, 2020(165), 49–61.

Linville, P.W., Fischer, G.W. and Salovey, P. 1989. Perceived distributions of the characteristics of in-group and out-group members: empirical evidence and a computer simulation, *Journal of Personality and Social Psychology*, 57, 165–188.

Mensah, S.N. and Benedict, E.E. 2016. Managing root causes and effects of xenophobic attacks in South Africa: a relative deprivation approach, *Journal of Contemporary Management*, 5(4), 68–82.

Misago, J.P. 2019. Political mobilisation as the trigger of xenophobic violence in post-apartheid South Africa, *International Journal of Conflict and Violence (IJCV)*, 13, a646.

Mojisola, A.O. 2019. Xenophobic attacks and its implication on human resource management, *Afro Asian Journal of Social Sciences X*, III, 1–11.

Montagu, A. 1973. *Man and Aggression*, 2nd ed., New York, NY, Oxford University Press.

Murray, C. 1996. *Charles Murray and the Underclass: The Developing Debate*, London, IEA Health and Welfare Unit.

Murray, C. 2001. *Underclass + 10*, London, Civitas.

Piper, L. and Charman, A. 2016. Xenophobia, price competition and violence in the spaza sector in South Africa, *African Human Mobility Review*, 2(1), 332–362.

Rasila, B.N. and Musitha, E.M. 2016. The lack of effective communication influences xenophobic attacks in South Africa, *Journal of Education, Society and Behavioural Science*. Available at: https://www.semanticscholar.org/paper/The-Lack-of-Effective-Communication-Influences-in-Rasila-Musitha/572260ff81da0e1594b3a59d587e097 e7bf045f2 [Accessed 12 March 2017].

Wurzel, J. 1986. The functions and forms of prejudice. In *A World of Difference: Resource Guide for Reduction of Prejudice*, Boston, MA, Anti-Defamation League of B'nai B'rith and Facing History and Ourselves National Foundation.

Chapter Three

# Xenophobia, Media and the "Forgotten Dimensions"

Perceptions regarding xenophobia and the media's falsified, adverse, biased reporting on xenophobia in Durban will be the major theme of this chapter. Xenophobic populism by politicians and traditional leaders will also be dissected. In addition, xenophobic factors and dimensions that have been overlooked by government agencies and the media will feature in this chapter. The viewpoints of a number of informants who have been directly involved before, during and after the xenophobic attacks will be presented and analyzed, including government officials, media reporters and members of civil society groups.

Researchers' practical knowledge and experiences will be shared by following ethnographic principles. Furthermore, print and electronic media articles will be analyzed to ascertain the tone of reporting during the 2015 xenophobic attacks in Durban. This chapter depicts the extent to which the rhetoric and inflammatory and negative tone of reporting by media platforms contributed to the xenophobic attacks in the city. A significant contribution can be made to the study on xenophobia and the media by tapping into overlooked methods and targeting the existing literature. This chapter further touches on the hotspots that have not been empirically researched thus far, a fact which challenges the current status quo and could influence future researchers to seek further interrogation of realities.

The print media has shared narratives of attacks on foreign nationals which have been inconsiderate, negative and anti-immigrant. This has resulted in aggravating the ferocious tensions and supporting certain ideologies which are anti-government. In their reporting, media houses have communicated toxic information to the public and propagated divisive ideologies and discourses through their shallow analyses, thus arming these warring factions and instigating them to attack one another. It has been observed that destitute young locals, foreign black men and other designated groups have been victimized by such incidents, especially since the South African Government has inadequate contingency plans in place to proactively respond to xenophobia. The government has reacted to avoid, prevent, prepare, mitigate, respond to and recover from the effects of the xenophobic violence, and to rehabilitate and reconstruct those communities that have suffered from the catastrophe.

Addressing Xenophobia in South Africa:
Drivers, Responses and Lessons from the Durban Untold Stories, 61–81
Copyright © 2022 by Bethuel Sibongiseni Ngcamu and Evangelos Mantzaris
Published under exclusive licence by Emerald Publishing Limited
doi:10.1108/978-1-80262-479-320211004

Insensitive media reporting by journalists has contributed to the injury, death and displacement of vulnerable people (black women and children) and tarnished the international standing of South Africa. The dehumanization of immigrants across the globe through the use of divisive and discriminatory language has a history of causing genocide in countries like Rwanda (the Interahamwe) and Germany (the Nazis). The increase in nationalism and xenophobia has been seen even in developed countries such as the United States, where former president Donald Trump rose to stardom through dehumanizing immigrants. This is the kind of behavior that led to the establishment of concentration camps. The rise of the far right in countries such as Hungary has observed its prime minister (Viktor Orbán) spewing xenophobic language against immigrants as well as India's prime minister (Narendra Modi), which saw fatal attacks against the minority Muslims at the hand of his majority Hindu nationalists. This situation was the trigger for this study.

The current research has been conducted using different instruments in order to investigate known and overlooked dimensions of xenophobic violence in South Africa and the way this has been reported in the media. There are a limited number of scholars who have attributed xenophobia to reckless reporting by the media. However, a study by Ngcamu and Mantzaris (2019a), which maps and examines the relationship between xenophobia and the media in the KwaZulu-Natal province, has espoused the hidden dimensions that exist. These include the fight for territory, the state's covert and overt strategies, foreign nationals outperforming locals in terms of skills in committing crimes, youth boredom, the absence of police and the distortion of facts by reporters.

In addition, the same authors exposed the theory of the "third force" to be a fallacy, as well as the private sector's preference for employing immigrants as cheap labor. These issues have been put forward as being the causes of xenophobic attacks against foreign nationals. However, there have been a number of researchers who have published studies linking xenophobia to the competition among foreign nationals who are shopkeepers or between South Africans and foreign nationals. Some business people have even used local unemployed youths to intimidate their competitors (Ngcamu and Mantzaris, 2019b).

Ngcamu and Mantzaris (2019b) have also uncovered the competition of existing technical skills between citizens and immigrants as it relates to committing crime. Kerr et al. (2019), however, argue that the violence perpetrated against foreign nationals was justified due to the discourses of liberation struggles against the apartheid government.

## Article Information

Conversely, in the last two decades, Hadland (2008, p. 7) has disputed the adverse influence of the media on xenophobia by suggesting that fictionalized violence through media platforms and aggressive behavior does not exist. Neocosmos, meanwhile, attributes xenophobic violence to extreme poverty, inequality in communities and "the politics of fear" (Neocosmos, 2008). Nonetheless, at the beginning of the twenty-first century, South African society was regarded as being extremely xenophobic due to the fear of migrants whose human rights citizens did not value or respect. In addition, foreigners were identified by local residents as being the key perpetrators of social ills such as crime committed in urban areas (Leggett, 2003, p. 52). Landau et al. (2005, p. 2) assert that foreign nationals have been discriminated against by local people and government agencies, including the police. Private organizations that manage detentions and deportations centers have also ill-treated immigrants.

This narrative has been supported by Desai (2008) who has written that foreign nationals have been exceedingly harassed through the xenophobic culture created and perpetuated by print and digital platforms through stigmatization and stereotyping of immigrants in townships. Within this broad historical and present context, the media's coverage of xenophobia in South Africa and internationally is directly and indirectly connected to the social crisis and the thinking processes, understanding and actions of very significant social and political groups representing affected communities, civil society and the state. This is because members of the media shape opinions, ideas, beliefs and actions. Previous research concerned with xenophobic violence and similar issues has been chiefly impressionistic, providing a qualitative analysis based mostly on a small sampling of press clippings.

On March 30, 2015, South African Police (SAPS) received a number of messages from colleagues patrolling the Isipingo CBD, who were reporting a protest on Subjee Road in the vicinity of Jeena Cash and Carry in Isipingo. Although it was initially difficult to assess the reason for the protest, it became known that it was being staged by striking employees of Jeena Cash and Carry against "scab" labor consisting of foreign nationals. During the protest, there were a few skirmishes and this initial demonstration resulted in altercations between locals and foreign nationals, which then spread to the Isipingo CBD. The confrontations and retaliations resulted in three injuries and damage to five taxis and several houses. The houses targeted and attacked by South Africans were those that belonged to citizens and who were known to rent rooms to foreigners. Such acts indicated that the attackers were very familiar with the local situation. Most of the shops run by foreign nationals that did manage to close were looted by groups of between 50 and 70 attackers. As time passed, their numbers increased.

While the attacks and the commotion continued, all the foreign nationals in Isipingo who had not disappeared into various side roads and toward Isipingo beach and Umlazi fled to the Isipingo Police Station, where they took refuge while they waited for assistance from the government. Those who took refuge included men, women and children who were all affected in terms of their social lives and business operations. While dealing with the Isipingo matter, reports were received of attacks on foreign nationals residing in other parts of Durban. The first consideration of the police leadership at that moment was whether the attacks were coordinated and planned by specific groups before the incidents began.

Although the violent attacks on foreign nationals started in the Isipingo area, situated in the south, it spread to the smaller townships in the south and south-central areas, such as Umlazi, KwaMakhutha, Malagazi, Clare Estate/Sydenham and Chatsworth. The violent incidents spread farther over the next two weeks to the northern areas, including Greenwood Park, Lindelani and KwaMashu.

In Isipingo, locals engaged in violent protest action in support of the retrenched South Africans and Umlazi became the epicenter over the next two hours. The attacks developed a momentum of their own, with opportunists and criminal elements capitalizing on the situation. The role of the youth as perpetrators was regarded as a serious concern while the accidental shooting of a South African woman in Umlazi prompted further mayhem. The Isipingo looting was described as being organized by the Umlazi business owners (organized as the South African Traders Association), supported by the South African National Civil Organisation (SANCO) eThekwini regional and provincial structures and a group of homeless people. A number of instigators were arrested and kept in police custody. The use of social media was noteworthy in terms of mobilization and incitement. The victims of the xenophobic attacks were mainly Congolese, Zimbabwean, Malawian, Mozambican, Ethiopian and Somali nationals:

*Chatsworth: 1,000*

*Isipingo: 280*

*Cheron Drive Community Hall (Greenwood Park): 200*

As the police and other relevant state departments began intensive investigations, detailed verifications and assessments on the ground indicated that the foreign nationals who were the victims of these attacks were mostly Congolese and Zimbabwean, while other foreign groups from Mozambique, Burundi, Malawi, Tanzania and Somalia were also victims but in smaller numbers. Police investigations confirmed the vast majority of victims from Mozambique and Malawi were illegal immigrants. The senior management of all affected police branches, the Disaster Management Centre, the eThekwini Municipality and other national and provincial departments recognized and agreed that the xenophobic violence was a crisis created deliberately. It was up to the collective state machinery to take decisive steps to address the matter seriously, effectively, efficiently and expeditiously. The police and national intelligence undertook to uncover the causes, reasons, factors and leaders or individuals that may have been behind the attacks, with a special focus on the primary causes. Following a few days' investigations, the following factors were put forward as the primary causes:

- Socio-economic competition between the warring groups (the locals and the foreigners) as well as turf wars among the immigrants themselves;
- The eThekwini Municipality's failure to regulate and enforce the by-laws for small enterprises;
- Competition over access to resources, for example housing and employment;
- The failure of foreign nationals to register their businesses with the eThekwini Municipality and a lack of penalties for unregistered or expired licenses. The majority of businesses owned by the immigrants are not registered with South African Revenue Service (SARS) or local banks;
- The involvement of foreign communities and individuals in criminal activities (not only drugs);

- The misrepresentation of the speech by King Goodwill Zwelithini by the media and its opportunistic exploitation by South African nationals, including small businesses and competitors of foreigners;
- The payment of protection monies by foreign nationals to people in government and members of SAPS; and
- The spreading of misinformation on social media.

Inevitably, such information given to the state apparatus led to the belief that these were the fundamental reasons that had led to the widespread acts of violence, with the attackers displaying a culture of impunity and complete disrespect for authority. The violence led to the short- and medium-term displacement of many in the community; the disturbance of local peace; the disruption of law enforcement, including the police, local authorities, disaster management, foreign affairs, the UN, foreign African nations, intelligence and other state services; and the complete or partial disruption of the informal sector's economy, which supports indigent communities. It also resulted in the weakening of harmony and social cohesion in the affected communities, an increase in opportunistic criminal activities and reputational damage to South Africa as a country in the African and global terrain. This latter consequence was confirmed by the SAPS senior member:

> The situation provided the opportunity for organisations such as [the] UNCHR and other United Nations' affiliates to enter the country and interfere in our country's affairs, especially at a time when these situations created animosity and even turmoil in our communities. [This] had very negative repercussions [on] our informal economic systems in the townships and had very negative effects on social cohesion and unity amongst our communities and their relations with our African displaced people.

The local representatives from the UN had a relationship with the press and community members, who provided them with reliable information on future attacks directed at foreign nations. This was supported by eThekwini Municipality member who was a member of Provincial Joint Operational and Intelligence Structure (PROVJOINTS) and present in these strategic meetings:

> In [the] south they came from the second day when the situation started in Isipingo. Mahlangu a key man in the UN in South Africa was there, he spoke to the newspapers [on the] same day ... and told them that the UN was very worried about the attacks on foreigners and called for decisive intervention and solving the problem through [the] collective efforts of all stakeholders and role players in stopping the attacks everywhere. They also said that they were worried by the fact that there were fears that the attacks will escalate and expand to other places. The question we asked was how these people could really make [a] statement about the expansion. This told us that in reality they had inside information from a number of sources because of the

contacts they had throughout the years ... there was really nothing wrong with their call for collective interventions in fighting [the] violence against migrants.

The official attached to the Disaster Management Centre mentioned that the UN had relationships with a large number of stakeholders who assisted them in responding to the xenophobic attacks had this to say:

> They became involved from the first day; they are very well connected with some people in the police, the Premier's Office and a number of ministries in KZN. This [is] because they pump money [into] a number of activities like lectures, seminars and things like this. Then they have important connections with the various embassies and consulates throughout the country and this helps them connect with the high levels in government. They also have networks in municipalities that they have interests in like Msunduzi and uMgugundlovu in Pietermaritzburg because the legislature and all government departments are there. They have established good connections; they have a very good operator, Ntokozo Mahlangu, the key man for their main organisation here, the International Organization for Migration, that is in charge of the foreigners; this exists in most counties, especially those that face problems with violence against foreigners and refugees. Mahlangu was telling us how well they train the people who deal with governments because the problems with attacks on foreigners and the refugee crises are throughout the word and a major problem for the UN.

For a number of days, more than 170 foreign nationals, including children, remained at the premises of the Isipingo Police Station, as they were afraid to leave. A number of Non-Governmental Organisations (NGOs) provided cooked meals and raw food supplies for the displaced. They were visited at the station by SAPS Cluster Commander Major General D.J. Chiliza; Transport, Safety and Community Liaison MEC Willies Mchunu; and eThekwini Mayor James Nxumalo in an attempt to address the situation. The state officials were accompanied by several others from the Member of Executive Council's (MEC's) office and the eThekwini Municipality. The meeting was also joined by a group of 10 representatives of the displaced people.

There were several agreements reached during the meetings, despite the fact that there were a number of different opinions expressed by the representatives of the displaced, especially regarding the verification of the displaced by the Department of Home Affairs. It was stated during the meetings as a matter of fact that the department was working on the verification process in order to ascertain the residential status of the displaced. There was an undertaking from the South African team that food and other supplies would be immediately available to the displaced. Generous donations from a variety of NGOs had ensured continuous and sufficient food and other necessary supplies such as mattresses, blankets and personal hygiene products. A mobile kitchen was supplied by an NGO to facilitate the preparation of meals on-site using raw supplies donated by other NGOs. The provision of temporary accommodation, access control and policing was guaranteed.

Three marquees were set up at the Isipingo Beach Sports Ground to accommodate initially about 180 men, women and children on day one. As at 7 April, there were 276 people accommodated in the temporary shelter, consisting of 231 adults and 45 children. A mobile Community Service Center was supplied by SAPS. Metro Police was also represented at the site, with 16 private security officials on night and day shift (8 per shift). The site was supplied with electricity, water, sanitation and waste bins.

A mobile clinic was made available for two hours a day to provide primary healthcare, while the Department of Social Development would provide psychosocial support on demand. The Department of Environmental Health would inspect all food to ensure it met the required standards and the community reintegration program would begin immediately.

The affected foreign nationals were from the DRC (102), Malawi (65), Burundi (36), Mozambique (24) and Tanzania (1). They lived in Isipingo, Malukazi, KwaMakhutha, Umlazi S Section and Unit 9 Chatsworth.

## Hidden and Overlooked Dimensions of Xenophobia

There is a multiplicity of well-known dimensions of xenophobia that have been overlooked by the government and its agencies as well as other interested stakeholders: businesses, civil society groups, religious communities, international agencies and organizations for foreign nationals. These dimensions include the socio-economic causes emanating from poverty, extreme unemployment levels, inequality, competition for scarce resources, issues of labor and competition concerning employment opportunities, and the informal economy. These dimensions are mostly social and economic as identified by Kerr et al. (2019) who repeated the reality that the perpetrators of xenophobia felt that the foreign nationals undermined citizens' socio-economic standing.

## Poverty and Unemployment in Peri-Urban and Township Communities

Government agencies, scholars, media channels and civil society groups have failed dismally to link poverty and unemployment with the triggers of xenophobia in the townships in the Durban metropolitan area. While the current unemployment rate in South Africa stands at 29%, with the KwaZulu-Natal province at 29% and Durban at 21.8% (Statistics South Africa, 2019), the unemployment rate of the youth aged between 25 and 34 in 2019 was 35.6%. The majority of the residents (mostly youth) in townships in Durban are unemployed. They mostly live in the informal settlements in close proximity to industries – but in terms of employment, these businesses tend to favor foreign nationals. Gordon (2019) concluded that xenophobia is concentrated among the lower socio-economic groups and that is it rife among the unemployed. The majority of the xenophobic attacks are believed to be the result of the rapid rural–urban migration and the influx of immigrants from poor neighboring countries in search of employment. These immigrants escape the poverty of their country of origin – often rural – but are met with extreme poverty in South Africa's urban areas, exacerbated by the absence of basic needs being met. Many of these migrants, who are mostly young, engage in criminal business for their daily survival. This includes becoming dagga merchants, drug traffickers, shack lords, izinkabi (assassins) or getting into prostitution, car hijackings, human trafficking or kidnapping. Some immigrants are even used by local business-people to intimidate and attack their competitors.

There is a myriad of negative perceptions and stereotypes leveled against foreign nationals. For instance, it is alleged that the size of their sex organ is bigger than local men, that they have money to attract local girls (whether they are young, old or married), that they use powerful traditional medicine and that they spread disease. These were the results of a survey conducted by Gordon (2019). This researcher revealed that a total of 75% of the adult interviewees believed that foreign nationals escalate crime rates, steal jobs and spread disease. Such beliefs have been supported by the research findings of Masikane et al. (2020) who assessed leaders' responses to xenophobia, determined by locals' violent history and responses, culture in communities, denialism, people's stereotypical attitudes and the economic inequalities in the country.

The majority of migrants live with their parents, their siblings and their own children. The local peoples' income from social grants is deemed too little for their daily survival. While poverty abounds in the urban townships, the residents also pay a "black tax" to their families in rural areas, sending them financial support to help them survive. The shortage of basic necessities and poverty leads to the sad reality that "opportunities" are taken when there is xenophobic violence toward foreign nationals who own small businesses in the townships. Stores are looted and valuables are stolen. Such attacks have been labeled by some as the action of a "third force."

Boredom and issues with anger have been observed in South African youth and perpetuate xenophobia as these young people are both energetic and underutilized. The majority of them are involved in drugs, either as traders or using them to alleviate boredom. The only way to sustain their drug habit is through stealing from their own households, local businesses (including foreign nationals) and macro businesses. The entities that are mostly targeted by such groups are spaza shops, taxi drivers, delivery trucks and ATMs. The security apparatus such as the police have also been seen colluding with the alleged perpetrators of xenophobia in committing these crimes. While the government agencies who are responsible for rooting out these illegal activities are silent, they are the ones who have created the myth of the "third force."

## Economic Competition at a Local Level

There are a myriad of factors that play a role in influencing South African citizens and immigrants to attack each other, but the reasons appear to be mainly economic. For instance, foreign nationals have taken serious advantage of the weaknesses of the existing but inadequate by-laws of the eThekwini Municipality, opening lucrative businesses in the townships including spaza shops and tuck shops, specialized car repairs (including panel-beating), construction, and legal and illegal electricity connections. These are enterprises that cannot be operated by locals because they do not possess either the skills or the funds to bribe officials. The existing by-laws have not been enforced by municipal law enforcement agencies in the townships' informal sector and there are evidently limitations in the regulation frameworks regarding small businesses. Recent research has indicated that immigrants have been involved in entrepreneurial activities in central business districts of the country's urban and semi-urban areas, which have been instrumental in job creation. It is estimated that 52% and 45% of businesses are owned by foreigners in Cape Town and Limpopo, respectively, and employ mostly South Africans in their enterprises. It was also reported that foreign workers continue to be attracted to traditional sectors such as mining, but there are other industries that attract newly arrived immigrants such as information technology and finance.

In the same townships, casual or menial jobs that do not require special skills have been dominated by foreign nationals as they accept low wages and do not embark on labor strikes. In addition, macro companies are believed to favor migrants as these employees are regarded as trustworthy, skillful, reliable, non-unionized, accepting of low wages and any employment condition and do not challenge unfair labor practices. There is also fierce competition that has been called "entrepreneurial violence." This emanates from competition among foreign nationals themselves and between foreign nationals and local businesspeople in the informal sector. This sector in South Africa is almost forgotten even though it creates jobs, reduces poverty, provides income to some 2.5 million workers and business owners, and contributes 5% to the country's GDP (Statistics South Africa, 2015).

The small business sector (also called the informal sector) is over-represented by foreign nationals who have been accused of unfair pricing (as their products are generally cheaper when compared to those of their South African counterparts). They are also accused of selling counterfeit and expired goods although many South African customers favor these stores because of the low prices and the shopkeepers' responsiveness to the needs of their customers. For instance, on 19 May, the online news portal Eyewitness News reported that a total of 15 undocumented foreign nationals had been arrested in Durban who were found to be operating unregistered businesses. These shops were closed immediately. In addition, over 200 immigrants were apprehended in the notorious Durban Point and over 100 shops closed during the COVID-19 lockdown. During the operation, the municipal enforcement agencies had the goal of eradicating the trade in illegal and illicit products. Furthermore, expired goods and counterfeit goods were also confiscated during the raid. This swift operation was spearheaded by different government departments and agencies including the provincial Economic Development Department (enforcement agencies) and the department of consumer protection (inspectors), with business regulations also playing a pivotal role.

There was an outcry from local businesses because it is well known that the majority of migrants in informal businesses are not registered with the municipality and do not pay taxes or municipal rates. Due to the fact that the municipality is regarded as an unethical entity run by corrupt political and administrative officials, migrants pay bribes both to provincial security agencies and municipal officials. The eThekwini Municipality's officials are known for their corrupt dealings over the years, as the Manase Report in 2012 showed, with senior municipal officials and politicians involved in financial irregularities, fraud and corruption estimated at R2.2 billion.

During the 2019/2020 financial year, the city mayor and senior administrative officials were released on bail in the multi-million rand criminal case. There were also charges of fraud and corruption laid against Durban Solid Waste over a contract of R430 million (Erasmus, 2020). Apart from migrants receiving illegal support from corrupt municipal officials, they also receive preferential treatment from wholesalers due to their religious affiliation and beliefs. In addition, they open their shops for longer hours and are in close proximity to immigrants' shops owned by South Africans. To worsen the situation, landlords who rent their houses for business purposes prefer foreign nationals because they accept the price given and condition of the building.

## Rapid Urbanization and Lax Immigration Policies

An increase in immigration numbers followed by unprecedented high numbers of people who are urbanized but with limited resources to cater for their needs has created a myriad of challenges. This has led to the majority of the urbanized dwellers residing in informal settlements and rented rooms where they face problems related to affordability as the landlords raise prices regularly due to the demand. Migrants are preferred by property owners because foreign nationals tend to be in a better financial position and pay their rent on time. Furthermore, many recipients of Reconstruction and Development Programme (RDP) houses (free government houses) sell them to foreign nationals despite government's policies. Such illegal transactions occur despite the strict conditions in respect of selling RDP houses as per the Housing Amendment Act, 2001 (Act 4 of 2001) (RSA, 2001). This Act states that the beneficiary of an RDP house may sell it, but only after eight years and first option is to be given to the government. Due to this situation, the state is sitting with more than 30,000 cases of illegally sold RDP houses (Magubane, 2020).

Another challenge is the lack of service delivery – millions of our citizens reside in shack settlements where there is an inadequate supply of basic needs including clean drinking water, electricity, proper sanitation and shelter. Much of the available water and electricity are illegally connected and many such inhabitants are harassed by law enforcement agencies and private security agencies since their shacks are built on municipal or privately owned land. These unstable living conditions result in conflict among shack dwellers. Due to these frustrations, municipal law enforcement and locals are driven to attack foreign nationals.

Inadequate service delivery has been associated with xenophobic attacks according to Gordon (2019). This author asserts that poor service delivery has led to immigrants' businesses and homes being looted. This has been aggravated by the mushrooming of informal settlements as a result of foreign nationals arriving in the country. These individuals originate from sub-Saharan Africa and come in search of brighter opportunities in a country where opportunities have become scarce. The porosity of the South African borders together with lax immigration and refugee policies have left locals without the option but to view migrants as the deterrents to economic freedom in their lifetime. The soldiers who are trusted to safeguard South Africa's borders have been accused of being involved in criminal activities and being bribed by migrants in various ways (such as exchanging money or sexual favors to cross into South Africa).

Citizens have been complaining that the South African Government has weak and inappropriate systems and control measures in place to screen and record illegal immigrants in the country. The majority of them obtain residency or identity documents illegally. This they do by bribing government officials in Home Affairs, border control or immigration, which enables them to compete equally with locals for the existing scarce resources. The control measures in the latter agencies are flawed, with corruption being rampant. The absence of reliable and valid statistical data on undocumented and illegal immigrants, refugees and asylum seekers in the country has created discontent for some black South Africans. Furthermore, the lack of information on the rights of both legal and illegal immigrants, asylum seekers and refugees has contributed to the 2015 xenophobic attacks.

## Human Trafficking Syndicates

The majority of illegal immigrants entering South Africa are either being trafficked by syndicates in their countries of origin or at the country's borders by vicious gangs. This is evident with the majority of "Zimbos" as they are fondly known (the Zimbabwean diaspora) who brave peril to reach South Africa. Along the journey they face gangs, crocodiles in the rivers and the possibility of deportation. These immigrants face many hazards to escape abject poverty in their war-torn, politically unstable and economically imploded countries. Along the Limpopo border, they have to negotiate the possibility of starvation, crocodiles in the infested Limpopo River, razor wire and heartless gangs called "maguma-guma" (derived from the Shona indigenous language and referring to organized groups of criminals). These gangs patronize Zimbabweans and facilitate immigrants illegally entering other countries, and South Africa is no exception, with people entering through the Beitbridge border post. These ruthless crooks, known for extorting a myriad of valuables from illegal immigrants – goods, money, sex and other items like mobile phones – offer safe passage and protection.

The border jumpers (illegal immigrants) seek assistance from these criminal gangs to unlawfully pay off Zimbabweans security officers, bypass immigration, and enter into South Africa. These "jumpers" are said to pay R120 (US$16) to the maguma-guma. This money is used to pay the soldiers and security guards from both borders. For those who do not have money to pay the gangs, the consequences can be dire. These lunatics (who are mostly Zimbabwean men) in their hundreds are feared for their ill deeds including theft, rape and murder of those who do not use their services. These syndicates of con men normally steal money and belongings under false pretenses. Lately these thugs have included women who also target people from Zimbabwe who come to purchase goods in South Africa. Mpondi and Mupakati (2018) consider the emigration of Zimbabweans to South Africa as being informalized and perilous. The authors cite specific instances where border jumpers' misunderstandings over money with the maguma-guma has led them being deliberately drowned in the Limpopo River.

A recent cruel incident where illegals tried to enter South Africa ended tragically on March 24, 2020 when a total of 64 undocumented immigrants from Ethiopia were found dead in Mozambique, crammed inside a freight container. There were a total of 78 in the container; the driver having been promised R6,400 to transport them to South Africa (UPI, 2020).

All the immigrants were destined for South Africa, and Mozambique is considered to be a smuggling corridor for migrants to the continent's industrialized nation (i.e., South Africa).

## Inactive Policing in the Townships

The government's security agencies are considered to be embroiled in politics, leadership succession, government tenders, corruption, bribery, murder and extortion, with less focus on using the existing financial and other resources to combat the extreme levels of crime in townships (and much of this is associated with xenophobia). The xenophobic attacks have been linked to corruption, with intelligence agencies and operatives in the country failing to detect such criminal elements which are perpetrated by both locals and foreign nationals. The local police are known to be beneficiaries of foreign business owners as they provide protection from competitors, law enforcement agencies and their illegal dealings. During and after xenophobic attacks, the police are known to take part in the looting of local businesses owned by foreign nationals. The shortcomings in policing by the state's security agencies have been conspicuous before and during xenophobic violence and there is evidence of their members working collaboratively with South Africans in fueling the violence. However, there have been ethical police officers who have acted decisively and honestly during the course of attacks against foreign nationals, leading to perpetrators being arrested, although the Department of Justice has delayed the process in prosecuting those who have been charged.

## The Effect of Print and Digital News on Xenophobia

A total number of 48 media articles published by the popular printed media were analyzed. There were 19 (35%) of the newspaper articles with a positive tone, followed by 23 (43%) with a negative tone and a total of 12 (22%) with a neutral tone. Xenophobia is exacerbated by fake online news stories that have led to extreme hatred and tensions between the warring factions. This has resulted in South Africa's brand reputation being slandered internationally, the country's Constitution being disrespected and people being misled. These stories have been posted, published and circulated via bogus websites and WhatsApp, Twitter and Facebook. False narratives and propaganda by the print media have been disseminated by misinformed people including politicians, cultural leaders, media reporters and invisible yet organized individuals. This is done through social media platforms, with inflammatory rumors and a wave of misinformation spreading via videos, voice notes and photographs (most of which are old and unrelated to the violence).

## Propaganda and Inaccurate Reporting by the Print Media

The respondents from the municipal and the KwaZulu-Natal Provincial Government have deliberated on the questionable part played by media channels during the xenophobic attacks. The reporting was done in a "planned, middle of the road," mediocre manner – in such a way as to narrate the political agendas of media moguls. This kind of reporting is associated with a weak analysis that is based on perceptions – such as those who believe that foreigners are stealing South African citizens' jobs and distributing drugs. This has been attested to by a senior provincial government official who said that

> this means that "middle of the road" is not neutral; it is adopted in order to misguide the people and confuse them in regard to the real cause of these events and processes, the unemployment and its roots, poverty, the lumpen proletariat.

Many of the informants pointed out that journalists do not report accurately on the situation and circumstances, the reasons for the belief that locals "refuse menial jobs" and that there is a preference for foreign nationals in terms of employment in these jobs by employers at all levels and sectors of the market.

This has been posited by the senior policy specialist in the provincial government:

> The fact of the matter is that the refugees, asylum seekers and the illegal immigrants in South Africa are preferred by the industry as they are cheap labourers. The menial jobs are dominated by them and they do not challenge such labour malpractices. This is not covered in the popular media ... why the locals are not preferred [for] such jobs [while] the foreign nationals are exploited. The business sector understands that by employing the locals, the trade unions will fight for the unfair practices at workplaces and low remunerations. The struggle credentials and tradition of the South Africans to fight for the discrimination in wages and salaries does not find a place in the press as a reality.

The preference for immigrants and South Africans being overlooked in terms of job opportunities has been averted by the state's development of the White Paper on International Migration for South Africa (RSA, 2017). This paper is implemented through the Immigration Act of 2002 and the Refugees

Act of 1998. The migration policy, which was enacted in 1999, is considered to be outdated and having a myriad of limitations which has necessitated the state to develop the White Paper on International Migration (RSA, 2017). This paper safeguards the sovereignty of the country, public safety and national security. The Department of Home Affairs has identified three major gaps in the previous policy on migration which evolved around asylum seekers and the management of refugees, emigration and the integration of international migrants. The points-based system of work permits determines whether the applicant qualifies for a short- or long-term residence visa. (The number of years spent in the country would not qualify an immigrant to apply for naturalization.) However, this White Paper on International Migration (RSA, 2017) has received condemnation from different stakeholders and has been labeled as being discriminatory against unskilled immigrants and the poor. For instance, the Pan Africanism Today Secretariat (2020) suggests that this paper aims to target the highly skilled workforce by granting points-based work permits. This only accommodates skilled immigrants and marginalizes asylum seekers and refugees in the informal sector (Pan Africanism Today Secretariat, 2020).

The perception shared by the respondents from the provincial government has stated that the derogatory and unwarranted choice of words used by journalists has been instrumental in exacerbating tensions between local people and foreign nationals. One interviewee in a senior government position pinpointed the fact that the use of derogatory names even when in inverted commas inevitably "creates a social identity," in most cases unacceptable to a social group associated with it. The use of the term "amakwerekwere" (foreigners) is considered derogatory and denigrating to all foreigners irrespective of their background, social position in society or geographical roots. It was stated that these were issues of common knowledge that are part and parcel of journalistic knowledge and ethics at all levels of the profession. The key question arises, then, while such realities and truths are known to everyone, why the perpetration of such terms in the printed media by journalists and whether or not such realities of perpetuating such negative stereotypes can be described as one of the reasons for xenophobic attacks throughout the years including 2015.

The research participants eloquently concluded that the print media has been disseminating propaganda and casting aspersions against the warring groups, exacerbating the tensions. This was accentuated by a senior disaster management official who believed strongly that journalists with a number of exceptions have been for years victims of propaganda that can be described as the root of ethnic or national prejudice that leads to violence. This reality, it was stated, was rooted on the "undeniable fact" that an ideological agenda instrumental in the division of locals from foreigners was behind the journalists' stories. This ideology was the root of the reality that journalists had no respect for either South Africans or foreign immigrants.

A member of the strategic committee from the eThekwini Municipality provided a background regarding the recurring xenophobic attacks in Durban. This municipal official indicated that

after a couple of days, they went on TV and gave a press conference and interview with a few selected journalists, including *Isolezwe* and other local papers, making statements about their strong
views about these attacks that do not happen for the first time and
continue to spread.

## Pro-immigrant, Selective, Distorted and Sensational Reporting

The government's informants shared similar sentiments, stating categorically that
the reporters were biased in their articles. They were seen as pro-immigrant, providing false information and consequently worsening the xenophobia. A senior
municipal official strongly believed that journalists fueled xenophobia especially
through the Zulu King's false interpretation of his public call for foreigners to be
repatriated. Such a reality, he indicated, was reinforced by their false reporting
following their interviews with immigrants in the shelters. It was felt that the situation in the establishment was blown out of proportions.

Such a position was corroborated by the shelter coordinator who stated that
the analysis undertaken by experts pinpointed the newspapers' misinterpretation
of the King's speech. It was felt that such a reality was used as an excuse for the
attacks on immigrants.

The interviewees at the municipal level unanimously believed that the print
media negatively shaped locals' perceptions by selectively reporting on a correlation between violence and xenophobia, disseminating a negative perception of
migration, and made empty promises to the government to provide assistance to
curb the violence.

An eThekwini Municipality official who was a member of the strategic committee expressed a wider understanding and background to the realities of the
situation chronologically and meticulously. He indicated that there was a common theme in the press that at the initial stages of the events there was a general
agreement that the attacks and violence were a problem for the nation in its total-
ity and not the government's alone. This meant, he said, that the initial message
was seen as a sign that journalists and publishers were critical supporters of a
national unity that could lead to a peaceful return to normality and end of the
violent attacks. In what was described as a complete turn-around attitude toward
foreign immigrants reinforcing violence and attacks at a number of levels.

There was a general belief among the government officials who were present at
the shelters that the press distorted information and misreported the day-to-day
operations and difficulties faced by all the stakeholders. These government practitioners believed that the articles published in the print media were fabricated – lies
meant to be sensational. This was supported by the disaster management senior
member who indicated that while journalists were welcome to visit the immigrant
shelters and were free to interview the immigrants in the establishments ended
authoring pieces both in printed and social media that were all devoid of truth.
It was accepted that the conditions in the establishments were problematic at
times, but such realities and dynamics in place were just ignored. The fact that

such conditions and circumstances were accepted as acceptable by international organizations such as the United Nations were ignored by journalists. Interestingly, it was confirmed that journalist only interviewed foreign citizens but not state officials in charge of the establishment.

Such realities exposed in the interviews have been widely reported in the isiZulu newspaper *Ilanga* and *The New Age*, with a negative response to the Zulu king's alleged speech (2015), such as the headlines *Abase Nigeria babopha iSilo sama Zulu* and *Mozambique, Congo quit tourism Indaba.*

## Government's Tireless Efforts and Invisible Groups

One of the informants from the provincial government, a senior disaster management official expressed the following views on reporters:

> It is not balanced, and shallow because they [reporters] were taking things at face value and reporting on things that they [saw] at face value without giving themselves time to interview both sides ... involved and they were [therefore] very shallow. They were unable to go deep in their stories to inform objectively so that people can make a fair judgement.

A provincial communications coordinator cited numerous initiatives undertaken by government departments with the only aim of curbing the violence. He maintained that following debates taking place daily and for many hours the "publicity machinery" was very active in the production of masses of pamphlets in English and isiZulu that were distributed throughout the city, all African townships and informal settlements calling on everyone to stop the attacks, report attacks or attempted attacks to the nearest police station, defend migrants, and do their best to welcome back in their areas those attacked who wished to return and be re-integrated into their communities.

The above-mentioned evidence has been attested to through key messages from the KwaZulu-Natal government and the eThekwini Metro leadership through the media through the messages such as:

- "Stop the attacks! This is not who we are as a nation";
- "Negative perceptions that African immigrants are using resources meant for South Africans are invalid";
- "We must not forget the hospitality and support we received from fellow Africans";
- "We all have a role to play to ensure peaceful co-existence in communities."

The daily newspapers *The Mercury* and *Isolezwe*, meanwhile, published 11 articles with a negative tone between April 20 and April 30, 2015 with titles such as:

- *The curse of xenophobia*
- *Government did not act on March warnings*

- *Wave of reprisal*
- *Government must be blamed on the immigrants*
- *Millions are to be lost because of the immigrants.*

Conversely, a provincial coordinator shared a number of negative letters by invisible groups counteracting the efforts that were being made by the provincial government. The coordinator confirmed that there was a serious and well organized movement for a number of days that employed a number of young people to distribute thousands of pamphlets in a form of a letter in isiZulu demanding all foreigners to leave the country immediately. The pamphlets were distributed in townships such as Ntuzuma, Inanda, Kwamashu, KwaNyuswa. Once the SAPS realized the seriousness of the situation, there were attempts to uncover the people or organizations behind the initiatives. They failed.

The government officials suggested that the media portrayed a complex analysis of xenophobia while the ruling party's position was ambiguous and contradictory. This was exemplified by a senior government PROVJOINTS member who said:

> On occasions there were attempts on the part of the media to portray some sophisticated analysis and positions, but, given the present realities, there was no unified position on key issues and this can also be realised by the position ... of the ruling party which is ambiguous and contradictory. It is not easy to say one thing if one knows our country's people historical relations with Africa during the liberation struggle and then understand today's policies and politics towards African brothers and sisters.

The government departments that formed part of the provincial strategic committee during the 2015 xenophobic violence raised serious concerns regarding how the press inaccurately reported on the root causes of the attacks. Further, they planted "spies" in the shelters to provide them with information, which was unverified. The provincial disaster management official gave the following views:

> It can be my own assumption. The SA media is not responsible enough especially when it comes to issues of national concern; they are reckless, senseless, biased, anti-state ... even [in] matters of national interest. During these attacks, [the members of the] media were focusing on locals attacking foreigners; they [the news stories] were fine; we are not condoning such attacks and it is not something that we can encourage. However, the media failed to go down to the root causes of these attacks and they also failed to report the casualties, the accurate causalities, and they were also using people in some instances; they will deploy people to observe in the shelters, to observe the wrongs not the rights. [At] some point at KwaMashu in Block A (hostel), the Somalians were attacked and the media failed to report that there were 15 causalities with gun wounds ... two were Somalians and the rest

were South Africans. Even if I was on-site, they were rude (the foreigners) and there were rules that we have implemented on-site ... most of them were for the intelligence and some of these people were organising themselves with foreign countries and the media was putting some pressure and working with these guys on their rights. For instance, they were asking for telephone connections and Vodacom offered that they [could] have open lines; they ended up abusing them and when we took [the] decision to close those lines, the media was reporting the government as being abusive to the displaced. Unfortunately, in the country the whole media is sick; [the reporters] have failed to prioritise matters of national interest and [be] objective.

## The "Third Force" and Unverified Media Reporting: Perceptions of Civil Society Groups

There were prominent civil society group members and activists who were directly involved and effective in their relations in communities during the xenophobia. These individuals formed part of the research participants and cast a negative light on the press, who reported unfounded and unverified information. A community activist held the following view of the media:

> The township residents know the daily happenings in their respective areas and they are open about their plans to attack the foreign nationals. The media reporters visit the areas susceptible to the xenophobic attacks after [the] events and pretend as if they know everything. The community leaders consult with communities formally and informally on a daily basis in order to discuss and deliberate on various matters in the location and the media reporters are informed on the resolutions taken regarding the immigrants and they will thereafter report falsified information. When they are confronted on the lies and innuendos and reasons which motivated them to publish incorrect stories, they claim that they are afraid for their lives in publishing truthful stories.

The social activists in the areas affected by xenophobia have strongly disputed a "third force," claimed to be a "Bible truth." This is the ideology mostly shared by government and the media regarding the xenophobic attacks. One of the activists who described himself as a leader argued that:

> there [are] numerous theories advanced by government agencies, politicians, the media and the civil society groups regarding the causes of attacks against the foreigners in these communities. As a respected leader in the community, it is quite difficult to understand the situation which has fuelled the attacks, as the situation changes [from] time to time and the environment we know very

well is complicated. The state agencies call it a "third force," while the unemployed are in the struggle against the government to access resources and job opportunities. As community leaders we are bribed by the media reporters ... [they] buy us beers to report [to] them, give them stories, [but] when the attacks take place, they are nowhere to be seen.

The social activists in the areas affected by xenophobia had disputable Bible truth shared by government and the media – that the narrative of the "third force" which is shared by different stakeholders does exist and that it is responsible for the attacks against the foreign nationals. One of the activists argued that:

it is difficult to deal with these theories because the situation on the ground is sometimes complicated, most of the time simple, but as the situation evolves it becomes more complicated. We who are called community leaders, because we have participated in these areas of contention amongst different groups, know that such terms are given by either the state agencies or journalists. This because in the struggles against the state by the leadership of the poor, the unemployed, etc. are themselves the creation of a "third force," the state or the press; then journalists keep on calling you for news. They are either scared to come to townships or they say they are too busy they have no time.

The civil society activist who had been in the trenches with the poor in the affected communities disputed the stories reported by journalists and their sources in the communities, something regarded as a publicity stunt. Another grassroots social activist indicated that a number of community members had relations with journalists and a cohort of activists who understand existing dynamics and these are the reasons journalists are in contact with them when the attacks begin. It was felt that this fact alone pinpointed the ignorance of the majority of even accredited journalists regarding realities in the townships, the mjondolos (informal settlements). This, was said, made a number of journalists connect with police people for information. The problem with such people and relations established is that the day-to day journalist is not interested in the heart and soul of the information and its deeper realities. They care for photographs, not the realities and analysis of the situation, the foundations of relationship s and what leads to violent attacks. The average journalist, it was said, is interested in sensations, not understanding.

### The "Third Force" and Unverified Media Reporting: The Perceptions of Civil Society Groups

Prominent civil society group members who were directly involved in communities before and during the xenophobia and who formed part of the research participants depicted the print media reporters in a negative light, reporting unfounded and unverified information. It was strongly felt that the key problem with journalists at large has been that they have not been interested for the heart and soul of the information and its deeper realities. Most of them mostly care for photographs, not the realities and analysis of the situation, the foundations of relationship s and what leads to violent attacks. The average journalist, it was said, is interested in sensations, not understanding.

An association between rhetoric media reporting and the escalation in xenophobic attacks against foreign nationals cannot be disputed in view of the above empirical findings. The media has been used in different countries as a form of instigation for the warring groups to attack one another and to perpetuate ethnocentricity, tribalism and racism in different countries and regions. For instance, the Rwandan genocide is a typical case where the news media led to the killings, torture and displacement of people in their thousands.

In such countries, the media was supported by government agencies, and South Africa is no exception. Terms such as the "third force" have been created by the state and disseminated through the media. There are existing discourses of the so-called "third force" as being behind the attacks against foreign nationals.

The manner in which the media treats and disseminates information about xenophobia in South Africa can have a lethal influence. Most scholars have failed to question the tendency of reporters and their bosses in escalating xenophobia through their propaganda machinery, which is spread through print and digital publications. However, since the academic space (through publication in journals and books) on xenophobia in South Africa is led by immigrants with an anti-state stance and narratives depicting locals as being behind xenophobia, this blind approach toward the media is not surprising.

However, the South African Government has failed dismally to set a precedent that enables it to hold journalists and their handlers accountable for inciting xenophobia through their derogatory, stereotypical, reckless, biased and misguided reporting. Nonetheless, this chapter clearly depicts the media as dehumanizing the victims of xenophobia and reporting unverified and sensational stories in order to be respected by their handlers and media bosses. It is noteworthy in this study that the media has been anti-government and pro-private companies who indirectly contribute to the crisis by preferring to employ foreign nationals and regarding South African citizens as lazy, unionized and untrustworthy.

# References

Desai, A. 2008. Xenophobia and the of the refugee in the rainbow nation of human rights, *African Sociological Review/Revue Africaine de Sociologie*, 12(2). doi: 10.4314/asr. v12i2.49834

Erasmus, D. 2020. eThekwini municipal manager to join Zandile Gumede in court, *Daily Maverick*, March 1. Available at: https://www.dailymaverick.co.za/article/2020-03-11-ethekwini-municipal-manager-to-join-zandile-gumede-in-court/ [Accessed 21 May 2020].

Gordon, S. 2019. A violent minority? A quantitative analysis of those engaged in anti-immigrant violence in South Africa, *South African Geographical Journal*, 101(2), 269–283.

Hadland, A. 2008. *Shooting the Messenger: Mediating the Public and the Role of the Media in South Africa's Xenophobic Violence*, Council for the Development of Social Science Research in Africa. Available at: http://www.codesria.org [Accessed 23 March 2014].

Kerr, P., Durrheim, K. and Dixon, J. 2019. Xenophobic violence and struggle discourse in South Africa, *Journal of Asian and African Studies*, 54(7), 995–1011.

Landau, L.B., Ramjathan-Keogh, K. and Singh, G. 2005. *Xenophobia in South Africa and Problems Related to It*, Johannesburg, Forced Migration Studies Programme, University of the Witwatersrand.

Leggett, T. 2003. Rainbow tenement: crime and policing in inner Johannesburg, *Institute for Security Studies Monographs*, 2003(78), 100.

Magubane, T. 2020. Department of Human Settlements concerned over illegal sales of government houses, *The Mercury*, April 14.

Masikane, C.M., Hewitt, M.L. and Toendepi, J. 2020. Dynamics informing xenophobia and leadership response in South Africa, *Acta Commercii*, 20(1), 11.

Mpondi, D. and Mupakati, L. 2018. Migration trajectories and experiences of Zimbabwean immigrants in the Limpopo province of South Africa: impediments and possibilities. *Africology: The Journal of Pan African Studies*, 12(1), 215–235.

Neocosmos, M. 2008. The politics of fear and the fear of politics: reflections on xenophobic violence in South Africa, *Journal of Asian and African studies*, 43(6), 586–594.

Ngcamu, B.S. and Mantzaris, E. 2019a. Xenophobic violence and criminality in the KwaZulu-Natal townships, *TD: The Journal for Transdisciplinary Research in Southern Africa*, 15(1), 1–8.

Ngcamu, B.S. and Mantzaris, E. 2019b. Media reporting, xenophobic violence, and the "forgotten dimensions": a case of selected areas in the KwaZulu-Natal province, *International Journal of African Renaissance Studies- Multi-, Inter- and Transdisciplinarity*, 14(1), 131–146.

Pan Africanism Today Secretariat. 2020. *Xenophobia in South Africa Fractures International Working-Class Solidarity*. Available at: https://peoplesdispatch.org/2020/07/07/xenophobia-in-south-africa-fractures-international-working-class-solidarity/ [Accessed 17 November 2020].

Republic of South Africa (RSA). 2017. *White Paper on International Migration for South Africa*. Available at: https://www.gov.za/documents/international-migration-white-paper [Accessed 27 November 2018].

RSA. 2001. Housing Amendment Act, 2001 (Act 4 of 2001). Available at: http://www.saflii.org/za/legis/num_act/haa2001187.pdf [Accessed 4 April 2010].

UPI. 2020. *64 Migrants Found Dead in Track Container in Mozambique*, March 24. Available at: https://www.upi.com/Top_News/World-News/2020/03/24/64-migrants-found-dead-in-truck-container-in-Mozambique/7131585060627/ [Accessed 21 December 2020].

Chapter Four

# Media Reporting of the 2015 Xenophobic Attacks in Durban

Media platforms in South Africa have generally been considered by government agencies to be inconsiderate and vicious in their reporting of xenophobia, which has aggravated the ferocious tensions between South African citizens and immigrants of African origin. The negative portrayal of migrants by influential leaders in South Africa – including traditional, political and business leaders – through the rhetoric of media platforms has fueled and armed locals with xenophobic slogans and reasons to attack nationals of African descent. Through their reporting, media houses have failed to uphold ethical values in reporting on xenophobia. Reporters rely on gossip and second-hand information and use baseless data, which further instigates various groups to attack one another.

In view of the above, the present study attempts to examine the reasons why the media plays such a critical role in understanding xenophobia. Second, the study aims to establish whether the initiatives of government agencies and of civil society groups influence the media so that journalists report in a responsible manner and tone. There is a serious gap in the current literature, which is biased against the government. The researchers of the current study have not tested the perceptions of journalists, government officials and members of civil society on the adverse effects of xenophobic attacks in hotspots – such as townships where attacks are prevalent. This study was triggered by the fact that there is a paucity of empirical published research on the relationship between the media and xenophobic violence at a local level in South Africa and the different perceptions of print media's reporting and how it fuels xenophobia. Furthermore, the existing studies are generic and anecdotal, lacking information that is reported in the popular media. This chapter provides empirical evidence where in-depth interviews regarding this catastrophe were conducted with relevant informants and triangulated with published media articles, where unknown themes emerged.

An interesting research study was conducted by Dahlback (2019) investigating the framing of both the victims and the perpetrators of the 2015 xenophobic attacks. The author analyzed six online newspaper articles and found the newspapers to have reported a combination of balanced and unbalanced content during

**Addressing Xenophobia in South Africa:**
**Drivers, Responses and Lessons from the Durban Untold Stories, 83–107**
Copyright © 2022 by Bethuel Sibongiseni Ngcamu and Evangelos Mantzaris
Published under exclusive licence by Emerald Publishing Limited
**doi:10.1108/978-1-80262-479-320211005**

the violence. Meanwhile, Ngcamu and Mantzaris (2019a), in their empirical study conducted in Durban on the 2015 attacks against immigrants, found the media's reporting was reckless and that journalists did not properly investigate the xenophobic phenomenon. The authors confirm the widely shared sentiments that media reporting is biased and reckless.

Another interesting study was undertaken by Moyo and Nshimbi (2020) who claim that the members of the media in South Africa portray and catalyze the ideology that immigrants of African origin are undesirable and do not deserve to live in South Africa. These authors further opine that the media's narratives contribute to xenophobia, destroying the basic fabric of social cohesion. There are some authors who have contested the association between inconsiderate reporting by the media and xenophobia in South Africa (Hadland, 2008, p. 7), with other authors arguing that such conflicts take different shapes, forms and manifestations (Nyamnjoh, 2006). In the xenophobic violence that took place in 2008, Neocosmos (2008) observed the politics of fear coordinated by the apparatus of the state. As early as 2000, the media was seen to be stoking xenophobic tendencies (Dube, 2000): journalists were the creators of certain perceptions about African immigrants (Smith, 2001). However, studies that dissect the triggers of xenophobia at a local level and how this is influenced by the media are lacking in South Africa.

The following sections are broken down into the literature review, which links criminality, the media and xenophobia. Furthermore, the results and the discussion are intertwined with the conclusions and recommendations at the end of the study.

## Triggers of Xenophobia in South Africa

False and biased reporting by the media has been perceived to have contributed to the injury and displacement of vulnerable people (immigrants, refugees, asylum seekers and black women and children in general) and tarnished the international standing of South Africa. Everatt (2010) observed the reporting of the xenophobic attacks to the newspapers with less effort pertaining to the broadcast media. The author believes that the 2008 xenophobic outburst were caused by the "ripe conditions" of the time which were linked to the combination of socio-economic and spatial inequalities, reliance on the cheap labor by employers, shortage of houses, economic competition in the retail sector, racism and the history of violence in the country.

Nkealah (2011, p. 124) partly concurs with the previous author, but further outlines the causes of xenophobia as interwoven with service delivery, access to housing, water and sanitation, high youth unemployment in the townships, crime and lackluster immigration laws. Furthermore, Ngcamu and Mantzaris (2019b) posit that scholars mostly link economic competition between the warring factions to xenophobia and overlook government's failures and poorly enforced legislations. These authors further conclude that economic competition among immigrants, criminal businesses, the state's poor contingency plans and security agencies' failure to detect attacks against foreign nationals as being behind the violence. The literature reviewed above clearly paints a picture which points to the reality that media houses are basically producers of anecdotal data which are mostly one-sided and filled with the perceptions of civil society groups, community activists and government officials who are directly implicated in this catastrophe.

Bennett (2009) highlights the role of the media in covering substantial issues of public interest, such as political and/or moral crises, questioning their stand-points, analyses, accuracy and effects on society and affected populations. Such research analyses of the direct and indirect effects of communicative practices, where state functionaries and institutions feed the media their own centralized messages regarding existing or future crises, ensure that a particular message will be transmitted to the public. It was only in the mid-1980s that researchers in different disciplines began exploring and analyzing the social realities conveyed to society through news content and wider communication coverage. In so doing, an attempt was made to dissect and interpret communication messages, especially those dealing with a wide variety of crises (Entman, 2010, pp. 390–391; Wilkins et al., 2014).

In this particular case, the research by Charman and Piper (2012, p. 81) indicated that the attacks targeting foreign nationals were mostly driven by "anti-foreigner sentiments," criminal activities and economic competition between locals and foreigners. There has been research indicating that xenophobia is both a direct and indirect result of the government's failure to control its borders with its neighbors and the economic, social and political crisis in the country, together with poverty, homelessness and unemployment (Crush and Ramachandran, 2014). Piper and Charman (2016) saw that the attacks were directed mostly at Somalians who are considered to be more successful compared to Bangladeshis. This espoused another form of xenophobia that arose between competitors and foreign nationals not originally from Africa. A host of researchers have associated the triggers of xenophobia with "denialism" of government officials and their ineffective policies as well as the scapegoating of foreign nationals due their inabilities to provide quality services to the locals. The socio-economic and socio-political negative repercussions of the attacks the immigrants have been at the center on the research writing in this subject of xenophobia with very few focusing on xenophobia in universities.

Meanwhile, Rasila and Musitha (2016) attribute the causes of xenophobia in South Africa to the lack of communication between foreign nationals and locals. The authors acknowledge economic competition as being behind xenophobia; however, what they singled out as the trigger of the xenophobic attacks was the lack of effective communication in integrating foreign nationals into local communities. Piper and Charman (2016), meanwhile, have argued that attacks against spaza shops owners (immigrants) in the townships have occurred as a result of the belief that foreigners have taken over informal businesses in various areas. The authors' survey among 1,000 spaza shop owners revealed a fascinating finding, pinpointing the fact that those with expensive goods experienced less violent attacks than those with cheaper goods. Piper and Charman (2016) concluded that violent attacks have nothing to do with nationalities but are linked to the pricing of the goods.

Crush and Ramachandran (2014) termed both administrative and political officials "denialists." They also confirmed that media reporting in the townships is insufficient, even invisible even though such areas are the worst affected areas of xenophobia. These authors (Crush and Ramachandran, 2014) mention another form of denialism, mainly coordinated by state security agencies (including the police): the dereliction of duty by government through failing to safeguard and control its borders. The authors also characterize the xenophobic attacks as "minimalism." They consider the violence to be deep-seated in a country's social crisis and linked to economic competition.

Hence, in a book by Eliseev et al. (2008), Bishop Paul Veryn depicted the 2008 xenophobic attacks against the foreign nationals as an unexpected thunderstorm that was characterized by unprecedented horror and unabated anger. The Bishop alluded to the fact that the warning signs were evident before the full scale of the unprecedented xenophobic violence of the 2008 in South Africa which was exacerbated by an unprepared government unable to respond to such attacks against the most vulnerable people. The Bishop mentioned that the attacks were directed against the black foreign nationals without any evidence on the attacks against the Indians and Whites. The perpetrators only targeted the vulnerable and mostly poor foreign nationals.

Worby et al. (2008) provided a background on how the 2008 attacks against the foreign nationals and the South Africans who speak other languages than the dominant ones (Xhosa and Zulu) were viciously attacked on a Sunday of May 11, 2008 which was sparked by murder, rape and looting which had also spread to other provinces (such as the KwaZulu-Natal [KZN] and the Western Cape). The then President of the country (Thabo Mbeki) distanced his people from embarking on xenophobia rather associated such attacks to criminals. The president accentuated that the "authentic South Africans" cannot harbor such xenophobic sentiments and motives as they are imbibed to the struggle to African university.

In 2008, Gelb (2008) suggested that numerous commentators have associated xenophobic violence in the informal settlements (Townships) with existing difficulties encountered by poor people. The author argued that when the journalist pressed them on the main causality of such attacks against the foreign nationals, the residents cited the issues of shortage of work, crime, lack of housing and access to basic services. Meanwhile, Minister Essop Pahad linked the xenophobic violence as the act of the "Third Force" by claiming that the government of South Africa has delivered more for the poor when compared to other developing countries. Landau (2012) posits that although 60 lives were lost and 700 people wounded in the 2008 xenophobic attacks against the foreign nationals in South Africa, the government of South Africa consistently denied the existence of xenophobia and rather blamed the criminal elements, third force, opposition parties and the civil society groups. Resentment and anger, nationalist tendencies, and anti-immigrants' rhetoric by the locals were the key reasons identified by Landau (2012) to be behind the attacks against the shopkeepers by community leaders, gangsters and the business associations.

Whilst, Pillay (2008) posits that a simple narration of xenophobia as an issue of "identify" or identification ("South Africans have foreigners" or South Africans have African foreigners') is misleading.

Landau (2008) provided some realties that, the government of South Africa and the civil society groups have long overlooked the marginalization of foreigners as well rapid and rabid murders at the hands of the locals. In addition, these important organs of state and Non-Governmental Organisations (NGOs) have turned a blind eye the culture of naming the foreign nationals with derogatory names such as illegals, illegal immigrants, jumpers, displaces, aliens, *amakwerek-were* and Nigerians.

There were a number of concerns raised by local entrepreneurs who reported that foreigners were "killing their businesses by selling goods cheaper" and that the foreign nationals "were operating their businesses without licences or permits." However, such statements were disputed by the reference group led by Judge Navi Pillay, which concluded that it was unfortunate that a number of foreign nationals operated outside the legal confines of the country. The reference group was set following the attacks. It was an enquiry undertaken by a group of experts in a variety of fields, called the Special Reference Group on Migration and Community Integration in KZN and was appointed by the then provincial premier.

The team of experts was chaired by the internationally respected Judge Navi Pillay, and included the reputable NGO African Centre for the Constructive Resolution of Disputes (ACCORD) which operated as the initiatives as the secretariat aimed at supporting the group's operational work. Its aim was to investigate the causes and consequences of the March and May 2015 xenophobic attacks in the province as well as to assess the shortcomings and successes of present and past efforts. The purpose was to focus on the reduction of tensions between communities and to propose tangible and achievable short- and long-term solutions that would lead to a peaceful coexistence between communities.

Within this broad historical and present context, the media coverage of xenophobia in South Africa and internationally is directly and indirectly connected to the social crisis: the thoughts, understanding and actions of very significant social and political groups that represent affected communities, civil society and the state. This is because the media shapes opinions, ideas, beliefs and actions regarding certain significant situations. Previous research concerned with xenophobic violence and related issues has been essentially impressionistic, providing a qualitative analysis based mostly on a small sampling of press clippings. Different commentators (Smith, 2001, 2008) have in previous years observed media reporting as being shallow, with xenophobic, anti-immigrant stories being published which shape ideologies and discourses. However, researchers have mostly relied on secondary sources of literature without interrogating the viewpoints of the stakeholders who were directly involved in the planning, response and mitigation of the impacts of xenophobia in selected, affected communities. These stakeholders who have been overlooked include government officials and agencies, the police, civil society groups, NGOs, media reporters and community activists, who have been sidelined in a process of testing their perceptions regarding the occurrence of xenophobic attacks in South Africa.

## Media Frames and Xenophobic Violence

The available literature on the issue of the media and xenophobia has been dominated largely by a number of media and printed newspaper articles that predominantly characterized by impressions and anecdotes passing as analysis. Accordingly, in the past two decades, media platforms have been seen to be propagating certain ideologies and discourses, showing bias toward specific powerful individuals (Smith, 2008, p. 2) and publishing xenophobic stories that give a shallow analysis of the phenomenon (Smith, 2001, p. 3). A plethora of researchers have highlighted the adverse impacts of the media in various ways, such as Hadland (2010, p. 119) who argues that journalists perpetuate attacks against migrants by publishing inflammatory stories.

An example of this is the lack of communication between the state and communities noticed in Alexandra in the 2008 xenophobic incidences (Gomo, 2010) and the shallow and inadequate information fanning ethnic hatred and violence observed in countries such as Kenya and Rwanda. Interestingly, Hadland (2010), in his study on the 2008 xenophobic violence (collected in Alexandra, Tembisa and Mamelodi), found that the perpetrators of the xenophobic attacks participated aiming to attract media attention in order to be seen and become famous. Meanwhile, anti-immigrant perceptions about cross-border migration to South Africa was negative; the statistics were unfounded and non-analytical (Danso and McDonald, 2001, p. 2). These findings support the latter conclusions by Smith (2008, p. 3) – that views of the media are one-sided and anti-immigrant, dominated by negative comments and using derogatory words against migrants such as *criminals*, *illegal immigrants* and *thieves of jobs*.

This type of research examines the direct and indirect effects of communication practices, where state functionaries and institutions feed the media their own centralized messages regarding existing or future crises, ensuring that their particular message will be conveyed to the public.

The South African Foreign Affairs Minister in 2008 was highly critical of the African media pointing fingers at what was called the lack of deep investigation into xenophobic attacks and the "sensational pattern" of reporting these incidents and their roots and causes (*The Times*, 2008). In addition, the Department of Home Affairs called on both editors and journalists to be brave enough to accept personal liability for the "inflammatory content" of articles that appeared in their newspapers (Hadland, 2010, p. 123). An empirical research study conducted in 2005 by the Institute for Democracy in South Africa (IDASA), a highly respected NGO, concluded that xenophobic reporting by the South African media is problematic.

## The "Seminal" Empirical Works on Xenophobia: A Brief Exploration

There has been a number of academically and researched –based works that have paved the way to new modes of thinking through the utilization of old and new theories and innovative methodological paths to a deeper and wider understanding of the realities of xenophobia at all levels. Although pioneer works on the issue such as those of Misago, Desai and Vahed and Neocosmos amongst others have been utilized extensively in this book, there are a few deeply empirical works that deserve to be briefly acknowledged as they have opened deeper and newer ways leading to the understanding the complicated and challenging nature of xenophobic attacks, violence, realities and their repercussions for human relations.

Von Holdt et al. (2011) collective work on insurgent citizenship, collective violence and what they call "the struggle for a place in the new South Africa" has paved the way to new and important information on xenophobia and its relationship with community protests and many of its realities, challenges and characteristics.

Their research project, an innovative, even pioneering one consisted of research studies of community protests and xenophobic violence as expressions of "collective action" and "insurgent citizenship." The CSVR (Centre for the Study of Violence and Reconciliation), a NGO and a Witwatersrand University based research institute, SWOP (the Society Work and Development Institute) collaborated in a research project aiming to empirically provide new knowledge on key issues of the underlying social dynamics of collective violence through an analysis of class formation and local life and politics.

It took place soon after the traumatic May 2008 xenophobic attacks and the feeling of analyzing and understanding social fragmentation, anger, exclusion, violence and death were transformed into a rich on the ground empirical effort that paved the way forward to a large number of research practitioners.

The research project was set in Gauteng and attempted to explore the linkages and differences between two dissimilar collective and occasionally violent actions through the utilization of a broad qualitative methodology aiming at the analysis of relationships, contestations and their meanings. The researchers utilized a snowball sampling methods and participant observation that took place at political rallies, taverns, and parties as well as a large number of interviews in street corners and informal focus groups in taverns.

It was an overall comparative analysis comprising of diversified case studies, which begun by pinpointing that the role played by the police in such events was characterized by a combination of either provocative and unnecessary violence or absolute absence. In terms of the latter attitude the researchers showed that during the period of xenophobic violence there was a serious lack of effort on the part of the police in preventing the attacks or protecting foreign nationals in the early stages of violence.

There are evident similarities between xenophobic attacks and community protests against government in their levels of violence according to the researchers and this can be found in their claims, impact targets and a number of their repertoires, including the similarities of organizations that may be involved, repertoires and commonalities, such as violence and grievances in regard of state inactions or actions.

In many ways, however, the researchers have shown that such similarities are founded principally but not exclusively on the fact that both xenophobic attacks and anti-government protest meetings follow common roots in terms of the organizing processes. This despite the fact that it has been extremely difficult to ascertain the key organizers of xenophobic attacks. The research has shown that on many occasions informal networks and groups have played a key role especially when anti-government protests turn into xenophobic attacks. The research has shown that almost all xenophobic attacks occurred primarily in informal settlements, where municipalities are ineffectual or have no presence. This means that the settlement's inhabitants take the law into their own hands.

This reality was evident in two areas where xenophobic attack occurred (Gladysville and Slovoview). The violence begun with mass meetings. The meeting in Slovoview was called by the settlement's leadership in order to debate and make plans in respect of the influx of foreign nationals fleeing violence in other areas. On the other hand, the meeting in Gladysville was called for decisions to be made in the process of organizing a protest march regarding housing and other services targeting the municipal offices. In both cases, the local civic organizations were instrumental in calling the meetings, but participants held different opinions in regard to the real mobilizers against foreigners. The crowd in Slovoview barricaded the entrances leading to the informal section of the settlement and identified foreigners systematically and expelled them, while parts of the participants left the meeting, attacked and looted foreign-own shops. During the next day in Gladysville large crowds congregated, abandoned the protest march and systematically looted and burnt foreign shops and their shacks in the whole area.

In the last case, there was strong evidence of an ambiguous role of formal organizations supplemented by the activities of South African business networks and young, unemployed youth group gangs organized in tavern meetings. They began the attacks and looting of shops and shacks and were immediately followed by man and women of all ages joined in.

In the Trouble area, the African National Congress (ANC) and the Community Police Forum (CPF) called the meeting, but isolated groups of young people began attacking the foreign shops, but they were repelled by well-armed foreign shopkeepers. In the meeting that took place both the ANC and the CPF opposed vehemently the community members demanding that the residents should arm themselves and drive the foreigners out. This was possibly a position justified by the fact that the majority of foreigners were very well armed.

A similar position was advocated by the ANC and the CPF in Slovoview. The organizations mobilized against xenophobic attacks together with the police and were supported by those residents in Reconstruction and Development Programme (RDP) houses while the ones living in shacks were absent.

The research has shown that such existing divisions have been rooted on internal political and organizational divisions leading to perpetual struggles amongst organizations, local councilors and ANC factions in serious conflict situations (such as the struggles between South African National Civil Organisation [SANCO] and the ANC) over control of specific areas. There has been evidence that SANCO leadership has been divided and under community pressure to lead the attacks against foreigners, while the ANC was instrumental in containing it. The evidence shows that in Gladysville, the massive protests that resulted in xenophobic violence were mobilized by the South African Students Congress

(SASCO) while in the Trouble area despite the divisions both within SASCO and the ANC none of these organizations supported the xenophobic violence.

The research has shown that despite the distinctions that exist between xenophobic attacks and violent community protest, the interplay between them cannot be ignored because on many occasions xenophobic attacks have taken place as an adjunct activity to the main focus on community protest. These are obvious in both the cased of Gladysville and Slovoview as the similarities are evident.

At another case study in an urban township (Ndabeni), the coalition of Rastafari groups, a coalition of local political activists and popular residents were successful in mobilizing against xenophobic attacks. In the same vain in the rural informal settlement of Bokfontein, the empowerment of local leadership through a public employment program and the process of community building were instrumental in resisting attempts to organize xenophobic attacks.

In general terms, it has been shown that community protests and xenophobic attacks overlap; that xenophobic attacks have been generally organized by a combination of informal networks and groups including South African business people, unemployed youths and formal organizational and political leaderships; the main tendency in these attacks shows that in most cases their most organized and violent attacks occur in informal and semi-formal settlements; such settlements have been characterized by weak state structures and communities are mostly characterized by perpetual competition over the control of existing resources; local organizations implicated in xenophobic attacks that are generally present themselves as civil society activists, tend not to dissolve themselves in the violence aftermath; they remain durable structures because of their control of resources outside the state; there have been informal networks and formal organizations who have opposed xenophobic violence and work to strengthen the rule of law and the state's monopoly over coercion.

Manson's doctorate on xenophobia, citizenship and "collective mobilisation" situated in a South African settlement attempted to analyze and dissect the "politics of exclusion" at the "threshold of the state".

Through the utilization of a very wide range of theoretical and methodological tools, the researcher attempted to explore political identities defined by history and space and the processes of "shaping exclusionary collective mobilization" in an informal settlement, thus countering notions of "xenophobia" as an effect of elite manipulation, racism, poverty or psychological pathology.

Theoretically, the work provided an understanding of "local belonging" built on political involvement and explores the relationship between exclusion, "threshold space" and "agency and bare life." The key aim was the effort to illuminate tensions between exclusion and inclusion and citizens' and human rights.

In the effort to develop a theoretical, ethnographic and historical analysis of informal residence in South Africa and "xenophobic" mobilization, the researcher moved from the national to the local scale, and utilized methodological tools such as archival data, documentary analysis, and ethnographic field research in the effort to periodize the history of a South African squatter camp as a site for the insurgent claiming of citizenship from 1994.

The case study that took place in the Mshongo settlement in the Tshwane township of Atteridgeville points to the reality that after the democratic transition starting in 1994 the settlement transformed into a "threshold space" that permanently existed neither outside nor inside citizenship.

In such a situation, the institutional structures of collective violence and mobilization rooted on political and spatial inequalities perpetually produced a form of (infra-)citizenship that led to a resurgence of Mshongo's traditions of collective action. It was argued that individualistic political and economic practices introduced and perpetrated by foreign newcomers ("non-citizens") became strong transgressions of this tradition, especially at periods of protest.

Within such a reality the researcher utilized a constructivist perspective in the attempt to capture the conceptual realities of the place, politics and history and their "material forms and fabric." Such realities are related to collective action, social interaction and are shaped by material forces that are connected to the center of state power. Within this context, the squatter settlement is described as a setting and a process because its world is shaped by specific social, economic and historical factors. The knowledge of such factors was strengthened through the exploration of government archives and similar material relating to squatting over time and across all state levels. Comparative studies in regard of squatter camps in South Africa and internationally were scrutinized especially in terms of establishing the realities of political identities associated with sanctions and rights including categories such as voting rights and citizenship.

In these processes, informal settlements' populations were described as "political communities" whose trust networks and common interests have led to collective action despite their individual characteristics and classifications such as religion, language, class or lineage. These realities meant that the case study planned should be based on a process of exploring hypotheses based on a comparative dimension enabling the exploration of causal mechanisms and reflection of the existing theory.

These are the key reasons for the selection of an informal settlement where "xenophobic" mobilization had taken place a reality that could lead to a knowledge-based dissection of realities. In the process, a wide variety of cases that took place in the 2008 outbreak, as over 100 incidences during the 2008 period were assessed and dissected through the media with emphasis on interfering variables during these periods. Such initiatives were supplemented by case study-based secondary data including personal interviews produced over the years by a specialized research unit based at the university of the Witwatersrand and the secondary data from case studies they had carried out in previous years.

The analysis of data begun with a description of collective mobilizations against foreigners based on the links to social and material changes in the residents' lives that led to emergence of insurgent practices, collective action and violence as well as the denunciation of non-participants. There was a demonstration of how noticeable tensions emerged between the what was described as the "communitarian politics" of squatters and the apparent individualism of foreign newcomers in the area as the latter performed political indifference during collective action, reinforcing the "polarizing effect" of foreign dominance in the existing retail market. In the researcher's analysis, the "politics of place" is illustrated in the existence and perpetration of the existing tension and contention.

There is no doubt that the thesis can be considered as a serious contribution to the understanding of vital components of historical and existent social realities of xenophobic violence in South Africa. The thorough empirical component at all levels is supplemented thoroughly by its connections not only with Von Holdt et al. (2011) pioneer research work, but also an abundance of theoretical justifications of almost every aspect of the many angles of the research terrain. The findings indicating that the mobilizations against foreigners have arisen because of socio-political tensions between South African citizens living a life sinking into a perpetual collective obligation, lack of social mobility and material decline, and non-citizens advancing materially, enjoying individual freedom and have opened the doors of a "good life."

The contribution of the researcher also lies in the fact that her findings have open new paths of understanding of realities within the confines of a "specific public place," with emphasis on the differences between established and "newly arrived" foreigners and the established foreigners, scapegoating, leadership roles power and legitimacy.

Sally Peperby's 2016 research on international migrants in Johannesburg's informal economy is one of the highly important undertakings of the Southern African Migration Programme (SAMP) Migration Policy series that has produced a wide variety of thoroughly researched projects dealing with most, if not all, aspects of the realities of the sector (Peperby, 2016).

The research undertaking was a collaboration of SAMP, the African Centre for Cities (ACC), Gauteng City-Region Observatory (GCRO), the Eduardo Mondlane University (Maputo) and the International Development Research Centre (IDRC).

The GIS methodology was selected and migrant entrepreneurship survey questionnaire was debated, planned and designed for use in Johannesburg. Tablets were utilized for the interviews allowing the GPS coordinates to be captured and the interview locations were determined by the knowledge of areas where migrant entrepreneurs were operating, including the Central Business Districts of Cape Town and Johannesburg, African townships residential areas in the inner city as well as informal settlements.

The research comprised of 618 interviews amongst international migrant entrepreneurs in Johannesburg in May 2014 including a small number of interviews that took place just outside the official municipal boundaries of the city but were included in this analysis. All informal business in the sample were not registered for VAT and with a turnover of less than 1 million South African rands per year and businesses in the finance, mining, and transport were excluded. Most of the participants were in Alexandra (76), the Johannesburg Central Business District (63), the Baragwanath Hospital (50), Westbury (47), Bellevue (42), Bruma (37), Yeoville (32), Rosettenville (31), Chiawelo (24), Berea (23), Hillbrow (23), Maponya Mall (22) and Lenasia (21).

The research was undertaken bearing in mind the reality that the informal economy has played over the years an important role in the entrepreneurial terrain of

Johannesburg and has been patronized by the majority of the city's population. A survey of Johannesburg residents that took place in 2013 showed that 11% owned businesses of which 65% operated in the informal economy. Contrary to the beliefs and wide speculation regarding the "penetration" of migrant entrepreneurs in the city's informal economy, only 20% of informal economy business owners had moved to the Gauteng province from their countries. This statistic reality, then, meant that existing fears amongst local informal entrepreneurs have been seriously exaggerated. Despite this statistical reality the local entrepreneur's competitive intensity had been instrumental in the proliferation of the violent xenophobic attacks in the 2000s that was followed by the January and April 2015 outbreak of violence against foreigners that led to murders and razing of homes and business premises.

The report has shown that politicians' rhetoric during and after the 2015 attacks were hostile to immigrant entrepreneurs. Such an attitude was similar to the local government's actions in 2013, when the City of Johannesburg began the *Operation Clean Sweep,* that swept all local and foreign traders off the street. Following the operation, the "re-registration" of entrepreneurs in the area tried to limit access to South Africans only. This did not deter immigrant entrepreneurs from operating their businesses in the city.

The research showed that the majority of the entrepreneurs were men (70%), while 30% were women with 96% been between 20 and 49 years of age; 29% had completed primary school or less, almost 40% had attended secondary schools while 23% had completed it and 9% had at least some tertiary education. Their origins were in 27 countries, 21 in Africa and the majority (65% of them) originated in Southern African Development Community (SADC) countries especially Zimbabwe (30%) and Mozambique (14%). Seven percent of them were from Nigeria, 5% were from the DRC, Lesotho, and Pakistan, and 4% from India.

At least 46% were asylum seekers, refugees, or permanent residents with permits that allow them to own and operate businesses in South Africa. Another 20% held work permits, mostly Zimbabwean Special Dispensation Permits which again allowed them to operate a business. Another 12% held visitors' permits, while only 12% had no official documentation.

There has been a perception that migrant entrepreneurs have advantages in business skills and experience compared to their South Africans counterparts, while the general belief is that those involved in the informal economy, irrespective of nationality, are often described or/and thought to be survivalists, lacking entrepreneurial skills and aspirations.

The survey discovered that 56% of the participants were unemployed before coming to South Africa; 5% of them were involved in informal entrepreneurial activity; only 2% owned a business in the formal economy in their own countries; 47% of them were unemployed in South Africa before opening their own business; over a quarter of them had performed semi-skilled or unskilled manual work, while 5% were professional workers. These realities suggest clearly that the informal sector of the economy offers opportunities not always found in the formal economy.

It was shown that a minority of the entrepreneurs had prior experience in an enterprise in South Africa, as 13% had operated a previous informal economy business and 5% owned a business in the formal economy before starting their present business. 56% of the participants indicated that their skills were self-taught, 19% had learnt from relatives and friends and relatives, and 10% had learnt from operating as apprentices. Finally, 37% indicated that they did not need any particular skills.

The survey researchers interviewed migrants in the wholesale and retail (59%), services (30%) and manufacturing (12%) sectors. The findings relating to their business operations and success indicated that for most, there has been a considerable time lag between the arrival in South Africa and the time their business begun; three-quarters of the enterprises were established after 2005 although 55% of respondents had arrived in South Africa long before that date; 85% utilized personal savings as the main source of start-up capital, while 32% accessed loans from relatives and other individuals; only 1% obtained a bank loan.

In terms of amounts of start-up capital 39% of the participants had invested less than 5,000 rands, 21% between 5,001 and 10,000 rands, and 19% between 10,001 and 20,000 rands. Only 18% had businesses valued less than 5,000 rands while 52% valued them at over 20,000. This even though only 21% had invested more than 20,000 rands as a start-up.

The general feeling most amongst South Africans is that immigrant and refugee entrepreneurs have a negative economic impact on the South African and the livelihoods of the local population. The findings of the survey showed that migrant entrepreneurs have created jobs for locals as they have employed 1,586 of them (i.e., 2.6 jobs per business); South Africans held 503 (32% of all employees and 41% of all non-family employees) of these jobs; 41% sourced their supplies from formal wholesalers, 27% from factories, 17% from supermarkets, and per cent from small shops and retailers, all of them South African owned.

These findings clearly show that they are instrumental in creating jobs in the economy and pay VAT. In addition, 31% paid rent to a South African company or individual for their business property; are providers of goods and services to South Africans at affordable prices and in convenient geographical locations.

On the other hand, the entrepreneurs face a number of problems and challenges including the inability to get bank credit for start-up and ongoing investments, mostly because they are "foreigners"; the police (mainly spearheaded by the Johannesburg Metropolitan Police Department) possessed a negative impact on their businesses because they confiscated items, demanded bribes, and exercised physical assault (cited by 19%); prejudice because of their nationality (54%), verbal insults against their business (46%), and physical attacks by South Africans (24%); one in five respondents indicated that acts of xenophobia had affected seriously their business operations.

The survey report provides through empirical research the importance of refugee and migrant and informal business-persons operating in the informal and formal sectors of the economy of the City of Johannesburg.

The researchers have pinpointed the need to develop policies that will enable the growth of the Small, Medium and Micro Enterprises (SMME) and township economies, and manage fairly and professionally the informal economy and street trading instead of trying to sweep the streets clean of these small businesses.

It is believed that the research has shown the need for the incorporation of the businesses owned by migrant entrepreneurs, instead of them exclude and demonization because they are a seriously valuable contribution to Johannesburg's economy despite the fact that they operate in non-enabling policy and political environment.

The originality of Orkin's book in 2019 (Orkin, 2019) lies in the fact that his empirical research attempts to investigate possible predictors of xenophobic attitudes. These attitudes and the research subjects' underlying causes, which have been experienced by the local population in the longer term must be according to the researcher distinguished from the short-term, context-specific triggers of outbreaks of xenophobic violence.

Orkin's work is founded on the belief that attitudes, causes and "triggers" have been what he considered to be the separately necessary conditions which when they occur simultaneously are "jointly sufficient" for xenophobic outbreaks to take place.

Based on existing research realities and findings, the researcher opines that "triggers" that are particular to sudden moment or place are very difficult to predict as on many occasions they involve local shopkeepers who are threatened by foreigner competition or campaigning national or provincial politicians, encouraged and supported by media coverage, an issue that has received serious attention in the present book.

The key fundamentals of the research were rooted on "objective" and "subjective," proximal and distal factors such as demographic or structural, peoples' dispositions, perception and moods regarding xenophobic attitudes and intentions to act, triggers such as mobilization of "violence entrepreneurs," acts of xenophobic violence as well as macro-culture are: foreigners; policies, legislation, media, etc., social and economic situation and governance shortfalls providing opportunities.

The main objective of such a research, Orkin believed, was to open a new original and fresh understanding and identification of the more enduring causes leading to xenophobic attacks and the instruction of policy interventions enabling the likelihood and reduction of such outbreaks of violence and destruction.

It is a statistically based analysis rooted on attitude surveys attempting to "correct" three already published similar scientific efforts whose final findings indicated that poverty, unemployment, illiteracy and residency in informal settlements, were found not to have correlations with xenophobic attitudes in the process of a multivariable regressions analysis. It is then such findings that made the researcher to attempt a deeper, more comprehensive and multiple regression analysis.

The analysis was rooted on the Quality of Life Survey produced by GCRO (GCRO, 2016). The detailed report of the Observatory contained comprehensive information of 27,820 South Africans who participated in the large sample of 30,002 respondents living in the 529 wards of the Gauteng City-Region that included the urban metropolitan areas of Tshwane (Pretoria) and Johannesburg.

Orkin pinpointed the existence of three statistical models in the analysis in order to "mediate" in between intervening variables and predictors as well as an outcome and the realities of their suitability in the analysis and dissection. One of the two models incorporated the particularities, strengths and methods of social sciences including psychology, sociology, ad philosophy as well as the "everyday intuition." According to him, qualitative research was based on a "causal chain" found in these social sciences. Such a reality evident in this type of research creates an explanatory pathway based on peoples' objective circumstances and leading to their specific attitudes and actions.

In order to justify the usefulness of this methodological choice, he used the opinion of a local homeless interviewee who believed that houses that should be owned by local people were sold to foreigners. This, despite the fact that according to him foreigners bring illnesses and drugs to South Africa.

The three statistical models used were based on the utilization of different variables associated with a variety of questions with the first one addressing responses to questions in the GCRO data set. One of them contrasted the opinion of the respondents who felt that foreigners should be sent back to their countries of origin. 25% of interviewees agreed with this position, while 75% accepted or welcomed foreigners in case they were "legal" (75%).

Eighty percent (80%) of residents in informal settlements residents were more likely to possess more hostile attitudes toward foreigners than formal residents a reality pinpointing the existence of the mediator of depression. On the other hand, 44% of the unemployed were more likely to have a hostile attitude when compared the employed because of the existence of depression, worries, or dissatisfaction with their everyday lives. In addition, those in the database whose households had to skip one meal in the past were 31% more likely highly dissatisfied with their lives as well as their local authorities.

Another statistical model was based on most likely the most extreme survey question, dealing directly with the "readiness to attack foreigners." Only 3.6% assented, hence the researcher used the data at the individual level. The findings indicated that those who did not feel better off in comparison to those living near them were 63% more likely than those who did feel better off.

According to the researcher, the three statistical models in the literature, were found to be inadequate in suggesting that objective circumstances are "generally not significant determinants of xenophobic attitudes." In this process, he pointed out, the force of these predictors, such as life's realities of personal or social hunger, unemployment, or/and life in informal settlements becomes evident in path analysis. This uncovers the reality that attitudes, beliefs and actions work through a multiplicity of subjective mediators such as dissatisfaction with life and personal depression. Such individual and social situations and feelings make people who experience such realities and face the consequences of their distressed circumstances are more likely to entertain xenophobic attitudes as a matter of empirical realities. It has been mentioned that there could be possibilities of mitigation of such circumstances if they are "tackled by social development."

# Results

### *Print Media Propaganda and Inaccurate Reporting*

The respondents from the municipal and the provincial government have considered the role of the media during the 2015 xenophobic violence to be the:

> *"planned, middle of the road"* and that the media disseminates
> *anti-immigrant ideologies which drive certain political agendas."*
> "Planned, middle of the road" reporting is associated with weak
> analyses based on perceptions such as foreigners stealing citizens'
> jobs and distributing drugs."

This has been attested to by a senior provincial government official who
believes that the reality of the so called "middle of the road" is not rooted in
political or social neutrality, but on its adoption by propagandists in order to mis-
guide the majority of the South African people, to confuse them and make them
forget or become blind-folded instead of meeting face to face the real causes,
homelessness, poverty and hunger.

The above research findings coincide with Moyo and Nshimbi (2020) arguments that the media depicts immigrants of African descent as undesirable and
not welcome to live in South Africa.

Several of the research subjects pointed out that the print media does not
report accurately on realties and rationales of why locals refuse to take on menial
jobs and business owners' preference of employing foreign nationals for such
jobs. This has been posited by the director in the Office of the Premier:

> The question that never appears in the press is ... not why South
> Africans do 'not want menial jobs' but the reality that all busi-
> ness sectors in South Africa want refugees and immigrants
> because they are cheap labour, they do not fight back, they will
> not join unions.

The narratives presented above have been echoed by numerous researchers
(Crush and Ramachandran, 2014; Dahlback, 2019) that during the 2015 xenophobic attacks against foreign nationals, the media reported unbalanced content.

The derogatory and unwarranted choice of words that have been used by
the press exacerbates tensions between citizens and foreign nationals, a perception that was shared by the interviewees in the provincial government sector. A
comment by a senior member in the Office of the Premier pinpointed the fact
that newspapers used derogatory terms for African immigrants and denigrating.
These were acts divided people on the ground and the stereotyping was at the
center of the perpetration of the attacks.

The above sentiments were also shared by Dube (2000) and Neocosmos (2008),
that government agencies were observed in the early part of the twenty-first century as encouraging xenophobic tendencies.

A government leader in the Provincial Disaster Management Center strongly
believed that journalists were victims of an ideological agenda based on hatred
against immigrants and refugees because deep inside were really afraid of an alliance of the African and South African poor that could lead to united action
against the state. These beliefs were behind their writings.

This has been confirmed by Hadland (2010), who stated that the media aggra-
vates attacks against immigrants through its inflammatory publications.

### *Pro-immigrant, Selective, Distorted and Sensational Reporting*

The government subjects who were interviewed shared similar sentiments – that the print media reporters were biased in their reporting. They were seen as pro-immigrant, providing false information and consequently worsening the xenophobia. The view held by a manager at the eThekwini Municipality was rooted on his belief that the escalation of attacks was due to the journalists' descriptions and "analysis" of key events such as King Zwelithini's "attacks" on foreigners and their "false impressions" created to the public in their reporting of the conditions of the shelters. It was described as false information.

The false information by publishing houses has been supported by Ngcamu and Mantzaris (2019a) who found that the 2015 attacks against foreign nationals were perpetuated by the media's reckless and one-sided reporting.

An eThekwini municipality official and member of the strategic committee indicated that despite the fact that in the first period of violence journalists accepted the fact that this was a "national problem," they abstained from the collective efforts and distorted realities on the ground as they occurred.

Such positions were reinforced by a senior disaster manager who described the negative reporting associated with the refugee shelters and their realities. It was stated that the description of the life in these institutions in the printed and social media was completely distorted in an open sensationalism and "clear distortions of reality." Such a position was reinforced by an eThekwini Coordinator of activities who believed that the journalism of the time was fueling violent attacks, especially in terms of the "misrepresentation" of King Zwelithini's speech on immigrants.

### *Criminal Business and the "Territory Dichotomy"*

A community activist from the informal settlement Bottlebrush, who recorded almost all the attacks against foreign nationals, had this to say:

> One of the reasons for the attacks on foreigners is related to the fight over "territory" in respect of electricity cable theft and illegal electricity connections that have become a lucrative trade for foreigners and South Africans alike. Foreigners have been described as much more advanced operators, in comparison with locals. eThekwini Municipality and the South African Police Services have failed to solve the electricity cable theft over the years. The theft has pitted South African [against] foreign thieves who compete over the lucrative loot. eThekwini [Municipality] did something to stop [the] theft, but they have been attacked violently by communities who defended the illegal connections.

The association between criminality and xenophobia mentioned above concurs with the findings of Charman and Piper (2012, p. 81) – that the violence perpetrated against the immigrants in Cape Town was fueled by criminal activities, anti-foreigner sentiments and economic competition.

This was also mentioned by a member of the ward committee in Chatsworth:

> The reality is that cables that supply power to homes have become a valuable commodity and fetch top prices; while illegal connections are rife in disadvantaged and underdeveloped areas and due to the high rate of copper and cable theft, the eThekwini relevant departments are forced to do replacements almost every day. This forces the municipality, with the help of the police, to send teams that are deployed in groups of five [to] the informal settlements and other areas [to] set about dismantling the illegal connections. The electricians cut through cables of different sizes that are connected to electricity supply boxes on wooden poles. Poles holding up these illegal connections must also be brought down. Street lights are easy targets for thieves and this happens because informal settlements have no electricity and this provides criminals and thieves with opportunities that otherwise would not exist. Foreigners, especially Mozambicans and Zimbabweans, are more skilled and operate not only as thieves but also as illegal contractors who get paid by residents to make these illegal connections. This obviously puts them in competition with locals who are seen as second best and have over the years [been] instigating attacks against foreigners. This has occurred on many occasions, including several group attacks in Dassenhoek and KwaNdengezi, two predominantly African townships, where these incidents have taken the form of xenophobic attacks.

This position, expressed by a community activist who has dedicated his life to serving his community for decades, is similar to the findings of Crush and Ramachandran (2014) and Charman and Piper (2012). These authors coined the term "violent entrepreneurship" and confirmed that this is behind the violence that takes place in the townships.

### The Effects of Boredom and Youth Unemployment on Xenophobia

A former United Democratic Front (UDF) activist, who recorded eight attacks in a suburb outside Pinetown (KwaNdengezi) between the latter part of March and June 2015, cited boredom, especially among young people, as one of the key reasons behind the xenophobic attacks. This activist opines that:

> I believe that xenophobic attacks in this area [KwaNdengezi] are the result of a combination of factors such as unemployment, boredom, drug and alcohol abuse and lack of service delivery. The key foreigners attacked were Zimbabweans and Mozambicans and the attackers were always 10–15 young people armed with baseball bats, stones and knives. Those who were attacked were accused of stealing cables [and] jobs from locals and were threatened with

death if they did not leave the place within the next two days. The attackers told them they knew where they were staying and they will follow them until they go. Their cellular phones and money were stolen from them before the attackers fled. Police arrived from the KwaNdengezi station an hour after the event [even though] they were notified earlier. No one was found at the place of attack.

Numerous authors (Crush and Ramachandran, 2014; Nkealah, 2011) have confirmed this, attesting to the fact that the xenophobic crisis in South Africa revolves around competition and access to scarce resources.

### *Unethical Media Reporting*

A civil society activist pointed out that such realities exist because

> we as community leaders can only consult and talk to the community, but on most occasions, no one listens; we talk to journalists, telling them the truth as we know and see it and they print what want because they do not care and they are also afraid for their lives if they write the truth.

Another civil society activist with vast experience and knowledge of the community began by saying that community leaders are respected because everyone knows they are at the forefront of their communities, what newspapers and state agencies have openly called the "third force." According to this respondent:

> The state and the press have created the myth of the "third force" that attacks communities and the leadership in the press and the streets. This means that the state and the press have directly and indirectly portrayed the struggles of the poor as the "third force." On the other hand, journalists tried to befriend civil society and community leaders and they would call immediately after major situations arise and ask questions because they had no time to drive to the places where violence and attacks took place. In both the community and civil society groups, it was admitted, there have been leaders who, because they loved publicity, dealt with journalists, analysts, academics and other people "who talk big but are liberals." However, it was admitted that there have been a few … journalists and analysts who understood the dynamics of the places where the attacks took place, mainly in the poorest areas, "where people attack and ask questions later." A handful of journalists called before violent events, making me think that they had prior information.
>
> This means that one would not expect every journalist to "be like Marinovitch" [a world-renowned South African journalist and photographer], "who is everywhere when there is a need."

> The reality is that some journalists have connections with the police and send them the photographers and get the stories second-hand. Even when we talk to journalists about the realities of the situation they say they have investigated, but they did not seem to be very interested in analysis and understanding; they wanted the sensational stuff because this is what sells. In most cases, according to the community's stories, the truth falls on deaf ears, but academic research-ers are meticulous: they listen very careful[ly], make notes, etc. and present their findings according to what they believe, their own ideas. This is also wrong, but they – especially women – are more insistent and braver than journalists. Journalists love and promote sensational stuff; they do it because they believed it would give them a bigger name and people would love them and they would win awards.

The above experiences have many similarities with numerous research find-ings which state that the media's reporting in the country instigate and promote xenophobia (Dube, 2000; Smith, 2008). This previous finding has been echoed by numerous authors (Hadland, 2021 and Smith, 2001) who claim that the media publishes stories that are anti-immigrants which also distort public discourses.

### *Media Response: The Politics of Tone*

In addition to the above, a senior municipal official mentioned that:

> these realities never find themselves in the press. Of course, a name that is given to a person or a group by the press of other people and then reported verbatim in the press creates an identity [like] "Bantu," "amakwerekwere." This [is] because, as the history of Africa has shown, a united collective action of the lumpen prole-tariat consisting of the immigrant, refugees and the South African can destroy the status quo.

This is in agreement with Gomo (2010, p. 48) who argued that those who own production businesses prefer to employ foreign nationals due to the fact that South Africans allegedly believe they are entitled to all jobs and are lazy and dishonest once employed.

On May 5, 2015, the media reported the following:

> The name kwerekwere (foreigners) brings out evil, hate, intoler-ance and xenophobia in the hearts of a growing number of uned-ucated, illiterate South Africans. Have we forgotten our African neighbours who were our loyal friends during the fight against apartheid? (Ntuli, 2015, May 5)

The quotes below encapsulate the opinions of the eThekwini Municipality DMC:

> The media was pro-immigrants. The situation was blown out of proportion – when you go to the ground it was not a true reflection. There were assisting municipalities by conveying information while siding with [the] foreigners.

This finding has been corroborated by an article published in a local newspaper (*The Mercury*, 2015). The article was titled *Refugee misery at Isipingo camp*, and concluded that "the situation at the Isipingo interim shelter has escalated from desperate to inhumane after the eThekwini Municipality dismantled marquees and left destitute foreigners on an open field on Friday" (Ntuli, 2015, May 5).

The above analysis is in agreement with a study published in the early part of the twenty-first century (Fine and Bird, 2002), which found that the focus and coverage by the media in the country is simplistic and contains minimal in-depth discussions.

There was vociferous confirmation of the above positions by the Manager: Disaster Risk Reduction (KZN), who had the following opinion:

> During these attacks, [the members of the] media were focusing on locals attacking foreigners while knowing that the majority of South Africans do not condone such attacks and it is not something that they encourage or tolerate. The media failed to go to the root causes of these attacks and failed to report the casualties, the accurate casualties And they were also using people in some instances; they will pay people to observe in the shelters, to observe the wrongs not the rights. For instance, there were asking for telephone connections and Vodacom offered that they [could] have open lines; they ended up abusing them and we took [the] decision to close those lines, the media was reporting the government as being abusive to the displaced. Unfortunately, in the country the whole media is sick; [the reporters] have failed to prioritise matters of national interest and [be] objective.

### Inaccurate and Falsified Information

An official from the eThekwini Municipality and emergency center had this opinion of the media:

> [The members of the] media were escalating xenophobia. Through the media, the announcement by the King of the Zulus that foreigners should go [back] to their countries triggered the violence. The media went to the shelters (humanitarian) and they were interviewing foreigners and report[ing] on their conditions [in] the shelters and they reported false information.

The local popular newspaper concurred with this by a comment on April 29, 2015 (*Daily News*, 2015) in an article entitled *Journalists must consider the impact of their reporting (Merten, 2017)*. The Member of Parliament argued that:

journalists were South Africans first and foremost, and must consider the impact of their reporting. The [members of the] media have a right to report on issues. The media has a responsibility to think about the possible consequences of the angle they take on issues. Bhengu turned her attention to media reporting of King Goodwill Zwelithini's comments last month that African immigrants should pack their bags and go home. The King has maintained that he was quoted out of context and that he never said African immigrants should be attacked.

The negative tone was noticed in popular printed newspapers such as *Isolezwe* and *The Mercury* as compared to other newspapers that reported on xenophobia. Although the majority of the newspapers did cover the xenophobia, the following was reported by one of them:

> There is a wide view from the peripheral areas of the city that the government departments and agencies are ignoring the early warning by community activists on the looming attacks against the immigrants and their businesses. The perpetrators are mobilising to violently disrupt a peace march against xenophobia within eThekwini Municipality in the past two weeks.

A senior official in the Provincial Disaster Management Centre said that the fact of the matter was that the media was replete with imbalanced and shallow reporting. This occurred despite the fact that journalists were in a position to deepen the stories. It was believed that positions published in the newspapers were dictated to them.

Speaking about the media, the director of the Provincial Disaster Management Centre in KZN said:

> The lack of balance of their descriptions and analysis was indicative of the journalists' shallowness and this was one of the key reasons for mediocrity and lack of independence. Our department was there when the attacks took place and we were there in the aftermath ... experience in the field [has] shown us [that] the journalists ... dictated to [victims of xenophobia according to] their pre-determined positions. They do not interview all the sides [about] who [is] behind a story and this means that their mission to be messengers and distributors of the objective truth is betrayed.

These comments have been corroborated with findings numerous researchers, who have confirmed that the media reports inflammatory stories with negative connotations about immigrants (Fine and Bird, 2002; Hadland, 2010; Smith, 2008).

## Conclusion

This book chapter dissected the hidden dimensions and triggers of xenophobia in Durban. The hidden role of the media in fueling xenophobia has been unearthed. This study has unveiled the causes of xenophobia in Durban which are inter-woven with the lucrative criminal business in the form of illegal electricity connections and cable theft, where locals are being outperformed or outsmarted by foreign nationals, leading to violent confrontations. Nonetheless, boredom and unemployment among the youth, who are involved in criminal businesses through theft, fuel the xenophobic attacks. The narratives by government and media on the existence of a "third force" in peddling xenophobia in Durban have been refuted by all the informants. It is noteworthy that unethical journalists report unreliable information from the community leaders, civil society groups and the police. Furthermore, the biased imbalanced, subjective, predetermined and shallow reporting by the media exacerbates the incidences of xenophobia. The themes that emerged in this study show that xenophobia is linked to corruption. This suggests that the local police and the intelligence operators develop and implement solid strategies to arrest organized syndicates, the recipients of illegal electricity connections and those who purchase the cables. The government should criminally charge media reporters who report fake and inflammatory stories as a form of censorship. The media houses and reporters who promote social cohesion activities and projects, changing xenophobic behavior, should be rewarded. However, the findings of this study cannot be applied to other areas within the KZN province and beyond as the dimensions and causes of xenophobia can be understood only at the local level. This necessitates future researchers to focus on other areas in order to interrogate the visible and invisible dimensions of xenophobia.

## References

Bennett, W.L. 2009. *News: The Politics of Illusion*, 8th ed., New York, NY, Springer.

Charman, A. and Piper, L. 2012. Xenophobia, criminality and violent entrepreneurship: violence against Somali shopkeepers in Delft South, Cape Town, South Africa, *South African Review of Sociology*, *43*(3), 81–105.

Crush, J. and Ramachandran, S. 2014. *Soft Targets: Xenophobia, Public Violence and Changing Attitudes to Migrants in South Africa after May 2008*. SAMP Migration Policy Series No. 64. Cape Town, SAMP.

Dahlback, I.T. 2019. *Long Walk to Press Freedom: The Media Framing of the April 2015 Xenophobic Attacks in South Africa*. Doctoral dissertation, University of Cape Town.

Danso, R. and McDonald, D. 2001. Writing xenophobia: immigration and the print media in post-apartheid South Africa, *Africa Today*, *48*(3), 114–137.

Dube, P. 2000. Media berated for xenophobia. *Independent Online*. Johannesburg.

Eliseev, A., Maruping, R., Glaser, D., Nieftagodien, N., Gelb, S., Pillay, D., Landau, L., Coplan, D., Hornberger, J., Silverman, M. and Zack, T. 2008. *Go Home or Die Here: Violence, Xenophobia and the Reinvention of Difference in South Africa*, New York, NY, NYU Press.

Entman, R.M. 2010. Media framing biases and political power: explaining slant in news of Campaign 2008, *Journalism*, *11*(4), 389–408. doi: 10.1177/1464884910367587

Everatt, D. 2010. *Synthesis Report: Overview and Prospects*, Johannesburg, Atlantic Philanthropies.

Fine, J. and Bird, W. 2002. *Shades of Prejudice: An Investigation into South African Media's Coverage of Racial Violence and Xenophobia*. Unpublished research conducted by the Media Monitoring Project, Cape Town, Centre for the Study of Violence and Reconciliation.

Gauteng City-Region Observatory (GCRO). 2016. *Quality of Life Survey IV (2015/2016)*. Johannesburg, GCRO. Available at: https://gcro.ac.za/research/project/detail/quality-of-life-survey-iv-201516/ [Accessed 12 March 2021].

Gelb, S. 2008. Behind xenophobia in South Africa: poverty or inequality? In *Go Home or Die Here: Violence, Xenophobia and the Reinvention of Difference in South Africa*, Eds S. Hassim, T. Kupe and E. Worby, pp. 79–91, Johannesburg, Wits University Press. doi:10.18772/22008114877.9

Gomo, T. 2010. *Analysis of Media Reporting and Xenophobia Violence Among Youth in South Africa*.

Hadland, A. 2008. Shooting the messenger: mediating the public and the role of the media in South Africa's xenophobic violence. Paper presented at CODESRIA, 12th General Assembly: Governing the African Public Sphere, Yaounde, Cameroon, 7–11 December.

Hadland, A. 2010. Shooting the messenger: mediating the public and the role of the media in South Africa's xenophobic violence, *Africa Development*, *35*(3), 119–143.

Landau, L. 2008. Violence, condemnation, and the meaning of living in South Africa. In *Go Home or Die Here: Violence, Xenophobia and the Reinvention of Difference in South Africa*, Eds S. Hassim, T. Kupe and E. Worby, pp. 105–117, Johannesburg, Wits University Press. doi:10.18772/22008114877.11

Landau, L.B. 2012. *Exorcising the Demons Within: Xenophobia, Violence, and Statecraft in Contemporary South Africa*, Johannesburg, Wits University Press.

Moyo, I. and Nshimbi, C.C. 2020. The construction of African immigrants in contemporary South Africa and social cohesion: reflections on the role of the media. In *Pan Africanism, Regional Integration and Development in Africa*, pp. 181–197, Cham, Palgrave Macmillan.

Neocosmos, M. 2008. The politics of fear and the fear of politics: reflections on xenophobic violence in South Africa, *Journal of Asian and African Studies*, *43*(6), 586–594.

Ngcamu, B.S. and Mantzaris, E. 2019a. Media reporting, xenophobic violence, and the "forgotten dimensions": a case of selected areas in the KwaZulu-Natal province, *International Journal of African Renaissance Studies – Multi-, Inter- and Transdisciplinarity*, *14*(1), 131–146.

Ngcamu, B.S. and Mantzaris, E. 2019b. Xenophobic violence and criminality in the KwaZulu-Natal townships, *TD: The Journal for Transdisciplinary Research in Southern Africa*, *15*(1), 1–8.

Nkealah, N. 2011. Commodifying the female body: xenophobic violence in South Africa, *African Development*, *36*(2), 123–135.

Ntuli, N. 2015. Refugee misery at Isipingo camp, *Mercury*. Available at: https://www.iol.co.za/news/refugee-misery-at-isipingo-camp-1854166 [Accessed 24 April 2021].

Nyamnjoh, F.B. 2006. *Insiders and Outsiders: Citizenship and Xenophobia in Contemporary South Africa*, Dakar/London, CODESRIA/Zed Books.

Orkin, M. 2019. *Predicting Xenophobic Attitude: Statistical Path Models of Objective and Subjective Factors*, Johannesburg, Gauteng City-Region Observatory, September.

Pillay, D. 2008. Relative deprivation, social instability and cultures of entitlement. In *Go Home or Die Here: Violence, Xenophobia and the Reinvention of Difference in South Africa*, Eds S. Hassim, T. Kupe and E. Worby, pp. 93–103, Johannesburg, Wits University Press. doi:10.18772/22008114877.10

Piper, L. and Charman, A. 2016. Xenophobia, price competition and violence in the spaza sector in South Africa, *African Human Mobility Review*, *2*, 332–361.

Rasila, B.N. and Musitha, E.M. 2016. The lack of effective communication influences xenophobic attacks in South Africa, *Journal of Education, Society and Behavioural Science*, 1–11.

Smith, K. 2001. Hate crime: an emergent research agenda, *Annual Review of Sociology*, *27*, 479–504.

Smith, M.J. 2008. *Synthesis Report: The Media's Coverage of Xenophobia and The Xenophobic Violence Prior to and Including May 2008: A Synthesis Report*. Available at: http://www.atlanticphilanthropies.org/wp-content/uploads/2010/07/7_Media_c.pdf

Von Holdt, K., Langa, M., Molapo, S., Mogapi, N., Ngubeni, K., Dlamini, J. and Kirsten, A. 2011. *The Smoke That Calls: Insurgent Citizenship, Collective Violence and the Struggle for a Place in the New South Africa*, Johannesburg, Centre for the Study of Violence and Reconciliation (CSVR) & University of the Witwatersrand, Society Work and Development Institute (SWOP).

Wilkins, K., Tufte, T. and Obregon, R. Eds 2014. *Handbook of Development Communication and Social Change. IAMCR Series*, Oxford, Wiley-Blackwell.

Worby, E., Hassim, S. and Kupe, T. 2008. Introduction: facing the other at the gates of democracy. In *Go Home or Die Here: Violence, Xenophobia and the Reinvention of Difference in South Africa*, Eds E. Worby, S. Hassim and T. Kupe, pp. 1–25. Johannesburg, Wits University Press. doi:10.18772/22008114877

Chapter Five

# Biased and Falsified Reporting:
# The Government's Perspectives

Post-apartheid South Africa is characterized by a media democracy that has been instrumental in exposing constitutional violation, unethical conduct, poor governance and corrupt tendencies by government and political officials. Conversely, the media has also been blamed for fueling hatred against African immigrants in the country through its sensational reporting. A wide range of viewpoints are discussed and analyzed in this chapter, mostly from government and security agencies as well as civil society group members as it related to the print and electronic media's inaccurate, insightful reporting and misrepresentation of the facts by certain publishing houses and platforms. Furthermore, falsified information and omissions about shelters for displaced migrants is dissected by a host of stakeholders. The security personnel's perception of the effect of the adverse and unethical reporting during the 2015 events – influenced by bribery, crookery and careerism – is shared in this book chapter. Finally, we uncover how media houses have overlooked accurate government communications and reports. A total of 18 informants from various government departments, its agencies and civil society groups were targeted and interviewed in this study. The researchers acted as participant observers (ethnography) during instances of xenophobic attacks during the previous two decades. Their experiences and understanding of this subject becomes evident in this study. A qualitative analytical tool (NVIVO version 12) was used to search, classify, map, develop themes and code the data. As a result, a thematic analysis was used to develop themes, patterns and trends in this chapter.

The most potent themes that emerged in this study include the media's adverse framing of xenophobia, derogatory language used by reporters and their effects, and the media's shallow, unverified and unethical journalism. This book chapter has entered unexplored terrain and a hotspot that contributes to theory on ethical journalism by unearthing the government's and civil society's viewpoints. This study therefore has an impact on policy, decision-makers and security officials in terms of understanding the reckless media reporting and the impact this can have on the socio-economic development of society and communities in general.

The media democracy, which was first experienced in post-apartheid South Africa, has played a pivotal role in exposing government's irresponsible policies,

Addressing Xenophobia in South Africa:
Drivers, Responses and Lessons from the Durban Untold Stories, 109–123
Copyright © 2022 by Bethuel Sibongiseni Ngcamu and Evangelos Mantzaris
Published under exclusive licence by Emerald Publishing Limited
doi:10.1108/978-1-80262-479-320211006

maladministration, corruption and poor governance, providing voices to the voice-less. The media has been regarded as the backbone of the country's democratic direction and it has been widely acknowledged as connecting South Africa to the world: sharing pertinent stories, exchanging information and informing, criticizing and stimulating debates regarding the country's realities. Furthermore, the media have been recognized for its contribution to the political, cultural and socio-economic programs undertaken during the first years of the African National Congress (ANC) government, promoting the country beyond its borders. However, due to the fact that media houses have predominantly continued to be owned by the same moguls in post-apartheid South Africa, it has become noticeable that many support the previous oppressive regime. The media channels and platforms reporting on xenophobic conflicts have recorded anti-state sentiments.

Post-apartheid South Africa has seen an influx of African immigrants into the country, coupled with emerging violent tensions, which was covered in the print media fairly extensively. Media channels have failed in their mission to report honestly and accurately, and in the process to advise government in advance of its omissions and weaknesses in terms of immigration issues and looming xenophobic violence. Media reporters did not obtain accurate and factual information and they were not cognizant of how they should report ethically and accurately on conflicts such as xenophobia. Against this background, this book chapter dissects the government's and civil society's perspectives on ethical media reporting during the 2015 xenophobic violence in South Africa. The chapter questions the extent to which the media has contributed to xenophobia and increased the tension between key stakeholders by publishing inflammatory and discriminatory stories. There is a void in the literature soliciting government's and civil society groups' in-depth understanding of media reporting, which this study hopes to fill. We examine the effects media reporting has on initiatives and programs to combat xenophobia as well on the victims and the perpetrators.

According to Borman (2018, p. 62), social media divided locals and immigrants by causing confusion and spreading false information during the 2015 xenophobic attacks; however, it also assisted the victims in mobilizing and responding to the attacks. Meanwhile, Hadland (2010), in his study conducted in the informal settlements during the same period, concluded that the media cannot be solely blamed for fanning the xenophobic violence. The previous author linked anger and violence from the communities to the breakdown of communication between municipalities and residents. However, Hadland (2010) posits that the media's failure to respond to the latter communication breakdown and provide a voice to the voiceless has made the public consider the media to be more complicit in exacerbating xenophobic violence.

## The Media's Framing of Xenophobia

Since the beginning of the twenty-first century, the media's framing of xenophobia has tended to take an anti-immigrant stance, describing South Africans as having a legitimate right to attack foreign nationals and characterizing citizens and foreign nationals as warriors and barbarians, respectively. The perpetual movement of thousands of African immigrants (mostly from poor neighboring countries) into urban townships has been followed by a number of gruesome attacks on migrants. The anti-immigrant sentiments, stereotypes and antipathy have been mainly manufactured by the media, and supported by minimal facts. Such an appalling situation in the townships and the country at large has been exacerbated by the extreme denials by politicians and government officials, while the media and scholars have viewed the events as xenophobia without compelling evidence to support such a claim.

A host of media platforms, both print and digital, has relied on the old patterns of xenophobia being accredited to hatred against foreign nations, with immigrants being labeled as "job stealers" and "disease spreaders," or believed to be involved in criminal activities, with unrelated images widely shared and published in inflammatory headlines. Many media outlets, including newspapers, television, radio, as well as social media (including Facebook and Twitter) have attributed the spate of crimes in South Africa to immigrants. This position has been supported by the Department of Correctional Services calculations which depicted an increase in the number of foreigners being incarcerated in South African prisons since 2005 (Singh, 2011). While the research findings by Singh (2011) indicate that a number of foreigners do commit crimes, foreign nationals oppose the myth that most of them are offenders. The myth of large numbers of immigrants being involved in crime has also been aggravated by the fragmented and chaotic communication in South Africa, perpetrated by the rise of fake news.

## Derogatory Media Language and its Effect on Xenophobia

A study by Mangwiro (2018) establishing the role of the *Daily Sun* and *The Sowetan* local newspapers in Soweto, which reported on the xenophobic conflicts, concluded that the media is not responsible for the negative attitudes against foreign nationals. This researcher cited social factors and socio-economic challenges faced by locals as the cause, leading citizens to dislike foreign nationals. The research findings of Mangwiro were, however, contradictory as it was established that the media does *not* have influence on how foreigners are perceived, whereas the informants confirmed that they *were* influenced by the print media to attack foreign nationals (Mangwiro, 2018, p. 66).

Gordon (2018, p. 72) proposes that anti-immigrant sentiments and dangerous stereotypes promoted by the media, political leaders and politicians need to be scrutinized. He further argues that print media in the past have used pejorative terms in their publications, calling immigrants "job stealers" and "carriers of disease," which necessitates evidence-based research to be conducted in South Africa as well as xenophobic messages to be monitored (Gordon, 2018, p. 85).

This author further argues that the media can play a pivotal role in influencing the attitudes of the citizens. Such a position is in agreement with De Poli et al. (2017) who, in their study investigating the drowning of refugees in the Mediterranean Sea, depict how media coverage can shape the attitudes of locals toward immigrants. Meanwhile, in the last few years, European countries have not been spared from xenophobia. For instance, Galariotis et al. (2017, p. 5) mention that in Europe there are older patterns of xenophobia which are linked to non-violent discrimination and segregation, and which does not consider xenophobia to be a violent practice. These researchers analyzed vast amounts of texts from newspapers and websites over four decades (1996–2015), which espoused violent anti-immigrant behaviors coordinated and perpetuated by the Greek Neo-Nazi Golden Dawn Party and the police.

## The Media's Hidden Agenda

Media channels and their reporters have been considered to be complacent to the xenophobic attacks in South Africa for the past few decades as a result of their imbalanced and reckless reporting. This seems somewhat odd since it is believed that reporters are almost always alert and briefed by their informers in the townships or the police force prior to the outbreak of xenophobic attacks. However, they fail to inform government agencies about violence looming against foreign nationals' businesses. Furthermore, most media reporters are in cahoots with certain international humanitarian organizations that are active in shelters for displaced immigrants. Journalists consistently report negatively about the unpleasant conditions in the shelters and share the narrative that the country is opposed to immigrants. Their biased reporting, which is anti-state, depicts government's operations as being ineffective, inefficient, uncaring and intolerant toward foreign nationals. The government's tireless efforts to provide humanitarian assistance in the shelters and basic needs and services – with limited budgetary resources – are seldom reported by the media. The media mostly promotes international organizations' hidden agendas in South Africa, which can be traced back to the apartheid regime and which undermines the tireless efforts of civil society groups, Non-Governmental Organisations (NGOs) and Community Based Organisations (CBOs). These local non-profit organizations (NPOs) perform a sterling service, supported by their experience in dealing with humanitarian crises in South Africa and beyond, but they too are often overlooked by the media.

Immigrants are perceived by media platforms to be facing an uncertain future in the country although there is a total of 4,036,696 foreign-born people in South Africa (United Nations Population Division, 2017) against a total of 7,000 immigrants who were displaced in the shelters during the 2015 xenophobic attacks. Furthermore, the displaced immigrants lived in the shelters for exactly seven weeks from the onset of the attacks against them in 2015 (Doctors Without Borders [MSF] Southern Africa, 2015). The print media depicted the foreign nationals in the shelters as being traumatized and fearful of locals and security agencies. When the foreigners were attacked by citizens, the victims sought refuge at police stations for days. The information being disseminated by reporters, who were hardly seen in the shelters, was shameful. They widely publicized the "failures" of the government and its agencies despite there being a concerted effort to deal with the burning issues. The South African state's leading role was acknowledged by other countries. These government stakeholders worked collaboratively with national and international NPOs in providing and rendering various professional functions and services.

The print media's consistent criticism of the South African Government has worsened matters, despite organizations such as the United Nations High Commissioner for Refugees (UNHCR) acknowledging the state's concerted efforts to contain the wave of xenophobia. According to Gordon (2018, p. 8), the state's initiatives to build social cohesion among different groups and create spaces for positive societal integration of immigrants residing in the country are significant. While those uprooted during the attacks included refugees and asylum seekers, the media regarded and described them all as illegal immigrants – a position that developed a stereotype toward them. Journalists failed to report on the state's assurance of the support provided to the refugees and asylum seekers (in accordance with international laws and protocols). Furthermore, the government's interventions to curb xenophobia and improve the well-being of immigrants in the displaced shelters, with assistance from the UNHCR, received scarce attention from the media. Although the report authored by Human Rights Watch (2018) cited the government's lackluster response to xenophobia and its failure to acknowledge the realities and depth of the problem, the state's agencies and government officials did use a counterfeit goods raids as a cover for xenophobic harassment and attacks.

## The Media's Shallow Reporting: A Government Perspective

The government officials at the municipal and provincial communication departments, who were responsible for dealing with the media and analyzing their stories during the 2015 xenophobia, argued that the reporting of journalists was "planned, middle of the road" as their stories were underpinned by a political agenda and the influence of media moguls. The officials opined that news stories were informed by weak analyses and dominated by articles based on common "generalities"; for example, that immigrants steal jobs and traffic drugs without investigating both the perpetrators and the victims. In this particular case, the victims were not only the immigrants, but also the locals who were renting houses and rooms to the foreign nationals, who were their customers. The victims included immigrants' spouses, who were mostly South Africans, and the families of those murdered during the violence. This has been evidenced by the high number of South African fatalities during the xenophobic attacks. For instance, in the horrific 2008 xenophobic attacks, there were 62 fatalities, with 21 South Africans killed (Crush, 2014). In 2015, there were seven deaths from both sides.

There are overlooked stories being peddled by media reporters regarding claims by government officials that South Africans are unemployed but are overlooked by prospective employers. Such inaccurate stories have been cited by officials who claim that South African citizens are selected when it comes to employment opportunities, but that they refuse jobs that lack prestige. Furthermore, there are stories that have been circulated in the print media claiming that low-paying jobs are being turned down by South Africans, which is considered to be untrue by government decision-makers. The South African Government Minister of Labour tabled in Parliament on May 7, 2020 a policy planned to limit foreign nationals from being employed in particular sectors of the economy is currently being developed. The minister opined that there are sectors where foreign nationals are preferred over South Africans due to their skills or as a result of cheap labor being exploited. This includes restaurants and the hospitality sector, the private security industry and agriculture and necessitates the government to set quotas or targets (Ensor, 2020). The minister emphasized the fact that the country cannot allow millions to be unemployed while non-nationals are employed, without legislation being in place. The state will apply these quotas in the future without being xenophobic or violating international conventions, of which South Africa is a signatory (Ensor, 2020).

In fact, state officials have blamed the media for inaccurately reporting the reasons why foreigners are preferred by business owners over South Africans. One government official posited that that the realities of the labor market in South Africa has been distorted by the press producing the "myth" that South African are not prepared to perform "menial, lowly-paid jobs." This wrong perception created to the public hides the fact that foreigners are preferred by small, medium and established businesses because they are cheap, they do not go on strikes and do not join trade unions. In contrast South African workers were in the forefront of the struggle against apartheid through their unions and their activism in the United Democratic Front. Today's trade unions still fight for a better life for them, their families and the people as a whole, it was said.

The derogatory and unwarranted choice of words that has been used by print media reporters exacerbates tensions between local and foreign nations. This is the perception shared by informants in the provincial government sector. This comment was provided by a senior provincial official:

> Of course a name that is given to a person or a group by the press of other people and then reported verbatim in the press creates an identity [like] "*Bantu*" and "*amakwerekwere.*" These identities are derogatory; they denigrate different sections of people and the journalists and editors are aware that this is the case. Nevertheless, despite this reality they continue to use them, thus perpetrating denigration. This perpetuation of derogatory stereotypes is very instrumental in perpetuating violence against refugees and immigrants.

The research informants who played a central role in the 2015 xenophobic attacks eloquently concluded that the print media has been disseminating propaganda and casting aspersions against locals and foreign nationals, which has aggravated the xenophobic violence in South Africa. This has been exemplified by a government disaster management official in the leadership position:

> They [the members of the] press are victims of propaganda and are instrumental in pushing the prejudices. The press has a clear ideological agenda to denigrate and dehumanise the victims [and] divide the population from the refugees and immigrants. This [is] because, as the history of Africa has shown, a united collective action of the lumpen proletariat consisting of the immigrants, refugees and the South African poor can destroy the status quo. [The members of

the] media play an important role in informing people of what is happening. They were able to profile it to say there is a problem and let us address it ... it was not enough. I consider them as sell-outs. Even in America if you are talking about state matters, the country will deal with you. Let us protect our country.

The government functionaries shared similar sentiments – that the print media reporters were partial in their reporting. They were seen as pro-immigrant, proving false information consequently worsening xenophobia. The interviewees at a municipal level unanimously believed that the print media negatively shaped citizens' perceptions by selectively reporting on the correlation between violence and xenophobia, disseminating a negative perception of migration, and making empty promises to provide assistance to government to curb the violence. The eThekwini Municipality official who formed part of the strategic committee gave the following views:

> While initially they were correct by stating publicly that the violence was not a problem for the government alone, but for South Africa as a whole, and that everyone had a critical role to play to put a stop to this ... on national TV they announced that they [will] avail their professional expertise in assisting the government, [but] this never occurred ... On occasion [they] stated that the media in general and especially the local media has a key role to play in re-examining its role in shaping the public's perception of migrants; they criticised the media as selectively reporting [on] violence, thus creating negative perceptions of migration. This was done because the press failed to highlight the many positive contributions that migrants bring and thus reinforce the popular association between violence and migration. This was another ... distortion of reality in my opinion.

There was a general belief among the government officials who operated in the shelters that the print media distorted information and misreported on the day-to-day operations and difficulties faced by all the stakeholders. These government practitioners believed that stories written in the print media were fabricated, lies meant to be sensational. This was supported by a disaster management senior member who said:

> Let's start with the journalists ... a number of them came to the shelters spent some time and then went to write things in the newspapers and [on] social media that were all lies, from beginning to the end. It is difficult to understand why because there were problems in these places, but we were there and treated the displaced and their families with respect in all these shelters. Newspapers or TV channels and social media [representatives] did not bother to even understand the dynamics [and] realities of the conditions under which both the state authorities and the displaced operated

because there are international laws and obligations [that] a government must follow in these cases of attacks on foreign citizens. The average, even good, journalists here only care about sensationalist stories; they don't know or care about laws regarding what are the government's responsibilities towards the displaced [in] their communities and their countries.

An eThekwini coordinator for the xenophobic violence concurred with the previous respondents by stating that:

the media according to our analysis played a serious role in this behaviour especially after [it] was thought on our side to be a complete misrepresentation of that speech made by King Goodwill Zwelithini. It was felt that such misrepresentation provided an alibi for the South African attackers to attack and it was in other words exploited by them, [giving them a reason] to attack. There was also [the] spreading of misinformation on social media that incited especially youths to attack.

### Unverified Reports and Publicity Stunts

Prominent civil society group members who were directly involved in communities during the xenophobia and who formed part of the research participants depicted the print media reporters in a negative light, reporting unfounded and unverified information (civil society interviews).

The government departments that formed part of the provincial strategic committee during the xenophobic violence raised serious concerns regarding how the print media inaccurately reported the root causes of these attacks. Furthermore, they planted spies in the shelters to provide them with information, which was unverified. A provincial disaster management official gave the following views:

It can be my own assumption. The SA media is not responsible enough especially when it comes to issues of national concern; they are reckless, senseless, biased, anti-state ... even [in] matters of national interest. During these attacks, [the members of the] media were focusing on locals attacking foreigners; they were fine; we are not condoning such attacks and it is not something that we can encourage. However, the media failed to go down to the root causes of these attacks and they also failed to report the casualties, the accurate causalities, and they were also using people in some instances; they will pay people to observe in the shelters, to observe the wrongs not the rights. [At] some point at KwaMashu in Block A (hostel), the Somalians were attacked and the media failed to report that there were 15 casualties with gun wounds ... two were Somalians and the rest were South Africans. Even if I was on-site, they were rude (foreigners) and there were rules that

we have implemented on-site ... most of them were for the intelligence and some of these people were organising themselves with
foreign countries and the media was putting some pressure and
working with these guys on their rights. For instance, there were
asking for telephone connections and Vodacom offered that they
[could] have open lines; they ended up abusing them and when we
took [the] decision to close those lines, the media was reporting
the government as being abusive to the displaced. Unfortunately,
in the country the whole media is sick; [the reporters] have failed to
prioritise matters of national interest and [be] objective.

The social activist in the areas affected by xenophobia disputed the perceived
"truth" shared by government and the media – that there are hidden forces behind
the xenophobic attacks in Durban.
   He argued that:

it is difficult to deal with these theories because the situation on
the ground is sometimes complicated, most of the time simple, but
as the situation evolves it becomes more complicated. We who are
called community leaders, because we have participated in these
areas of contention amongst different groups, know that such
terms are given by either the state agencies or journalists. This
because in the struggles against the state by the leaderships of the
poor, the unemployed etc. are themselves the creation of a "third
force," the state or the press; when [a] journalist make[s] friends
with you, buy[s] you beers and when major situations arise they
call you to tell them what's happening because they have no time
to come when or where it happens.

The civil society activist who spent many hours monitoring the situation
throughout the areas and communities affected by the attacks pinpointed a number of gaps and half-truths appearing daily in both the printing press and social
electronic media. In this he made a number of points regarding both the quality
of the professionals and community sources, something regarded as a publicity
stunt. He stated that:

When journalists phone me and other people involved in communities, they ask "what's happening?" because many of them don't
go to these places, not like Marinovitch [a world-renowned South
African journalist and photographer] who has been everywhere;
there are no journalists and photographers like him. Some journalists have connections with the police and send them the photographers and get the stories second-hand; not all, but many of
them. On my side, because of my experience, I try to tell them what
the situation is based on my experience, but they are not interested
in analysis and understanding; they want the sensational stuff

because this is what sells. Whatever I and other people like me try to tell journalists falls [on] deaf ears. Academics are different, they listen very careful[ly], make notes, etc. and present their findings according to what they believe, their own ideas. However, they are more insistent than journalists and more brave, especially women. Generally, journalists love and promote sensational stuff; they love it because they believe it will give them a bigger name and people will love them [and] they will win awards.

### Invisible Journalism in the Displaced Shelters: Security Agencies' Perspectives

There was a belief amongst a selected number of members from the security cluster who had "direct information" who indicated that a number of the initiatives undertaken by the print media as well as those of CBOs, South African National Civil Organisation (SANCO) and civil society groups played a role in the attacks. These people consulted those in the "hot zones" and encouraged citizens to attack foreign nationals, advising them how to plan the horrendous acts. The South African Police (SAPS) officer shared this information:

> There were a number of information sharing and communication efforts in the media [that included] talking to people [and] denouncing the attacks, the violence and the hatred against fellow Africans through press conferences with national, provincial and local government leaders periodically ... there was [the] distribution of hundreds of thousands of pamphlets calling for social cohesion peace and tolerance. All politicians, councillors, NGOs [and] religious organisations used the printed and social media to denounce attacks and violence and even SANCO who helped local Umlazi traders to attack foreign spaza shops issued a press statement rejecting attacks on foreign nationals.

Senior officials from the security cluster shed light on the inaccurate, false and inconsiderate reporting of the print media, which played an active role during the xenophobic violence. For instance, the senior SAPS official suggested that

> they [the media] blame everything on the youth who are unemployed; they do nothing and see the situation with foreigners as an escape to loot. The journalist[s] and analyst[s] say that it is the youth who loot, but this is not true; when the looting starts, everyone joins [in], no age plays a role.

A number of members in the security cluster had a clear idea of who coordinated the xenophobic violence; these members shared similar sentiments regarding the strategies and tactics that helped journalists misrepresent the facts during the xenophobic violence. The senior SAPS official, who was a member of the strategic committee, put it this way:

People say that King Goodwill Zwelithini's speech had an effect
on the attacks, but very few people understand that this speech
was completely misrepresented in the printed and social media.
It is difficult to say whether it had an effect on the attacks, but it
could have played a role ... [by being] used opportunistically by
criminal elements and business people. It is just speculation. People do not mention it much, but there was serious incitement and
[the] spreading of misinformation on social media.

There was consensus among the security cluster members that the incorrect
perception of the xenophobic violence was mostly fueled by the print media. This
was accentuated by the SAPS official who was the overall coordinator:

eThekwini in that period was bad, but one reason there are wrong
perceptions, that the violence really took place in one or two
places, was guided and fuelled by the press and the social media.
A number of different areas within the municipality's boundaries
faced many attacks on a large number of foreign nationals.

The security personnel consistently felt that journalists reported falsely, claiming that victims of xenophobia were being ill-treated by the South African Government in the shelters without visiting the shelters themselves (even though they
had been invited to do so). The SAPS member who was occasionally based at the
shelters from day one disputed the previous allegations:

The perception [was] created by the journalists mainly, who refused
to see what was really happening in the centres although they
received invitations almost every day to visit them. A few of them
came and only spoke to the victims of xenophobia. Our orders
and instructions were clear; we never interfered with the interviews. Even from these 2–3 interviews at the time, nothing really
substantial resulted in the reports – only some vague accusations
on the part of the interviewees who complained about the food
that was halal and tasteless and there were not enough blankets.

The above finding regarding print media's distortion of the facts was supported by a supervisor in one of the shelters who said that

one hears a lot of stories about these things, and there are people
who were there who have forgotten these realities for different reasons; many who did their best, others who did not care, and journalists who tried to make a name for themselves as investigators
after visiting the places where the attacks took place, the shelters
and the police stations for 45 minutes.

The government media liaison officer who participated in the current research
study had similar opinions – that the print media omitted some crucial information in

the articles that were published. The senior police officer and coordinator confirmed the previous statement:

> Yes, [there were] omissions in all reports in the newspapers and the government's communications; nobody mentioned that there were 25 foreigners attacked in Ward 23 Reservoir Hills, and [that] there were 45 displaced persons from the New Germany informal settlements – mainly Mozambicans and Zimbabweans – and all of them sought refuge at Sydenham Police Station. So did 65 refugees from Quarry Heights, [who were] mostly from Malawi. There was nothing about these happenings during a period of three days in the newspapers. Journalist did not even know, they did not ask.

The research participants from the security cluster shared similar beliefs in that it was difficult for the media to understand the conditions in the shelters as the situation changed constantly with people who had different demands and needs. The senior police officer held this belief:

> Journalists, newspapers and the people in general really did not know what was happening there because [the] situation changed by the hour, not by the day. There were a number of people from various departments who were in charge and they had to deal with changing circumstances, different people with different needs and wants, because many of the displaced wanted it all, they were feeling that they were always under attack … [that] they are victims, no one cares about them [and] everyone wants to loot their shops. These are the feelings they pass on [to] the journalists, and journalists want big stories to make a name [for themselves], irrespective of the truth.

There was general consensus among government officials from the security cluster that journalists' stories were based on gossip-mongering and on local amateur photographers who sold them photographs. A SAPS member confirmed the above assertion by saying that:

> the key issues that have been in the newspapers and the press generally are things people talk and gossip [about] because you hardly see the journalists around – only a couple of amateur photographers who take photographs and sell them to the highest bidder.

A Shelter Coordinator regarded the journalists as biased in their reporting and visited the shelters with preconceived ideas. In his opinion,

> the journalist had their own games. When they visited the shelters – and it was not very often – they only spoke to the victims who obviously painted the situation in the worse possible ways and

these things were presented in the press, while the journalists only spoke to them. However, the journalists quoted them [the foreign nationals] in the papers, but did not talk to us [the shelter staff] while they had the opportunities to do and complete their job.

The majority of the security cluster personnel who performed an overall coordinating function during the xenophobic violence challenged the print media's impartiality which overlooked reliable and valid data that were collected by government departments. The senior police offices and overall coordinator was of the following view:

The newspaper and other social media coverage do not even cover the realities of the situation despite the fact that the police and state departments have very strong communication channels so that the people know what's happening. In 2015, a big number of KZN areas were affected by xenophobia, but the journalists were sleeping. The tensions were there the attacks were there, but the journalists were sleeping. The 2015 attacks were not only in Isipingo and parts of Umlazi as the newspapers continued reporting for days; the attacks spread to KwaMakhutha, Chatsworth, Malukazi, Clare Estate, Sydenham and Greenwood Park and elsewhere and continued for a few weeks. For two to two and a half weeks, attacks and looting took place and hundreds or even thousands of people were affected: refugees, displaced immigrants and local populations.

The members of the National Joint Operational and Intelligence Structure (NATJOINTS) coordinating committee assert that various arms of the committee distributed reports to the media and other organizations. This was alluded to by one of the chief coordinators of Provincial Joint Operational and Intelligence Structure (PROVJOINTS), who said:

One of the saddest situations the state institutions faced during and after the xenophobic attacks was the complete ignorance of their actions and activities planned ... taking place from the first hour of the attacks till the end of the problem. This, despite the fact that the various arms of the committees and action groups that were created were careful in distributing communications to the press, TV and all media through the legitimate channels available. There were open communication channels with all media, newspapers, TV stations, who were made aware [of] who was in charge where, which institutions, all their contact details, etc. What was the latest news [was] basically communicated [to] them in detail with the exception of sensitive, intelligence-driven and collected details; these were kept for the state organs.

Almost all the officials who were interviewed by the researchers confirmed that they had media briefings daily and all media houses were invited. This was confirmed by the senior police officer who said:

The government over the years has signed all the conventions, declarations of human rights from the United Nations regarding refugees; and has the Immigration Act, and the Refugee Act. All these signed conventions, agreements and legislation are not a dead letter because when attacks take place there always has been cooperation, coordination and mobilisation amongst the key role players. All these things were reported to the newspapers in the daily briefing; [this was] sometimes done twice a day so more news with fresh developments [could] be printed or be [shared via] social media. For example, when we organised the big march against xenophobia, over 10,000 people joined [in] and this time the newspapers reported it while their reports on the issues [of] what was really taking place were short and without details.

The police force disputed aspersions that were cast onto their members – that Operation Fiela was targeting immigrants. An official from SAPS suggested the following:

It was the newspapers and some lawyers who believed and spread the stories that the operation [was] targeting foreigners only; the operation was a well-planned, anti-crime initiative targeting all criminals and was successful. When journalists asked if Fiela was specifically initiated against foreign criminals, they … ascertained that [it] was a citywide and provincial initiative against crime in general, but when reporting they were not clear about the issue [which] we found puzzling.

This book chapter dissected the media's framing of xenophobia and examined the viewpoints of government, security agencies and civil society groups, focusing on the consequences of derogatory, shallow and unethical reporting. The hidden agenda and propaganda of media houses and their influence in fueling xenophobia were also uncovered. In this chapter, we have unearthed lies, innuendos, propaganda and false information shared by the media and the effects it has had on xenophobia. Furthermore, weak analyses informed by shallow reporting have perpetuated the divisions between media houses and government as well as holding opposing views on the causes of the catastrophe. This is in addition to the unfulfilled promises of the media to assist government to proactively respond to the violence.

The chapter also included a host of unverified, twisted and fake stories purported by the print media to be the truth about the Zulu king being behind the worsening xenophobia, local youths' unwillingness to occupy low-paying and unskilled jobs, and a failure to study the unemployment rate in general and the youth in particular (which is approximately 35%). In addition, reporters have blamed the youth for xenophobia – which is regarded as incorrect. These are perceptions created by journalists which are based on plain gossip. The current study suggests that media reporters should be held accountable for their reckless reporting, and security agencies capacitated to detect such stories and take action according to the laws of the country. The study's limitation is methodological as the target population was a government department, its officials and some members of civil society groups. It is recommended that future researchers conduct an empirical study using deductive-theory development, where the perceptions of the perpetrators and the victims are tested in the xenophobic hotspots.

# References

Borman, J.W. 2018. *The Role of Social Media in Immigrants' Response to Xenophobic Violence in South Africa*. MA thesis Masters in Migration and Displacement Studies, School of Social Sciences, Faculty of Humanities, University of the Witwatersrand, September.

Crush, J., 2014. Xenophobic violence in South Africa: Denialism, minimalism, realism.

Doctors Without Borders (MSF) Southern Africa. 2015. *Displaced by Xenophobic Violence, Foreign Nationals Face Trauma, Fear and Uncertain Futures*. Available at: https://www.msf.org.za/stories-news/news-our-projects/displaced-xenophobia-south-africa [Accessed 2 May 2021].

De Poli, S., Jakobsson, N. and Schüller, S. 2017. The drowning-refugee effect: media salience and xenophobic attitudes, *Applied Economics Letters*, 24(16), 1167–1172.

Ensor, L. 2020. Labour department to impose quotas for foreign nationals in some sectors, *Business Day*, May 7. Available at: https://www.businesslive.co.za/bd/national/labour/2020-05-07-labour-department-to-impose-quotas-for-foreign-nationals-in-some-sectors/ [Accessed 29 August 2020].

Galariotis, I., Georgiadou, V., Kafe, A. and Lialiouti, Z. 2017. *Xenophobic Manifestations, Otherness and Violence in Greece 1996–2016: Evidence from an Event Analysis of Media Collections*. Available at: https://cadmus.eui.eu/handle/1814/46565 [Accessed 29 June 2018].

Gordon, S. 2018. Who is welcoming and who is not? An attitudinal analysis of anti-immigrant sentiment in South Africa, *South African Review of Sociology*, 49(1), 72–90.

Hadland, A. 2010. Shooting the messenger: mediating the public and the role of the media in South Africa's xenophobic violence, *Africa Development*, 35(3), 119–143.

Human Rights Watch. 2018. *South Africa: Punish Attackers in Xenophobic Violence Government Should Protect Victims to Ensure Justice*. Available at: https://www.hrw.org/news?tags[]=910 [Accessed September 2019].

Mangwiro, M.J.S. 2018. *Role of Local Media Reporting on Xenophobic Conflicts in South Africa: An Examination of Print Media Coverage of the Conflict in Soweto from 19 January 2015 to 5 February 2015*. Master's thesis, Ankara, Sosyal Bilimler Enstitüsü. Available at: http://www.openaccess.hacettepe.edu.tr:8080/xmlui/handle/11655/6142?locale-attribute=en [Accessed 14 February 2019].

Singh, S. 2011. Xenophobia and crime: foreign nationals awaiting trial in a South African prison, *Acta Criminologica: Southern African Journal of Criminology*, 24(3), 31–47.

United Nations, Department of Economic and Social Affairs, Population Division. 2017. International Migration Report 2017: Highlights (ST/ESA/SER.A/404). New York: United Nations.

# Chapter Six

# Inter- and Intra-Governmental Response: Unreported Government Response Capabilities

This chapter will focus on the toxic climate that was experienced in the townships regarded as xenophobic hotspots and the militarization of both locals and foreign nationals. The processes, including the screening and acceptance of the victims of xenophobia in the displaced shelters, will be analyzed and challenges and solutions exposed. Different sectors, governments and other professional collaborators' roles and responsibilities will be identified and analyzed in conjunction with other contributions and aspects of impacts in the shelters for displaced migrants. The intergovernmental relationship challenges will be described and analyzed in this chapter together with the negative effects they have had in shelter coordination. The strategies and responses of South African Police (SAPS) during and in the aftermath of the shelters' existence will be explored. The intelligence-gathering processes, local communities' involvement and migrants' leadership consultation regarding reintegration will be further analyzed. Humanitarian initiatives at a local level by the municipality, Non-Governmental Organisations (NGOs) and Community Based Organisations (CBOs) will be assessed, as well as the community's involvement in the fight against xenophobia. Open-ended interviews were conducted with government officials in different spheres and sectors, in addition to members from SAPS, NGOs, CBOs and migrants' organizations.

As time passed following the first attack is Isipingo, the xenophobia spread to the surrounding areas; later, violence occurred in a wide variety of areas in and around Durban. A situation emerged that had only negative effects at all political, financial and social levels. This climate of fear was mixed with one of aggression, scorn and ignorance, even hatred. It was not a unanimous feeling or sentiment that led to the actions but was the outcome of a multiplicity of factors rooted in deep or shallow social realities and relationships. These issues are the focus of this chapter, which deals with the experiences of a number of key actors and institutions. We examine their experiences in the hotspots, many of which were basically ignored by the press for a number of reasons (explored elsewhere). The events in these hotspots were the direct and indirect outcome of social relationships built

Addressing Xenophobia in South Africa:
Drivers, Responses and Lessons from the Durban Untold Stories, 125–144
Copyright © 2022 by Bethuel Sibongiseni Ngcamu and Evangelos Mantzaris
Published under exclusive licence by Emerald Publishing Limited
doi:10.1108/978-1-80262-479-320211007

and destroyed by many plans and actions that took different forms and angles, but ended in a similar fashion: intervention by the police, a climate of fear and antagonism and further militarization on all sides.

In such a process, many plans and actions were evident from all sides. Those who had been attacked had to find a safe place to be screened by the police and Home Affairs officials. The victims then had to make the decision to be repatriated or reincorporated into local communities. The former was an easy option as foreigner nationals were helped by their consulates; the latter were mostly residents in displaced shelters. Various state organs made strategic decisions which were taken in their collective meetings. They were officials who decided the next steps after getting the reports was analyzing what had happened and facing the existing problems and challenges head on, both now and in the future.

This chapter attempts to dissect these realities, including the strategic and tactical realities of the state institutions and their roles, responsibilities and decisions regarding plans and implementation. This included the state of displaced foreigners' shelters – institutions that have received scant attention. Many of the activities that followed in the wake of the attacks were directly and indirectly related to the decisions, functionality and implementation of the intergovernmental decision-making bodies. In this sense, the existing relationships and challenges need to be dissected. While the decisions of such bodies were important, the significance of SAPS as a key instrument to ensure peace and stability throughout the city and hotspots cannot be ignored. Consequently, its leadership's strategies and responses during and in the aftermath of the shelters need deep exploration. The same is true of intelligence-gathering initiatives, successes and failures, local communities' involvement and migrants' leadership consultation in terms of possible reintegration: these are the key elements in understanding the dynamics of these historical weeks. The humanitarian initiatives evident from the first days of the events, spearheaded by the eThekwini Municipality, NGOs and CBOs, and the involvement of the community in the fight against xenophobia, need to be analyzed.

Given the fact that the bulk of the literature review in this work has covered the majority of theoretical and empirical realities of xenophobia throughout the years in South Africa, the present study will cover the key issues associated with migration, refugees and shelters for displaced people. The international landscape in the first 20 years of the new millennium is facing an unstoppable movement of tens of millions of people "on the move" – a massive movement comprising different types of people who relocate for different reasons. The World Health Organization (WHO), whose constitution of 1948 is based on prioritizing equal health services to all as a basic human right, is one of the human rights organizations for refugees and migrants throughout the world. The organization's latest research on international human rights for such groups has shown that the number of migrants in 2019 had reached 1 billion, of whom 258 million are international migrants and 763 million are internal migrants. The research also showed that 68 million external and internal migrants in the world are forcibly displaced today. It has been estimated that 86% of the forced displaced population is hosted in developing countries (WHO, 2019).

An international research report produced by the United Nations Human Rights Commission (UNHRC, 2020) showed that at least 79.5 million people throughout the world have been forced to flee their homes; 26 million of these were refugees, half of whom are classified as below 18 years of age. The vast majority of these people have joined the millions of "stateless populations": people who have had to deny their own nationality, accompanied by a lack of access to basic rights such as employment, healthcare, education, housing and freedom of movement. These figures mean that 1% of the earth's population have been forced to flee their homes because of war, politics and/or internal or external conflict (UNHRC, 2020).

Africa as a continent has over the decades been in the world news mostly for the wrong reasons, even after the struggles of her people led to independence from colonial powers. From the period of Nasser in Egypt to Nelson Mandela's inauguration as the first democratic president of South Africa, the Continent and her people have suffered from internal revolutions and counter-revolutions, military and civilian dictatorships and a wide variety of wars among various countries (Ake, 1985; Collier and Hoeffler, 2002; Mamdani, 1996).

These realities have given birth to continental migration, as millions of people flee their home countries and end up as refugees elsewhere – in most cases, countries that are or seem to be more peaceful and/or developed in comparison to their own. The latest research has put the number of African migrants in Africa at 30 million, a massive number comprising internally displaced persons and returnees as well as refugees. A scientific research sponsored by Deutsche Welle (2019) has shown that these numbers have increased substantially over the last few years and that there has been a growing trend: more and more migrants choose the same destination. For example, by the first week of May 2018, 2.3 million citizens of South Sudan had fled their country, the highest number in Africa. Through the international borders they reached their destination, Uganda (10.4 million, followed by Sudan with 773,000 and Ethiopia with 422,000, the third largest refugee escape in the world after Syria and Afghanistan. A very large number of these refugees are children (United Nations High Commissioner for Refugees (UNHCR), 2018). The tensions and perpetual violence in the DRC has led to the displacement of 815,000 people in 2018, with civilians facing daily attacks by armed groups and inter-communal clashes between the south and the north, and Kivu, Haut-Katanga, Ituri, Haut-Lomami and Tanganyika. By the end of 2018, Uganda had received 242,000 refugees, Rwanda 83,000, Tanzania 76,000, Burundi 65,000 and South Africa 59,000 (UNHCR, 2018). The ongoing civil strife in Somalia has led to hundreds of thousands seeking refuge in Kenya, the most popular destination (284,000 out of a total of 809,000 by the end of 2018), followed by Ethiopia (284,000), Uganda (37,000), South Africa (31,000) and Djibouti (13,000).

The lack of a unified, cohesive, central government and the attacks of al-Shabaab in southern Somalia are instrumental in the refugee problem. The Dadaab camp in Kenya, one of the world's largest refugee camps, has been both a temporary and a permanent home. The camp is considered a "safe" haven by African refugees, many of whom see it as a place where they can have a home and build a new family, with all their children having refugee status for life. The settlement was built to accommodate 90,000 people, but by the end of 2018 it was home to over 200,000 refugees (Deutsche Welle, 2019). The Central African Republic (CAR) is one of the few African countries that have been unstable since its independence in 1960, mainly because of its occupation by Seleka Muslim fundamentalists in 2013 (despite the fact that they were forced to hand over power to a transitional government in 2014). At present, the country can be classified as "partitioned." Cameroon has received 254,000 refugees from CAR, followed by the DRC (182,000), Chad (77,000), Congo (31,000) and Sudan (2,000) (UNHCR, 2018).

Following disastrous civil wars among local ethnic groups, one of the poorest countries in the world – Burundi – is still struggling to recover. The Tutsis and the Hutus, the two main ethnic groups, began a civil war in 1994. This made the country, which gained independence in 1962, another victim of extensive and persistent conflict. April 2015 was another disastrous month, with President Nkurunziza announcing that he would run for a third term. The insecurity and instability created by political opportunism led to the country's economic collapse. The kidnapping and torture of citizens by the armed forces, the police and the ruling party's youth league have led 347,000 Burundian citizens to seek refugee status. A total of 276,000 of them sought refuge in Tanzania, 88,000 in Rwanda, 45,000 in the DRC, 41,000 in Uganda and 13,000 in Kenya (UNHCR, 2018).

Significant lessons about shelters for refugees and migrants can be learnt from the realities facing over 80,000 displaced people from Burundi, Zimbabwe, Ethiopia, Ghana, Mozambique and Malawi. Seven such establishments were opened in South Africa following the extensive xenophobic attacks in 2008. While large numbers of the victims preferred repatriation at the time, a significant number stayed in South Africa, hoping for well-planned and successful community reintegration. International migration law is clear on the responsibilities of host states, but the major problem facing South African authorities at the time was the number of "irregular" migrants – a seriously contested issue in international migration law, especially in terms of the UN Convention on Migrant Workers which extends rights to migrants without legal status (International Labour Organisation, 2003; Misago et al., 2009).

In the period that followed the 2008 xenophobic attacks in South Africa, the unacceptable circumstances in the displaced centers became public knowledge – family members were separated during the displacement and there was overcrowding, a lack of healthcare facilities and gender-based violence. As many of those in the camps had no documentation, their children had no access to education. There was a lack of consultation and information-sharing regarding the next step. One of the major reasons behind these realities in the shelters was the fact that a large number of migrants displaced in South Africa did not have a legally based status; they had not lodged asylum claims and there were no residents. Above all, they did not have documentation, a fact that made it impossible for the local authorities to identify legal immigrants from illegal ones. It was impossible for the foreign nationals to prove their claims of asylum (Forced Migration Studies Programme (FMSP), 2009).

The harsh reality of 62 migrants dead, 670 injured and tens of thousands violently displaced to substandard shelters in 2008 has raised legitimate concerns regarding the capacity of the South African Government to fulfill its commitments. The state kept silent on the issue of "forced repatriation," and no guarantee was given that displaced migrants would not be deported. This was despite the fact that the state's relevant authorities were aware that thousands of the shelter inhabitants had lost their documents during the attacks. This meant that they could not prove their legal status. There was also an evident reluctance on the part of government to work and cooperate with NGOs that were helping the displaced migrants. This included organizations such as the UNHCR, which, because of its experience and position, was able to process asylum claims at different levels (International Organisation for Migration (IOM), 2009). Because of its international standing, the UN could also create avenues that offered access to existing legal systems as well as the country's national courts in an effort to convince the government to apply existing international human rights law to cases that would eventually come before them.

Civil society organs that have been very active in helping displaced migrants at a number of levels had difficulties in their efforts to assess, monitor, evaluate and report on the existing conditions in shelters, to lobby for the human rights of those who had been displaced and to provide services and information to the public at all levels (Robins, 2009; United Nations Office for the Coordination of Humanitarian Affairs (UNOCHA), 2009a, b). Existing UN special mechanisms relevant to issues of migrants and refugees and who were in South Africa played no significant role in these key issues. These included the Special Rapporteur responsible for the human rights of migrants and the representative of the United Nation's Secretary General who deals with the issues of human rights of internally displaced persons (United Nations Evaluation Team, 2009). This is despite the fact that it was not the first-time xenophobic attacks and displacement had occurred in South Africa. The realities of the country at the time showed that these attacks would not be the last; it was more than evident that the state and its institutions could not fill the existing gaps in the country's normative framework (Forced Migration Studies Programme (FMSP), 2009).

## Multi-Stakeholder Response

The eThekwini Municipality was responsible for providing communication expertise to the shelter operations. The Government of South Africa was mandated by the Constitution (RSA, 1996) as well as by international obligations to protect the safety of both legal and illegal immigrants.

A plethora of departments were consulted to legally operate the shelters for displaced immigrants including the Justice, Crime Prevention and Security Cluster; the Social Protection and Human Development Cluster; the eThekwini Municipality; NATJOINTS; and the UNHCR (personal communication, senior member of SAPS). There was a multiplicity of NGOs and NPOs that responded to the dire needs and challenges experienced by the displaced immigrants, providing them with basic necessities. The organizations that responded timeously were both local and international, including the prominent Gift of the Givers, Al-Imdaad, the Red Cross, Food for Life and Doctors Without Borders. They were supported by private retail companies (Shoprite, Pick n Pay), religious organizations, the University of KwaZulu-Natal, the South African Democratic Teachers Union (SADTU) trade union, Ezempilo Publishing, CBOs, community members and youth structures (including the National Youth Development Agency). All of these organizations played a pivotal role during the catastrophe. The selfless members of these organizations provided clothing, cooked meals, groceries, blankets, mattresses, vanity packs, toiletries, cutlery, baby food, nappies and storage containers.

A host of senior officials from different government spheres visited the sites for the displaced. These included officials at a national level (the South African President and the Minister of Police and State Security), at a provincial level (the MEC: Community Safety and Liaison, the Member of Executive Council (MEC) Health Departments and the MEC Social Development) and at a municipal level (the eThekwini mayor and deputy mayor, eThekwini Exco members and the National Commissioner) levels. The official opposition political parties (e.g., the Inkatha Freedom Party (IFP) leader, Prince Buthelezi) and diplomats from different countries (including Mozambique, Zimbabwe and Malawi) visited the shelters for the displaced. In addition, members of NATJOINTS, PROVJOINTS and the National Disaster Management Centre visited the shelter (personal communication, member of PROVJOINTS).

## Government Officials' Deployment and Interventions

Government officials from different departments (the Department of Home Affairs, the Department of Basic Education, the Department of Social Development and the Department of Health) were deployed to perform various activities and tasks in the shelters for displaced immigrants. For instance, three Home Affairs officials were deployed to the shelters to document the displaced in terms of their status – to determine if they were asylum seekers or needed repatriation and validation. There were a total of five Burundian and 14 DRC citizens who were displaced. They were taken to the Department of Home Affairs for their papers to be stamped and were advised accordingly to leave before June 30, 2015. The Department of Basic Education sent four teachers from the University of KwaZulu-Natal, members of the Early Childhood Development and three social workers to set up a pre-school for 30 learners, with the social workers also providing counseling. The provision of education to the displaced learners is in accordance with principle 23 of the Guiding Principles on Internal Displacement of the UNOCHA (2009b). Principle 23 states:

*"1. Every human being has the right to education.*

*2. To give effect to this right for internally displaced persons, the authorities concerned shall ensure that such persons, in particular displaced children, receive education which shall be free and compulsory at the primary level. Education should respect their cultural identity, language and religion".*

The professional and enrolled nurses from the Prince Mshiyeni Hospital provided services to those with health-related problems. In addition, community caregiver volunteers,z Doctors Without Borders, paramedics, drivers, voluntary medical services, Emergency Response Services paramedics and water and technical advisors were on-site to provide professional services. There was also a mobile clinic twice a week and random checks were performed by an Emergency Response Services ambulance doing screening, psychosocial services and management of chronic diseases, outbreaks and acute conditions. Also, the Department of Social Development dispatched four officials to assist with trauma counseling, debrief individuals, offer psychosocial services and initiate an early childhood development program.

In total, there were 4,014 immigrants who were repatriated to their respective countries: 2,832 from Malawi, 453 from Mozambique, 17 from Tanzania and 712 from Zimbabwe (personal communication, NGO leader activist involved in the process until the closure of the shelters).

## The Politics of the UN Relief Voucher

The UN officials were present in the shelters for the displaced and played different roles, also offering assistance in the form of vouchers. In the Chatsworth shelter, UN officials recorded 200 immigrants who registered for these relief vouchers. These people had lost tools that were necessary for their businesses as well as basic necessities imported from other countries. They were offered two-months rental and a two-months food voucher. Furthermore, a total of 80 families' monthly rent was paid to their respective landlords. Some immigrants were provided with relief vouchers, but this gesture attracted criticism from government and others in the shelters. The UN indicated that many people were willing to take the UN package and leave the shelter and people came forward, wanting to be registered. The UN was also considering increasing the package by R500 for large families. Local people and their community leaders complained that the relief vouchers benefitted only immigrants, while there were also locals who were victims of the xenophobic attacks. For instance, houses belonging to South Africans and rented to immigrants were vandalized during the attacks, yet there was no assistance or support for them from the government or the UN.

The UN officials proposed a free capacity development program in order to train disaster management officials in a workshop setting. This was done in order to share the organization's experiences with government on how to manage such events and realities (including how to manage shelters for the displaced). The vouchers distributed by the UN representatives to the victims of the xenophobic attacks were openly biased as they only considered foreign nationals to be the victims. Such bias was expressed openly by both South African officials and citizens who faced the wrath of the attacks. Such bias violates principle 25(2) of the Guiding Principles on Internal Displacement (UNOCHA, 2009b), which states:

> International humanitarian organizations and other appropriate actors have the right to offer their services in support of the internally displaced. Such an offer shall not be regarded as an unfriendly act or an interference in a state's internal affairs and shall be

considered in good faith. Consent thereto shall not be arbitrarily withheld, particularly when authorities concerned are unable or unwilling to provide the required humanitarian assistance.

The officials of the South African Government asked the UN representatives to explain the realities and dynamics of the 20% grant available for South Africans. As government, the officials indicated that they were not against the services provided by the UN. However, they wished to have the opportunity to engage with the representatives in an honest and transparent manner so that both sides would not face new and possibly bigger problems (personal communication, member of PROVJOINTS). Such a position was exemplified by an official from the Provincial Disaster Management Centre who indicated that such contradictions led to serious challenges and problems facing the public service providers at all levels and operations as the pressure on the part of local communities increased. This because elements within the local populations agitated against civil servants accusing them of been providers of goods and services to foreigners and "illegals" while they ignored their own communities.

However, the UN representatives indicated that they had trouble identifying locals who might qualify for the 20% fund available from the UN, as these citizens were living in the community. The Community Safety and Liaison HOD indicated that his department, the Business Support Unit and the Department of Economic Development could also assist in identifying these people as the UN **was playing** an integral part of the integration process. The realities of the situation could be further confirmed by the displaced people not abusing the system. The UN representative mentioned that they were not providing business grants; it was merely a support package or token. The UN had not issued business support tokens to anybody at that time; they had only offered normal support packages such as food vouchers and rental support. These services were provided to asylum seekers on daily basis, and funds paid to landlords were monitored. The UN representatives were, however, willing to do away with the business tokens if there was a possibility that such an initiative could create problems to any of the role players (personal communication, PROVJOINTS negotiator).

There were also allegations leveled against government officials who were assisting in the shelters – for instance, that an official was having a romantic relationship with one of the displaced women and giving her special treatment. It was established that the allegations were false; the officials were providing special services to a woman because she was diabetic (personal communication, shelter manager).

## Food Shortages at a Shelter

It was very clear in the shelters that housing the displaced people for a longer period would lead to serious resource constraints. For instance, there was a food shortage at the shelters as most donors had exhausted their budget and further donations were not forthcoming. Speeding up the reintegration process and shutting down the shelter was emphasized in order to avoid dealing with the challenge of the food shortage. The plan was to progressively work toward shutting down the establishment (personal communication, Provincial Disaster Management Centre official).

There were serious challenges including security threats, the irregular movement of people in and out of shelters, the removal of "undesirable elements" from the sites, workshops on the shelter rules, the UN relief vouchers and transporting displaced people to Home Affairs. There were also reports that people of the same nationalities were fighting amongst each other. This was evidenced when a Burundian woman made an official statement that she had been threatened by her compatriots at the shelter. Furthermore, the trading and the use of alcohol and other illegal substances was noted; those who were displaced were persuaded to abstain from acts that were prohibited. There were some foreign nationals who used unauthorized and illegal methods to enter and exit the shelter, including cutting the "speed fencing," an act which was considered a criminal offense and could lead to the perpetrator's arrest (personal communication, SAPS official).

## Home Affairs Matters

It was established that the Home Affairs officials indicated that the printing of expired permits was to be activated via biometrics; this meant that the procedure could only be performed at the Refugee Reception Office. There were four people in the shelter with no permits; these individuals were taken to the SAPS office in order to open a docket. This meant that they were obligated to appear in court, otherwise they would be arrested. The chairperson wanted to know what the responsibility of the municipality was in terms of dealing with immigrants at the shelter who had no papers or papers that had expired. As the shelter official indicated:

> This is precisely what we did in these shelters when we were asked to provide these legal dictates and assistance to all people in the places we were obligated to turn into well-run places of peace in accordance with the country's laws the dictates of the United Nations and all other international organisations; it was the duties to look after all those in the shelters and this why we paid the most attention to children of all ages, mothers with small children, unaccompanied minors, expectant mothers, female heads of household, persons with disabilities and elderly persons, who were not many. These were difficult services because were not many and while we really did our best we never expected gratitude because these were our duties and responsibilities needed to be completed. All the time there was a great effort for us to ensure that we did our best according to the circumstances ... [we] never denied the request of displaced people to move to other settlements if they so wished. This was one of the problems we faced because, given the differences and diversity in the groups, if one of them dictated the conditions and the terms of other settlements, they communicated

and made decisions for their families, connections and compatriots. Most of them had the most expensive cell phones and massive bundles of data so communications were perpetual.

There were also a number of immigrants in the shelters who were arrested for misconduct and some individuals violated the shelter rules by consuming alcohol on the premises, which was prohibited. Furthermore, the coordination between security guards and SAPS was lacking which compromised the safety and security of the shelters. There were a number of ill-disciplined immigrants in the shelters who caused havoc and chaos which adversely affected the well-being of the rest of the shelter dwellers (personal communication, SAPS senior officer).

## Government's Strategic Response

The national, provincial and local spheres of government responded immediately when immigrants flocked to police stations after the xenophobic attacks began. A Provincial Task Team was established to coordinate the response, led by the MECs for Transport, Community Safety and Liaison, Health, Social Development, and Cooperative Governance and Traditional Affairs. The need for social cohesion interventions and the implications for trade and industry required the expansion of the responsible political leadership in the province dealing with a seriously complicated and multi-layered situation. A reference group led by Judge Navi Pillay was set up by the premier of KwaZulu-Natal to look into the matter. High-level meetings with relevant government ministers, embassies and the president were held. A number of ministers visited the province to provide assurance to immigrants and to support government's response plan.

## The Response Plan

A five-themed action plan was developed to coordinate the response:

Theme 1 – Humanitarian services

Theme 2 – Safety and security

Theme 3 – Immigration services

Theme 4 – Reintegration

Theme 5 – Social dialogue

### *Humanitarian Services*

Various government departments provided a great many basic services to the shelters for displaced persons. This included tents, fencing, electricity, water, ablution facilities and waste removal. Professional educators were sourced to provide lessons for the affected children. In addition, healthcare practitioners were present in the shelters to provide specialized services, while social workers and psychologists offered psychosocial support. Safety and security agents were also in place to protect the shelter residents who were visibly affected by the experiences of the xenophobic attacks. Basic necessities such as clothes, personal hygiene products, raw food supplies, cooked meals and blankets were donated by NPOs, private organizations and individuals. There were also medical supplies donated to the displaced persons in the shelters, which included specialized supplies, nappies and baby foods (personal communication, various NGO leaders).

**Humanitarianism at Local Government Level.** A senior SAPS member who was responsible for the coordination of the shelters from the inception of the xenophobic attacks confirmed that the premier had asked the former UN Commissioner for Human Rights to investigate the underlying causes of the attacks. This police officer further indicated that the eThekwini City mayor had offered humanitarian services to the affected and displaced immigrants. As a result, the shelters for the displaced immigrants opened in Chatsworth (which accommodated 100 people), one at Isipingo (276) and Greenwood Park (196) respectively, with the provision of 24-hour police protection.

A number of the informants consistently confirmed that the staff responsible for the shelters were always flexible in terms of civil society groups' access to the shelters as they were rendering services and providing the displaced with basic necessities. A provincial government expert who was in charge of communication indicated that apart from basic shelter and housing, there was always an effort to provide nutritious food and clothing and to fulfill other needs such as sanitary pads for women. In addition, immigrants were given viable contacts and connections for national and international humanitarian organizations, CBOs and religious organizations which offered the services they required. These organizations and individuals had free access to the shelters because of their efforts to provide humanitarian assistance.

The research participants unequivocally observed that the majority of the displaced immigrants were children, women and those living with disabilities, and that government officials were flexible in allowing them to move to other shelters.

An eThekwini Municipality official who was responsible for finance and mobilization indicated that all these services were intact – they were obligated by international law to pay serious attention to children of all ages, mothers, people living with disabilities, the elderly, infants, unaccompanied minors, female heads of households and expectant mothers. There was no expectation of gratitude because these were the duties and responsibilities expected of them. Accordingly, it was this official's duty to ensure that these responsibilities were fulfilled as per the circumstances and to facilitate the movement of residents to other settlements if displaced immigrants wished to do so. This was one of the problems encountered because the situation and conditions at one shelter needed to be applicable to all the shelters. This was due to the fact that most of the displaced immigrants had expensive cell phones and access to data, so they were able to communicate constantly with residents in other shelters and make decisions for their families, connections and compatriots.

**Community Involvement in Fighting the Scourge of the Attacks.**   A senior coordinating member of SAPS explained the strategic plans that were in place, as well as their successes and failures. She said that SAPS was immediately involved in extensive mobilization at least during the first week, and the priority of members was to communicate with communities and their leaders to win the local support. There was community involvement and cooperation between SAPS and other role players who were affected by the situation. This cooperation was widespread and in most cases there was a decrease in the xenophobic incidents against foreign nationals in the affected areas. This was the result of thousands of foreigners moving to the shelters. Following the instructions of the coordinating committee, all police stations needed to record and profile all spaza and other shops owned by foreign nationals in their district and patrol these shops to prevent any further attacks. Public order policing deployments in most areas continued, with ongoing visits to shops owned by foreign nationals. It was reported that, following this intervention, there was some stability in the region.

The involvement of local communities, who are hosts to immigrants, is considered to be central to the eThekwini Municipality's strategic committee's aim of curbing the scourge of xenophobia. However, SAPS did not get involved in planning or educating the local communities; they were only involved in assisting displaced foreigners in shelters. Such a connection with communities has been a success, as shown in different case studies. These studies indicated that in various areas, xenophobia can be prevented by communities and CBOs. These include Khutsong (Kirshner, 2012), De Doorns (Kerr, 2017) and Abahlali baseMjondolo in Durban (Clark, 2018). These communities mobilized to act against xenophobia and discourage xenophobic and divisive practices.

### *Safety and Security*

The Provincial Joints Committee (PROVJOINTS Committee) was activated under the ambit of safety and security, and was chaired by the provincial commissioner. An investigation team comprised of experienced detectives was set up, with its main aim to investigate all xenophobic incidents. Meanwhile, the police clusters affected were armed with operational centers. There was a wide deployment on a 24-hour basis of additional law enforcement personnel to flashpoint areas. They were backed by intelligence services that investigated all incidents and sought out perpetrators. All Provincial Disaster Management Centres throughout the district were put on high alert and were in charge of a 24-hour call center that was established specifically for receiving news of developments in the region and beyond. The process of verifying business licenses commenced and the process of verifying the personal status and documentation of immigrants in the affected areas also began.

According to SAPS, there were eight murders that were confirmed to be directly linked to anti-foreigner sentiments during the 2015 xenophobic attacks in Durban. A total of 432 incidents were reported, 265 criminal cases registered, 226 arrested and 57 court cases. These cases included murder, public violence, robbery, assault, intimidation, theft and possession of a dangerous weapon (personal communication, SAPS and NATJOINTS officials).

*Immigration Services*

The immigrants accepted into temporary shelters were registered and their status verified by the Department of Home Affairs. Undocumented persons were encouraged to make use of the voluntary reintegration into their home country. There was also constant liaison with embassies and consulates to process voluntary home country reintegration. The embassies and consulates were responsible for transporting citizens back to their country of origin. In addition, the biometric details (fingerprints) of all undocumented persons were taken and replacement documentation issued to those who had lost their documents.

The problems encountered in the shelters for the displaced included access control and the free movement of persons in and out of camps, which made it difficult to verify and record biometric details of individuals. Furthermore, South African citizens who were in a relationship with immigrants wanted to make use of the buses provided for residents.

There were a number of concerns raised by local entrepreneurs who reported that foreigners were "killing their businesses by selling goods cheaper" and that the foreign nationals "were operating their businesses without licences or permits." However, such statements were disputed by the reference group led by Judge Navi Pillay, which concluded that it was unfortunate that a number of foreign nationals operated outside the legal confines of the country. The local business people also complained that foreigners had longer opening hours for their businesses. These individuals gave several suggestion to authorities: that the existing fines they had incurred be withdrawn, that there should be a moratorium on the issuing of permits and licenses, and that capacity building and business skills training was a necessity and needed to be provided. Lastly, the equity participation for small local businesses in big businesses operating in townships and rural areas should become a tangible reality (personal communication, National Disaster Management Centre official and SAPS official).

The government officials followed their debates regarding the existing situation and future peace and development agreed upon and advanced the following initiatives (personal communication, NATJOINTS official):

- Hosting a business *izimbizo* in various regions;
- Investigating the possibility of a bulk-buying programme with Ithala Bank;
- Introducing business support programs and incubation from the Business Support, Markets and Durban Tourism Unit;
- Identifying and acquiring unused government and municipal buildings to house more businesses;
- Establishing a small enterprise academy;
- Seeking funding solutions from the Small Enterprise Development Agency;
- Introducing an intensified media campaign using communication and other proposed solutions;
- Implementing a business survey for the whole of KwaZulu-Natal by mid-May 2015;

- Prosecuting employers who employ undocumented immigrants, to be implemented with immediate effect; and
- Establishing a provincial local business association and a review of business permits and/or the Licenses Act.

### Reintegration

There was continuous notion to close the shelters and indeed an attempt was made, but government officials indicated that there were several problems hindering the process. For example, there were people who advocated different agendas and took the "opportunity created by the existence of the shelters to fulfil them." There were inconsistencies in the information provided by the displaced people. It was also noticed in crucial planning meetings that SAPS did not participate and NATJOINTS further invited PROVJOINTS to participate actively in the meetings. The operational plan for the reintegration process and the number of people who needed training was discussed in such meetings, during which officials of the security cluster indicated they were experiencing difficulties in opening cases and obtaining case numbers for immigrants who had been implicated in criminal activities. The reintegration process was facing another dilemma: some immigrants were not accepted back into their communities because they were not part of the community dialogue that had taken place (personal communication, PROVJOINTS official).

The roles and responsibilities for the reintegration of different stakeholders included government being responsible for facilitating the reintegration of displaced immigrants back into their communities. This was done in connection with the efforts of the authorities to build a profile of displaced persons in order to determine their living circumstances before and after their displacement. This exercise was related to a planned process of conducting an assessment of their readiness for reintegration. Simultaneously, both the communities and the displaced immigrants underwent a process of preparation through monitoring for reintegration, which was reinforced by community dialogue (personal communication, PROVJOINTS official).

**Social Dialogue.**    There was engagement with community structures by various government entities and consultative meetings which were held with affected local shop owners. Meetings were held with the media, resulting in more positive media reports. The political leadership continued to play a vital role in engaging with affected communities. Community meetings were planned with a view to facilitating reintegration and social cohesion. Programs such as Operation Sukuma Sakhe were used to promote reintegration, and pamphlets promoting unity between immigrants and local populations were distributed in affected communities.

On April 22, 2015, the eThekwini Municipality's Executive Council approved the reintegration processes for the displaced immigrants accommodated in the shelters. It was agreed that the immigrants' living conditions before and after displacement should be determined and profiled thereafter. The council also agreed that the municipality and other government agencies should have conducted assessments on the potential readiness of both the displaced immigrants and the host communities. It was clearly communicated that the victims of the xenophobic attacks who had been accommodated in shelters and communities where they would be reintegrated should be prepared and educated on various methods of reintegration. This process should be monitored to gauge the success of the project and to enhance sustainability through community dialogue in the form of izimbizo. This should involve community members and their leaders (constituting both citizens and foreign nationals), the political and traditional leadership, local business people and the youth (personal communication, eThekwini Municipality official).

A process of assessment and profiling were conducted where displaced immigrants indicated their preference for potential reintegration in terms of wards and areas. However, a total of 143 chose to be repatriated to their countries of origin, including Burundi and the DRC. Some of the displaced immigrants opted to be reintegrated into communities in other provinces, a preference that was vehemently refused by the National Joint Operational and Intelligence Structure (NATJOINTS) who were not willing to facilitate negotiations with other provinces.

The displaced immigrants initially refused to vacate the shelters and, following intensive consultations with their leaders and the UNHCR's revision of the reintegration voucher (R7,000 for families with more than five children and R5,000 for fewer than five), final agreement was reached between the parties. A total of 174 families and 95 individuals accepted the offer and subsequently vacated the Chatsworth shelter. The leaders of the displaced immigrants were dissatisfied with the UNHCR package, claiming that it was unsustainable and did not meet their basic necessities and needs. Nonetheless, the shelter closed officially on June 30, 2015 and approximately 67 adults and 65 children were moved by the farm owner to Hope Farm in Cato Ridge. The Provincial Technical Task Team took a resolution that they would not be responsible for the accommodation of the displaced immigrants on the farm as it contradicted the regulations for refugee camps. It was estimated that government departments (including the Department of Cooperative Governance and Traditional Affairs, the Department of Social Development, the Office of the Premier, Community Safety and Liaison and the Department of Health) spent R15 million and eThekwini Municipality another R15 million on the shelter operations (personal communication, PROVJOINTS official).

The reintegration processes followed after the re-profiling was complete, with the majority of people receiving assistance from RSS choosing to leave the shelter. The areas where the displaced immigrants were reintegrated into communities were profiled. Meetings were arranged with the councilors in the areas where incidents occurred as well as with community members. Furthermore, the reintegration processes were dealt with by all departments as a collective approach, but allowed the Department of Community Safety and Liaison to lead the process.

It was soon realized that the challenges associated with the reintegration processes were major, a fact emanating from the lack of capacity for facilitating dialogue with the community. To deal with the problems, the strategy of NATJOINTS was to recruit a service provider to assist with the process of reintegration. At the same time, a program to deport people with no valid documentation began, starting at Lindelani. Foreign nationals were scrutinized thoroughly for possible criminal acts such as rape, theft and other crimes. There were also some initiatives such as Operation Fiela, which dealt with foreign nationals among other responsibilities (one of its eight priorities was to deal with undocumented people) (personal communication, SAPS official).

The reintegration task team worked in collaboration with MSF (Doctors Without Borders) in order to fast-track the reintegration process. The group met all government departments and the UNHCR to arrange the resettlement in Pretoria, a decision that went against earlier decisions on the relocation issue. There were a host of challenges for the displaced people as the majority of them did not have legal documents; the Department of Home Affairs assisted with this. Buses were arranged to transport those with expired documents to the department. In addition, certain police stations in Durban had chased away foreigners who wanted to open cases against the perpetrators of the xenophobic attacks. The displaced immigrants had also made a number of unreasonable demands to the UNHCR including the arrangement of skills development and micro loans. A group willing to be relocated to Pretoria wanted to be in the care of UN in Pretoria, until a decision was taken to transfer them to a "third country" (personal communication, PROVJOINTS official).

There was a serious effort to accomplish the successful reintegration of the displaced into society; accordingly, the buy-in from municipal councilors was sought, but without much success. The group also engaged the eThekwini business unit and the Economic Development Department in order to ensure that the business issues were taken care of and the small businesses by-laws were enforced. While these processes continued, some immigrants were reintegrated into communities in other provinces.

Another hindrance in the reintegration program was favoritism by wholesalers that sponsored Somali businesses and spaza shops. This behavior resulted in the community threatening to destroy all the spaza shops owned by immigrants. Furthermore, it was stated that fees for municipal operational permits to start businesses were extremely high for locals, while immigrants could easily raise the money to start businesses (personal communication, eThekwini Municipality official).

As the days passed, there was a reduction in the number of displaced people in shelters, which was an indication of the progress of the reintegration process. The process started in the southern and western areas of eThekwini; the only areas that were still outstanding were the areas in the north, such as Verulam and Waterloo. The process will start soon in these areas. More than 1,000 displaced people were reintegrated into Mariannhill – mostly Malawians. The community in Mariannhill confirmed that they never had problems with foreign nationals and no attacks were reported in the area. This suggests that the xenophobic attacks were sporadic and that not all people in Durban can be regarded as xenophobic.

**Key Stakeholders.**   A large number of stakeholders who played an important role during the reintegration included traditional leadership, the Premier's Office, the Department of Cooperative Governance and Traditional Affairs, the Department of Home Affairs, community policing forums, community crime prevention associations, SAPS, the Department of Social Development, the Safer Cities project, local councilors, ward committees, community development workers, community mobilizers, civil society, FBO, businesses (formal and informal), the transport sector, volunteers and local multi-party leadership.

At the request of King Goodwill Zwelithini, the provincial government and the eThekwini Municipality convened an *imbizo* on April 20, 2015 at the Moses Mabhida Stadium, where he called for peace. The local political leadership on the ground followed the national and provincial governments' instructions and activated themselves in engaging affected communities attempting to lead them into negotiations of the reintegration of displaced immigrants (personal communication, PROVJOINTS official).

**Community Mobilization and Communication.** There was engagement with community structures by various government entities and consultative meetings which were held with affected local shop owners. Meetings were held with the media, resulting in more positive media reports. Political leaders continued to play a vital role in engaging with affected communities. Community dialogues were planned with a view to facilitating reintegration and social cohesion. Programs such as Operation Sukuma Sakhe were used to promote reintegration and pamphlets were distributed in affected communities.

Following the attacks, an enquiry undertaken by a group of experts in a variety of fields, called the Special Reference Group on Migration and Community Integration in KwaZulu-Natal, was appointed by the then provincial premier. Its aim was to investigate the causes and consequences of the March and May 2015 xenophobic attacks in the province as well as to assess the shortcomings and successes of present and past efforts. The purpose was to focus on the reduction of tensions between communities and to propose tangible and achievable short- and long-term solutions that would lead to a peaceful coexistence between communities.

The team of experts was chaired by the internationally respected Judge Navi Pillay, and included the reputable NGO African Centre for the Constructive Resolution of Disputes (ACCORD) which operated as the initiatives as the secretariat aimed at supporting the group's operational work.

The recommendations of this important group were well thought out and structured, touching on all aspects of the problems. This was based on well-researched processes guided by senior legal personnel and experienced NGOs that had dealt with similar situations in Africa and internationally. They recommended the following (Special Reference Group (RSG) on Migration and Community Integration in KwaZulu-Natal, 2015, pp. 173–178):

1. It is important to introducing innovative solutions enabling the reduction of tensions in informal and small trading sectors.
2. There is a need for everyone in the country to be treated with respect, as described vividly in the country's Constitution.
3. The thinking and processes of reintegration need to be strengthened through the directives of various government departments and the civil society groups.
4. There is an urgent need for civil servants at all levels to acquire a deep knowledge of all existing local and international legislation, rules and regulations affecting migrants and refugees.

5. A thorough chronological and documentary evidence needs to be collected of all processes leading to the attacks as well as those following them, including all the events from the first day to the last.
6. There is a need to strengthen all resources and capacity of state organs that deal with and manage asylum seekers, refugees and immigrants.
7. There is an urgent need for the physical infrastructure of the KwaZulu-Natal provincial borders to be upgraded.
8. A provincial intelligence audit is an urgent necessity for all structural imperatives, which should include all early alert systems operating through the operations and decisions of **PROVJOINTS** in KwaZulu-Natal.
9. There is a need to ensure accurate and clear information shared throughout South Africa regarding the exact number of foreigners in the country and the province.
10. The continuous promotion of new, progressive and united community relations at schools and neighborhoods is a necessity, which should be well-planned and implemented provincially
11. Local and provincial authorities should consider the possible benefits attached to the creation of local peace committees in all communities and regions of the KwaZulu-Natal province: platforms of open and honest dialogue as well as mechanisms enabling dispute resolution when it occurs.

An analysis and dissection of a complicated situation can take a multiplicity of forms because of the complexity of events, relationships, fake news, distorted stories and ideas discarded by ideologues and ideologies. Attacks on human beings take many forms: different people's "analysts" and "academic brains" use different lenses most, if not all, of the time.

The structure and depth of this chapter and the whole book in fact is based on truth, coming from first-hand participants' experiences and primary and secondary sources that cannot be disputed by anyone. This is because human histories deserve "the truth and nothing but the truth." Truth needs to told, even when it hurts people, families, communities, provinces, countries, continents or the world.

It was not a coincidence that the xenophobic attacks in Durban described in this book did not hit the national and international headlines like previous ones. After all, there were "only eight deaths."

The focus of this chapter has been on a number of dimensions of very different groups of people and individuals, all of whom could be described as "key actors" in a situation that began with attacks in certain "hotspots." This resulted in people "relaxing" in police stations, being repatriated, living in shelters and (mostly unsuccessfully) being reintegrated into communities. The situation called for countless meetings, delegations, decisions and contradictions in a tiresome daily effort to deal with the existing realities and the future, designing action plans at all levels and trying to change the character of a toxic environment. National and provincial government departments supported by relevant local government entities, security and intelligence operatives, disaster management experts and researchers found these groups in a conundrum of complicated realities on the ground and beyond as they attempted to dissect the facts in order to find solutions. Then there were the challenges of the UN local branch intervention and the selfless contribution of NGOs, CBOs and religious and civil society groups and their role in the maintenance and successes of the shelters for displaced migrants.

The key words and actions that needed analysis are *repatriation, community reintegration, shelters for displaced persons* and *intergovernmental relationship challenges*. The effort was based on all available sources that dealt with strategies and responses in managing a wide variety of key issues. These included intelligence-gathering processes, local communities' involvement (or lack thereof) and the tactics and strategies used by state entities (including their duties and responsibilities, and planning and implementing the decisions taken). Within this framework, the role played by what has been considered to be the unofficial "core entity" – SAPS – has been critical. The police service was considered to be the vital link in implementing, both directly and indirectly, the decisions of the intergovernmental decision-making bodies. This means that such important decisions highlighted the significance of SAPS as the key implementing body responsible for the maintenance of community stability and peace, not only in many hotspots but throughout the eThekwini Municipality.

Such a major responsibility could not be successful in the long run, not only because of the existing and known weaknesses of SAPS, but also because of the gaps that exist which are associated with the history of the turbulent weeks from the first day to the last. This includes the weaknesses of the intelligence-gathering initiatives, the lack of initiative from political leaders (e.g., to increase the involvement of local communities through consultation in the reintegration processes) and the widely acknowledged dysfunction of the Provincial Disaster Management Centre. These are very important elements in understanding the realities of these historical but sad weeks in the life and death of the city of Durban.

## References

Ake, A. 1985. The future of the state in Africa, *International Political Science Review*, 6(1), 105–114.

Clark, C. 2018. Why is there so much conflict between Abahlali and the state? Scarcity of houses is just one part of a problem that has its roots in the province's 1990s violence, *Ground Up*, September 20. Available at: https://www.groundup.org.za/article/why-there-so-much-conflict-between-abahlali-and-state-kzn/ [Accessed 14 October 2019].

Collier, P. and Hoeffler, A. 2002. On the incidence of civil war in Africa, *Journal of Conflict Resolution*, 46(1), 13–28.

Deutsche Welle. 2019. *Refugees and Migration in Africa Project*. Available at: https://www.dw.com/en/refugees-and-migration-in-africa-project/a-48817149 [Accessed 2 May 2021].

Forced Migration Studies Programme (FMSP). 2009. *Humanitarian Assistance to Internally Displaced Persons in South Africa: Lessons Learned Following Attacks on Foreign Nationals in May 2008*. University of the Witwatersrand, Johannesburg, FMSP.

International Labour Organisation. 2003. *UN Convention on Migrant Workers' Rights Enters into Force*. Available at: https://www.ilo.org/global/about-the-ilo/mission-and-objectives/features/WCMS_075619/lang-en/index.htm [Accessed 26 February 2018].

International Organisation for Migration (IOM). 2009. *Towards Tolerance, Law and Dignity: Addressing Violence Against Foreign Nationals in South Africa*, Pretoria, IOM Regional Office for Southern Africa.

Kerr, P. 2017. *Xenophobia, Social Change and Social Continuity: Changing Configurations of Intergroup Allegiance and Division Among Farm Workers and Farmers in De Doorns, 2009–2013*. PhD thesis, University of KwaZulu-Natal, South Africa.

Kirshner, J. 2012. "We are Gauteng people": challenging the politics of xenophobia in Khutsong, South Africa, *Antipode*, *44*(4), 1307–1328. Available at: https://onlinelibrary.wiley.com/doi/abs/10.1111/j.1467-8330.2011.00953.x

Kirshner, J. 2014. Reconceptualising xenophobia, urban governance and inclusion: the case of Khutsong. In *Urban Governance in Post-Apartheid Cities: Modes of Engagement in South Africa's Metropoles*, Eds C. Haferburg and M. Huchzermeyer, pp. 117–134, Scottsville, UKZN Press.

Mamdani, M. 1996. *Citizen and Subject: Contemporary Africa and the Legacy of Late Colonialism*, Kampala, Fountain Publishers.

Misago, J.P., Landau, L.B. and Monson, T. 2009. Towards tolerance, law, and dignity: addressing violence against foreign nationals in South Africa. *International Organization for Migration (IOM)*, November 13. Available at: https://www.atlanticphilanthropies.org/research-reports/towards-tolerance-law-and-dignity-addressing-violence-against-foreign-nationals-south-africa

Robins, S. 2009. Humanitarian aid beyond "bare survival": social movement responses to xenophobic violence in South Africa, *American Ethnologist*, *36*(4), 637–650.

RSA. 1996. *The Constitution of the Republic of South Africa*. Available at: https://www.gov.za/documents/constitution/constitution-republic-south-africa-1996-1 [Accessed 29 August 2012].

Special Reference Group (RSG) on Migration and Community Integration in KwaZulu-Natal. 2015. *Report of the SRG on Migration and Community Integration in KwaZulu-Natal*, October 31.

United Nations Evaluation Team. 2009. *Joint Evaluation of the Role and Contribution of the UN System in South Africa*, New York, NY, United Nations Development Programme.

United Nations High Commissioner for Refugees (UNHCR). 2018. *Global Trends*. Available at: https://www.unhcr.org/statistics/unhcrstats/5d08d7ee7/unhcr-global-trends-2018.html

United Nations Human Rights Commission (UNHRC). 2020. *Figures at a Glance*. Available at: https://www.unhcr.org/figures-at-a-glance.html

United Nations Office for the Coordination of Humanitarian Affairs (UNOCHA). 2009a. *Recommendations Stemming From Lessons Observed of the Response to Internal Displacement Resulting from Xenophobic Attacks in South Africa May–December 2008*, Johannesburg UNOCHA Regional Office for Southern Africa.

United Nations Office for the Coordination of Humanitarian Affairs (UNOCHA). 2009b. *Internal Displacement: Guiding Principles on Internal Displacement*. Available at: https://www.internal-displacement.org/publications/ocha-guiding-principles-on-internal-displacement [Accessed 23 March 2020].

World Health Organization (WHO). 2019. *Refugee and Migrant Health*. Available at: https://www.who.int/migrants/en/. [Accessed 18 March 2020].

Chapter Seven

# A Multi-Stakeholder Response on the 2015 Xenophobic Attacks: The Hidden Government Perspectives

Durban in the Autumn of 2015 (beginning on April 14) witnessed an upsurge in xenophobic attacks which had mostly been attributed to anti-immigrant sentiments allegedly expressed by the Zulu King in a public gathering, a labor dispute at Jeena Supermarket in Isipingo over the employment of foreign nationals and the shooting of a South African woman in Umlazi Township. It was also claimed that before, during and in the aftermath of this cataclysm, political and government leaders had been recorded in popular media expressing xenophobic and rhetoric views, promoting the language of hysteria, and demeaning African immigrants resulting in a climate of hostility and impunity.

This surge in xenophobia and the nub of the crisis was well known by all interested groups, the government has consistently denied the existence of xenophobia as a phenomenon blaming it on the existence of the "third force" and the right-wing tendencies which were mobilizing the lumpen-proletariat, particularly against the foreign nationals. The negative tendencies and attitudes have been exacerbated in the shelters for displaced victims set up by the authorities for the victims of xenophobia where the South African Police (SAPS) agencies have been accused of harassment, acting with impunity and a lack of concern for immigrants. Hence, those who indulged in xenophobic discourse have focused on the government agencies failure to proactively respond to the scourge and impact of xenophobia. This failure has triggered the researchers of this study to examine the government's claims of salient and solid plans and the activities of multi-departmental and sectoral agencies involved in the 2015 xenophobic attacks because existing empirical literature on the issue has ignored the government's viewpoints regarding their response capabilities. The *audi alteram partem* principle has been overlooked in the xenophobic discourse as researchers have been focusing particularly on the victims' perspectives without the viewpoints of government and its agencies.

The 2008 xenophobic attacks were relatively indiscriminate and focused on migrant and refugee business owners in the informal economy characterized by

Addressing Xenophobia in South Africa:
Drivers, Responses and Lessons from the Durban Untold Stories, 145–164
Copyright © 2022 by Bethuel Sibongiseni Ngcamu and Evangelos Mantzaris
Published under exclusive licence by Emerald Publishing Limited
doi:10.1108/978-1-80262-479-320211008

written or verbal threats, public intimidation through protests or marches, which have been regarded by Charman and Piper (2012) as "violent entrepreneurship." A host of authors argued that the locals dislike the presence of the foreign nationals and that the access to municipal services by the refugees was not monitored by the government. The current study, to account for the aforesaid drawback of previous studies, attempts to answer the extent to which responsiveness of the government systems and structures in the shelters for the displaced persons were appropriate, and whether the various government agencies collaboration and the SAPS strategies were beneficial to the victims through intelligence-driven information. Meanwhile, the article sought to investigate the processes, systems and structures, as well as the government departments and agencies' responsibilities, and the pitfalls in the shelters for the displaced persons. Furthermore, this study sought to determine the inter-stakeholder collaboration activities on responding to the humanitarian crisis arising from xenophobia. It further analyses the SAPS's responsive strategies regarding xenophobia and its effectiveness.

This article is primarily based on 21 qualitative interviews with key members of government officials following the visits made in the shelters for the displaced people by the xenophobic attacks. These government officials included eight SAPS members in different capacities such as coordinators for the National Joint Operations and Intelligence Structure (NATJOINTS), officers, communication, coordination and a senior member of the SAPS. The remainder was shelter managers, inspectors, eThekwini municipality officials, a KwaZulu-Natal (KZN) Provincial Disaster Management Centre (DMC) a senior official, and shelter supervisors. These subjects were directly involved in all operations in the shelters for the displaced. The shelters identified were located in Chatsworth (Westcliff Sports Ground), Isipingo and the Univale Sportground in Phoenix. Furthermore, government reports such as the Special Reference Group (SRG) (2015) and a report on the civil society coalition report on xenophobia were analyzed.

## Civil Society Group's Response to the Xenophobic Violence

The civil society was considered to have made a remarkable impact on their timely planning and response in providing humanitarian assistance to the victims of the xenophobic attacks. A qualitative research study by Desai and Vahed (2013) examining the Gift of the Givers (GoTG) role on the xenophobic violence which occurred in 2008 showed that the GoTG is playing a significant role in responding to such crises without engaging in long-term strategic planning. The authors argued that Non-Governmental Organisations' (NGOs) responses to emergencies transcend the nation-state in many instances and they need to be sophisticated in their operations as they are required to deal with donors, governments, ordinary people, as well as the protagonists. The 2008 xenophobic violence led the University of Cape Town's (UCT's) Faculty of Humanities to approach the Department of Social Development in order to offer psychological support to the displaced victims. Meanwhile, Minson and Misago (2009) cited a plethora of challenges in the shelters for displaced victims including the humanitarian response to the shelters, citing anxieties within government regarding public perceptions of aid to non-citizens, inadequate response to the protection needs of displaced foreign nationals, inadequate and inconsistent provision of shelters, unmanaged early departures and late departures from shelters, inadequate monitoring and evaluation of the re-integration process and tensions, and increasing politicization of the camp population.

Robbins (2009) interrogated NGOs' responses to the humanitarian crisis that was brought by the 2008 xenophobic attacks which resulted in 62 deaths and more than 30,000 people displaced, and the lack of necessities, such as food, clothes, blankets and legal aid. Peberdy and Jara (2011) examined the civil society organizations' responses to the xenophobic attacks of 2008 in Cape Town. They suggested that it is difficult to imagine the impact of the xenophobic attacks on the displaced people without the mobilization of resources by civil society through its humanitarian response and advocacy work. Nevertheless, the response revealed what appears to be significant weaknesses in sections of the society in the city. According to Crush & Ramachandran (2017), a psychologist who visited the shelters for displaced victims on behalf of the Médecins Sans Frontières (MSF) (Doctors Without Borders) observed that the kind of trauma experienced by the victims of the xenophobic attacks in Chatsworth is equated to the experiences he has seen in the Central African Republic (CAR) and in South Sudan where people were susceptible to such active conflicts. The literature above reveals a paucity on the notable role played by civil society groups in such attacks. Hence, this study interrogated the crucial role played by the NGOs in alleviating the humanitarian crisis in shelters.

## Disaster Risk Management and Xenophobia

Xenophobic attacks in South Africa have occurred in local areas previously. However, municipalities are still reluctant to consider them as a risk which qualifies the attacks as a local disaster depending on its severity, magnitude and propensity as well as its impact on communities. Such a declaration will enable the municipality to coordinate different sectors and departments with the available resources, including funding, infrastructure and human. Ngcamu and Mantzaris (2019a) have attributed the fight of xenophobia to the lack of coordination amongst the relevant state security clusters. The authors mentioned that the plans to mitigate and respond to xenophobia were non-existent, disaster risk assessment was lacking, and there was no planning for services for the displaced foreign nationals.

Meanwhile, Cabane (2015) considers the government's poor response to the 2008 xenophobic attacks against the foreign nationals in Cape Town as fueled by bureaucratic and political constraints which have led to the migrants' being displaced and vulnerable. The author further questioned the state's failure to comply with the international laws identifying who bears the responsibility for the protection of the foreign nationals. Cebane (2015, p. 57) who considered the attacks on foreign nationals as a disaster, asserts that the victims of the attacks are vulnerable, as vulnerable deserving protection, access to social relief, humanitarian assistance and long-term inclusion in communities. A study by Ruedin (2017) showing that South Africa is not uniquely xenophobic performed a regression analysis which depicted patterns of people who tend to be xenophobic including the people in vulnerable positions, and those who have less contact with the foreign nationals.

Monson and Misago (2009, p. 26) illustrate the government's ineffectual response to the 2008 xenophobic violence as characterized by failures to protect the victims during and after the attacks, prevent violence, prioritize prosecution of offenders throughout the judicial process, a reluctant approach to humanitarian assistance and integration, risk management and SAPS incapacity to manage risks. The previous finding was similar to Ngcamu and Mantzaris' (2019b) research study on the media and 2015 xenophobic attacks in KZN which revealed that the police were absent before, during and in the aftermath of the xenophobic attacks on foreign nationals even though the media had reported the unfolding of the attacks before they occurred. The above excerpt depicts a void in the literature regarding the role of the disaster management departments and other relevant departments at local and provincial government levels which is examined in this study by targeting relevant officials on the contingency plans available on xenophobia.

## SAPS' Ill-Preparedness in Fighting Xenophobia

SAPS agencies have been considered to be complicit in the xenophobic attacks as well as been seen, on occasion, to be working overtly and covertly in collaboration with the instigators and perpetrators of such violence. The brutal and callous way police agencies treat the foreign nationals was evidenced in South Africa in November 2000 when police officers were televised setting trained service dogs on three defenseless men originally from Mozambique (Desai, 2008; Palmary, 2002). Ngcamu and Mantzaris (2019a) study linking xenophobia to criminality has espoused serious weaknesses of SAPS, which makes them complicit in the attacks. The authors mentioned SAPS' reaction-based approach and inability to prepare for and respond to such violence, lack of intelligence collection and analysis, their involvement in crime and with criminals, incapacity to control the crowds and instigators, as well as the lack of communication. According to Ngcamu and Mantzaris (2019a), SAPS has been selective in dealing with criminality amongst the foreign nationals as they targeted specific categories and protected the Somalis who typically bribe them.

The data gleaned through the qualitative interviews by Minson and Misago (2009) support previous findings which also espoused the evidence that the police officials were aware prior to the 2008 xenophobic attacks. They were also regarded as reluctant during the attacks, under-equipped to respond to large-scale violence and intimidated by the prospect of opposing the general will of the people. They also assisted in the lootings of goods. An incoherent attitude of the Home Affairs bureaucracy and lack of effective communication with the police was observed. Victims of xenophobic attacks were arrested and deported by SAPS, an act in violation of the Minister of Home Affairs pronouncements that the victims and illegal immigrants would not be deported (Minson and Misago, 2009). The authors argued that the state agents actively protected those accused of xenophobic violence as well as existing informal leaders who were released due to community protests and mobilization. The researchers have identified existing gaps in the literature as empirical studies are absent in terms of exploring the security agencies' proactive role and strategies in responding to these attacks.

## Government Departments' Lackluster Approach on the Migrants

The Provincial Government of KZN established the rules for the management of shelters for displaced persons which are informed by the United Nations (UN) Guidelines on internal displacements to maintain law and order at the shelters by addressing their specific needs (Displaced Person Shelter Rules VII dated 08-05-2015). The Home Affairs in South Africa has been regarded as anti-immigrants through its broken and fragmented systems and processes in dealing with the asylum-seekers and refugees. Desai (2008, p. 53) espoused a host of descriptive words and phrases used by the South African judges during litigation against immigration and asylum procedures of the Department of Home Affairs as revealing. The words and phrases conveying a graphic picture of gross inhumanity as per Desai include "shameful," "horrifying," "dysfunctional," "unconstitutional," and "hypocritical nonsense." Murray (2003, p. 453) suggested that the Department of Home Affairs has deliberately stalled law reforms governing refugees and migration, which have led to the widespread knowledge of ill-treatment of foreigners. The previous claims coincided with a study by Kamwimbi et al. (2010) dealing with the violations of the civil, political, social, economic and cultural rights of refugees and asylum-seekers. The authors concluded that South Africa is not complying with international, regional and national standards of refugee law as they are victimized continuously, their human rights grossly violated and without social and economic rights and access to basic needs. A qualitative study by Ogunnoiki and Adeyemi (2019) on the relationship between South Africa and Nigeria has observed a violation of fundamental human rights as township residents have attacked foreign nationals in 2008, 2015 and 2019, respectively. The authors concluded that the long-standing relationship between the two countries had suffered because of the scapegoating of Nigerians in targeted attacks on African immigrants. Saleh (2015) has observed that South Africa is facing a crisis of image restoration because the local population does not like the presence of refugees, asylum-seekers or foreigners in their communities.

## Anti-Xenophobic' Attacks Initiatives and Strategies

A research study examining the relationship between xenophobia and urban violence by Tevera (2013) concluded that anti-immigrants' rhetoric and attitudes undermine the achievement of policy goals of promoting urban and national development, poison social interactions between the local and migrant groups, and result in economic and social costs due to the destruction of properties and the dislocation of some urban communities.

However, Kerr et al. (2019) cited several cases where anti-foreigner violence was averted such as in Khutsong; De Doorns (Kerr, 2017), and by Abahlali BaseMjondolo in Durban (Clark, 2018). The anti-xenophobic violence has been highlighted by Krishner (2012) where the local Community Based Organisations (CBOs) and the Merafong Demarcation Forum (MDF) outrightly discouraged communities from embarking on the attacks against the foreign nationals. Another noticeable anti-xenophobic activism was evident in De Doorns, which was undertaken mainly by the Zimbabwean members of the migrants' rights groups PASSOP (People Against Suffering, Oppression and Poverty). This activism was triggered after the Zimbabweans were forcefully evicted during the farm workers strike in De Doorns in late 2012 and early 2013. They tactically challenged the xenophobic, divisive tactics of some South African strike organizers while showing Zimbabweans that they too were participating in workers' struggles (Kerr, 2017). In Durban, the shack-dwellers' movement (Abahlali base Mjondolo) took a consistent anti-xenophobic stance stating that the attacks on the foreign nationals would not solve the problems associated with the delivery of quality basic needs and compared their living conditions to that of the migrants in the refugee camps and repatriation centers. Gordons (2016) suggested that in order to address xenophobia amongst the pro-immigrants, there is a need to focus on other areas such as intergroup contact, interracial attitudes and perceptions regarding the consequences of immigration which were found to be strong predictors of pro-immigrant sentiments.

### 1. Government Risk Reduction Strategies on the xenophobia

The violent attacks against the foreign nationals in the eThekwini Metropolitan Municipality was first reported on March 30, 2015 was sparked by a labor dispute over the dismissal of local employees (South African) in favor of the employment of foreign nationals at Jeena's Store located in the South of Durban (Isipingo). Geographically, the attacks commenced in Isipingo and spread to Malukazi, Umlazi, KwaMakhutha, Chatsworth, Clare Estate/Sydenham, Greenwood Park, Verulam and KwaMashu. The victims of the attacks were mainly from Congo, Zimbabwe, Malawi, Mozambique, Ethiopia and Somali. South African nationals who rented out their properties to foreign nationals were targeted during this catastrophe.

In the context of the above backdrop, the current study's purpose is to investigate the security agencies strategies applied to mitigate the impacts of the xenophobic violence.

Meanwhile, a Social Attitudes Survey conducted by Gordon (2019) on the three rounds of the xenophobic attacks of 2015–2017 ascertaining perceived threat of the xenophobic attacks driving past participation and potential participation in the future found the majority of people willing to consider participating in anti-immigrant violence.

The causes of the xenophobic attacks are multi-dimensional as the phenomenon and actions can be linked mainly to the economic competition, job opportunities as those who own the means of production prefer the foreign nationals as they are regarded as cheap labor, foreigners being perceived as attracting local girls and consumer's preferring the lower prices offered by foreign nationals. Hence, Ngcamu and Mantzaris (2019a, p. 1) argue that the government of South Africa's record on poor governance has been disassociated with xenophobia with the most focus on economic competition between the foreign nationals and locals.

A host of factors which aggravate xenophobia in the KZN province were found by Ngcamu and Mantzaris (2019b, p. 14) as including the fight for territory, the private sector's preference of immigrants for job opportunities and boredom. Other causes of xenophobia include inefficiency and ineffectiveness of relevant government agencies in eradicating crime in urban areas, mainly in Black African townships, which are prone to xenophobic attacks. The violent competition amongst the immigrants themselves and between them and local business men, unholy alliances with the police and unemployed youth, criminal endeavors, government's cover-ups for incompetence, corruption, minimal intelligence-driven and risk reduction analysis and planning has been considered by Ngcamu and Mantzaris (2019a, p. 7) as perpetuating xenophobic attacks in KZN. You need to punctuate your grammatical construction appropriately.

A host of researchers (Desai, 2008; Goddey, 2017; Landau et al., 2005) have suggested that the immigrants have been discriminated against by the security agencies. Note: You need to focus the review basically on the nexus between xenophobic attacks and security agencies which is the focus of the chapter with the police at the forefront. The police force has been regarded as reactive in dealing with a scourge of xenophobia by numerous commentators Bekker. The lack of adequate and serious intelligence services, including collection and analysis of reliable information on the ground has triggered and exacerbated xenophobic attacks in the KZN province (Ngcamu and Mantzaris, 2019a). The researchers concluded that the South African government should implement efficient, effective and appropriate crime-intelligence strategies that can detect, analyze and ultimately eradicate all forms of xenophobia in South Africa. The inability of the organs of state to detect the xenophobic attacks and porous borders has been cited by Ngcamu and Mantzaris (2019a, p. 5) as key reasons responsible for worsening the consequences of such evil deeds.

However, a study conducted by the latter authors in the KZN province linking xenophobia and criminality refuted theories of the "Third Force" which is widely shared by the government and the media. Instead, it was found that renting houses to the foreign nationals was seen as a serious problem and the immigrants' skills on illegal businesses such as illegal electricity connections can be considered as a trigger to xenophobia. A study performed by Ngcamu and Mantzaris (2019b, p. 14), within this analytical context, on the forgotten dimensions of xenophobia by the media showed the print media as untrustworthy, reckless and with serious bias in their reporting. A qualitative study by Cabane (2015) calling on xenophobia to be seen by the government as a disaster and the South African government's failure to manage disasters espoused several interesting findings. The author concluded that the 2008 xenophobic attacks were supposed to be declared a disaster by the South African government as the immigrants were vulnerable to such attacks, a reality which was seriously aggravated by bureaucratic and political constraints of disaster management. The author posits that following the 2008 xenophobic crisis, the Western Cape Provincial DMC acknowledged a new risk (xenophobic attacks) and developed a Social Conflict Emergency Committee responsible for such attacks.

Section 1 of the Disaster Management Act of 2002 (Act 57 of 2002) as amended to the Disaster Management Act of 2015 (Act 16 of 2015) defines a disaster as a:

> *"...progressive or sudden, widespread or localised, natural or human-caused occurrence which (a) causes or threatens to cause –*
>
> *(i) death, injury or disease;*
>
> *(ii) damage to property, infrastructure or the environment; or*
>
> *(iii) significant disruption of the life of a community; and [Sub-para. (iii) Substituted by s. 1 (c) of Act No. 16 of 2015. W.e.f 1 May 2016.]*
>
> *(b) Is of a magnitude that exceeds the ability of those affected by the disaster to cope with its effects using only their own resources."*

The same Act defines disaster management as a

> means a continuous and integrated multi-sectoral, multi-discipli-nary process of planning and implementation of measures aimed at- (a) preventing or reducing the risk of disasters; (b) mitigating the severity or consequences of disasters; (c) emergency prepared-ness; (d) rapid and effective response to disasters; and (e) post-disaster recovery and rehabilitation.

## 2. Legislative Framework

Sections 27, 41 and 55 of the Disaster Management Act of 2002 as amended in 2015 state that the national, provincial and local state of the country can be declared a disaster if the existing legislation and contingency arrangements do not adequately provide for the national, a provincial government and that municipality to deal effectively with the disaster; or other special circumstances warrant the declaration of a disaster. The abovementioned excerpts depict a significant gap in the literature that is attempted to be filled by this empirical study on the risk reduction strategies available to hamper and mitigate the impact of the xenophobic attacks.

## Research Findings

The government and the civil society group processes, systems and functions in the shelters for the displaced persons by the xenophobic attacks of 2015. The SAPS strategies and implementation plans are examined and pitfalls in this study.

## Township Climate, Societal Involvement and the Effects of the Xenophobic Attacks

A host of the provincial SAPS members described the situation during the xenophobic attacks as complex. A senior SAPS official indicated that after the Isipingo events Umlazi became the epicenter of attacks and many of its section (D, J, G, K, T and W) remained in turmoil for days. The attacks usually took place at night and SAPS had regular patrols of 30 to 40 policemen and women daily and nightly. During the nights it was challenging to stop the attacks which became more violent as properties that housed foreign spazas and residents were attacked with petrol bombs.

This was something new, as previously when the attacks commenced, only looting took place. Several South African locals from Umlazi who rented their properties to foreigners laid charges against "unknown people" who petrol bombed, attacked and looted their houses during the attacks. As time passed while there was a feeling that things would calm down because the displaced people had moved to the shelters, what really happened was that the levels of violence and the number of casualties increased. This situation worsened as days passed by because both South African and foreign nationals were well armed with machetes, firearms, knives, and baseball bats. The police knew that a significant number of foreigners were trained in military tactics, especially those from the DRC who participated in the civil wars in that country either with the government or the guerrillas. The DRC people in the shelters, especially the one in Isipingo, which was the most populous of the three were preparing to attack SAPS at one stage or another. One of the intelligence officials observed the negative sentiments shared amongst the foreign nationals toward the SAPS members resulting in them being attacked at the shelters as the majority of the foreign nationals amongst the Congolese displayed military expertise.

## Screening Processes and Acceptance in the Shelters for Displaced Victims

Several respondents indicated that in all the shelters for the displaced, processes were in place to screen the status of the displaced immigrants and consultation was conducted in locations where the attacks were prevalent by testing the victims' perceptions on possible re-integration. This was confirmed by one of the shelter managers who said that there was always a process of profiling those in the shelters, their paper documentation reflected, whether they were legal illegal or refugees. This was helped by representatives/leaders from the different countries who acted as recognized leaders/spokesmen. Communities in the areas where the attacks took place were widely consulted regarding issues of re-integration of those who suffered the attacks. The KZN provincial government mentioned a total of 1,179 immigrants who were successfully escorted by the SAPS and reintegrated into their homes without any incidents (KZN provincial government, 29 April).

Various government officials insisted that the displaced immigrants should be verified as there were opportunisms for access to free resources, including vouchers and processes that should be followed. The processes were shared clearly by the provincial coordinator in charge of communication who indicated that the first thing Home Affairs and SAPS had to establish was whether those in the shelters were really displaced after attacks because there were a few cases where people who had not faced attacks found the opportunity for free food, clothing and the occasional food and coffee vouchers.

The vast majority of displaced foreigners have been aware of the rules and regulations of such establishments because throughout the years there have been sporadic attacks on them by criminals or youths. The foreigners are aware that under such circumstances they must present themselves to a police station to open a case number. If there are shelters already in operation, the displaced persons are accompanied by the police, following the verification of their particulars. After their formal registration, they sign the document that sets the conditions and rules that are followed by the inhabitants of the shelter. These processes are compulsory and must be followed by all who live in the shelter, and it is the duty and responsibility of the displaced to ensure that all legal requirements are followed because this is the first step for good governance of the situation.

## Intergovernmental, Inter-Sectoral and Inter-Professional Collaboration on the Shelters for Displaced Victims and Activities

On April 21, 2015, there were 3,399 Malawian, 1,074 Tanzanian, 677 Zimbabweans, 324 who were un-coded, 44 Burundian, 35 from the DRC, 35 Ethiopian, 24 Tanzanian and 24 Kenyan foreign nationals in refugee shelters (RSG, 2015, p. 122). A senior coordinator of the NATJOINT mentioned government departments that were performing various activities and services in the shelters of the displaced immigrants. The Department of Home Affairs and the Department of Safety and Community Liaison were responsible for re-integration and verification status, operations and its implementation plan. The Department of Social Development was in charge of trauma response, social and statutory support, psycho-social support, counseling and the re-integration process. The Department of Justice and Constitutional Development provided dedicated courtrooms, prosecutors and foreign language interpreters.

Additionally, the Department of Health provided medical treatment on site, health awareness programs, condoms and support to the re-integration and repartition processes. The eThekwini Municipality was in charge of elevating the levels of community participation in the process of re-integration. A number of units and departments, including security and municipal fleet services were mentioned. The Municipal Disaster Management and Metro Police provided the temporary shelters, organized food at the shelters, controlled access measures and overall operations, managed incidents, prepared media statements and briefings, and facilitated the march against xenophobia. Traffic management provided visible policing and by-laws and general law enforcement.

The psychological and trauma assistance claimed to have been provided by the Department of the Social Development has been disputed by Crush & Ramachandran (2017) on their findings on the level of trauma experienced by the victims of the xenophobic attacks in Chatsworth (Durban). Similar conditions were reminiscent in the 2008 xenophobic attacks which influenced UCT's Faculty of Humanities to provide psychological support to victims at the shelters for the displaced.

Cooperative Governance and Traditional Affairs (COGTA) was in charge of developing a strategic work response plan and coordinating its implementation; supporting the re-integration and repatriation process; mobilizing the Community Works Programme to assist with community engagement meetings and response; coordinating emergency response measures and verifying trading business licenses. Furthermore, another NATJOINT member further cited the Disaster Management officials (emergency response); Municipal Health Department (Mobile Clinic 24/7 and offer medical treatment on site); EMRS (emergency response, transportation of patients and medical treatment on site); Durban Solid Waste (cleaning the shelters, grass cutting, provision of bins and plastic bags and waste management and control). The South African National Defence Force (SANDF) was to assist with additional temporary shelters; enhance safety and security and rescue operations as well as bolster humanitarian services and the Department of Education was there to ascertain the number of school children affected; the verification and assessment of schools affected and to report to the Department of Social Development.

An interviewee from the inspectorate mentioned that there were volunteers from government institutions such as paramedics from the RK Khan Hospital assisting people with chronic diseases and trained members from the Department of Social Development who played games with the children and other victims distracted from the element and assisted with the distribution of food. She mentioned that the Emergency Medical Rescue Service personnel performed random checks, and there were 12 Clinical Commissioning Group (CCG) for security from Social Development and Safer City.

A host of the informants have pinpointed a plethora of serious challenges at a number of levels regarding the planning and processes to be followed on the re-integration and repatriation of the displaced immigrants. The nature and propensity of the challenges were at the extreme even though the NATJOINTS with different state agencies were represented. This was exemplified by a senior member of SAPS who was mostly available in the shelter coordinating committee meetings. The SAPS member indicated that NATJOINTS was a key to the total functionality of the state at all levels because it is a coordinating mechanism for peace, stability and security because it puts all key law enforcement operations in perspective and action throughout the country. It deals with analysis, coordination and key deployments and plans, and designs and coordinates actions. The principal movers of the coordination, in this case, were the SAPS Service, the Department of International Relations and Cooperation, the National Defence Force, National Prosecuting Authorities, the Intelligence Coordinating Committee and the eThekwini Metro Police.

The government officials have revealed a proactive, well-planned and coordinated role performed by the multiple and diverse departments whilst Minson and Misago's (2009) contrary viewpoint suggested an inadequate response to the protection of the displaced and inconsistent provision of services in shelters.

This position coincides with Peberdy and Jara (2011) who indicated that the xenophobic attacks negative effect on the displaced immigrants would be severe if the civil society groups through its humanitarian response and advocacy did not mobilize the required resources.

A number of the interviewees echoed the role played by the Department of Home Affairs and SAPS in the shelters for the displaced immigrants. Their key responsibilities were mostly concerned with verifying their citizenship and possible repatriation. A total of 2,082 immigrants (from Mozambique, Malawi, Zimbabwe and Tanzanian) were repatriated to their countries by bus between April 16, 2015 and April 24, 2015.

A senior member of the eThekwini Municipality DMC confirmed that the Home Affairs department dealt with their citizenship, papers, and volunteered repatriation. It is intriguing that no Nigerians were in camps; the Malawians were in the majority. A number of Mozambicans and Malawians could not communicate in English or local languages.

Interviews conducted with shelter coordinators confirmed that various government agencies and departments were involved performing a number of activities such as the distribution of the Resident Support Scheme (RSS) vouchers. The Office of the Premier with the SAPS leadership were involved in the coordination of the situation and COGTA, Community Safety and Liaison, Home Affairs (dealing with people without proper documentation) the DMC and a large number of NGOs, and religious and business groups that helped throughout with food money. There was direct communication with the recognized leaderships of the displaced people who communicated with the Committee directly, but also through letters to the Premier and MEC Mchunu.

A senior DMC official noted challenges the government officials had experienced in the development of shelter-specific rosters for the division and the assignment of different responsibilities to various NGOs which proved to be a valuable tool in alleviating these specific concerns (Desai and Vahed, 2013).

The SAPS officer who performed leadership duties in the shelters confirmed that different departments in the shelter were coordinated by the SAPS and mentioned a plethora of challenges experienced during this period. The officer stated that all participants were equal partners, but the group was chaired by the SAPS Service that led the process of researching situations, making plans, delegating with people and groups and other state institutions throughout the affected areas and the whole of KZN and nationally. However, the unit witnessed a number of difficulties and challenges such as lack of capacity in the respective sections and departments of SAPS and the municipality, the small community attendance at meetings, the problem facing municipal councilors in their efforts to participate, and the final solution in hiring outside consultants/service providers to move the situation forward.

The interviewees clarified the widely shared perceptions that almost all xenophobic attacks were directed at African immigrants and refugees while the Chinese, Indians and Pakistanis were not violently attacked. One of the SAPS intelligence officials said that this occurred because of the vicinity and their operations and possibly because they were not considered opposition for local African establishment, although they had also faced problems with theft, burglaries and other criminal activities by the locals and from some from their own or other Africans.

A senior SAPS member who formed part of NATJOINTS argued that NAT-JOINTS was always a key to the total functionality of the state at all levels because it is a coordinating mechanism for peace, stability and security. She said that it deals with analysis, coordination and key deployments and plans, designs and coordinates actions. The principal movers of the coordination, in this case, were the SAPS Service, the Department of International Relations and Coop-eration, the National Defence Force, National Prosecution Authority (NPA), the Intelligence Coordinating Committee and the eThekwini Metro Police. The NATJOINT analysis and report pointed to serious challenges at a number of levels and key issues such as the planning and steps to be undertaken in the re-integration, which was the "ideal situation" together with repatriation.

## Intergovernmental Relationship Challenges

The provincial DMC had detailed their role before, during and in the aftermath of the xenophobic attacks. One of the senior disaster management officials argued that their function was based on coordinating and identifying the departments' response, provision for displacements, identification of facts and information, understanding of the capabilities and requirements of a specific situation and disaster risk reduction. He further mentioned that their primary role was commu-nity scanning, location of possible areas of attacks, risk assessment, sensitizing the structures, facilitating social dialogue, integrating communities, establish-ing community programs, and monitoring and providing humanitarian services according to the UN Charter. There were organizational and logistical challenges that were noted in the shelters including the allegations that government officials harassed immigrants and there was a breakdown in communication which led to unnecessary duplication of efforts and wastage of valuable resources (SRG, 2015, p. 126).

Cebane (2015) showed that the vulnerability depicted in the 2015 xenopho-bic attacks is similar to the vulnerability of the victims in the shelters for the displaced and exacerbated by bureaucratic and political constraints of disaster management. The previous finding supports the sentiments shared by numerous researchers that South Africans are regarded as anti-immigrant (Desai, 2008), have an extensive knowledge of ill-treatment of the immigrants (Murray, 2003) and do not respect national, regional and international refugee laws (Kamwimbi et al., 2010).

Almost all the respondents from the government departments acknowledged challenges which emanate from providing shelters to the displaced immigrants as a form of the humanitarian services according to the UN Charter which guides them on setting up a shelter and what is needed on a daily basis.

The government leaders' experiences indicated that they provided services to immigrants in these shelters; a process leading to the creation of a "comfort zone." Conversely, they were pressured by the locals who complained that the government provided quality essential services to foreigners at their expense.

Such dilemmas caused tensions as the foreign nationals came from the shacks where there were no basic needs including water, electricity and proper sanitation (Director: Disaster Management-provincial government). A report on foreign nationals compiled by the Disaster and Emergency Control Unit between March 30, 2015 to April 30, 2015 showed that there were infighting amongst émigrés over access to necessities such as food and beds. This was perpetuated by the expectations created by certain African embassies when repatriation was not fulfilled.

The SRG (July 30, 2015, p. 127) pinpointed allegations of incoherent management by government officials as leading to failure in resolving the humanitarian crisis, lack of accurate and timely information distributed by officials and ineffective division of labor. The failure of the government to resolve a humanitarian crisis in the shelters for displaced victims was mentioned in Minson and Misago's (2009) study, which revealed inadequate government response and a reluctant approach to humanitarian assistance.

## The SAPS's Experiences and Approach on the Xenophobic Violence

The interviewees from the security cluster mentioned a host of factors which were brought by the xenophobic attacks. These actors concluded that the impacts of these attacks not only affected SAPS but almost all the government departments.

The SAPS analyst believed that the situation had major consequences at all levels and the country has paid politically, financially and otherwise for the conditions that exist in most countries in Africa. It was stated that to manage these attacks is a difficult task because many foreigners are involved in crime. The present situation has led to very serious pressure on resources, money, staff, police stations and courts because in almost every attack there are dead or injured victims.

It was mentioned that South Africa repatriates 5,000 people who wish to go back in a month many of them and thousands more return. The statistics show that 80% to 85% of the immigrants arriving in South Africa are from the continent. It is known that millions of them are illegal, and it is almost impossible to control them because the government institutions like the Department of Home Affairs are unable to manage these situations. Resources are scarce so there is no knowledge of how many illegals are in the country.

## SAPS's Response Strategies

The lack of "communication and engagement" between the immigrants and government officials managing shelters was raised by foreign national representatives (Civil Society Coalition on Xenophobia, May 5, 2015), a reality that has been revealed by Ngcamu and Mantzaris (2019a) research study.

The reactions in the aftermath of the xenophobic attacks in Isipingo (Umlazi) and spreading toward Durban has been described by a host of research participants from the security cluster as involving mobilization of the resources and activation of the action plan and targeting of the instigators and perpetrators.

One of the SAPS coordinators confirmed that there was immediate mobilization based on an action plan designed by the SAPS, NPA and the State Security Agency (SSA), where the key decisions and initiatives were drawn and expected to be implemented. The plan was based on the essential expectations that the functions of the key state instruments would be followed. SAPS and NPA were expected to arrest and prosecute instigators and perpetrators of violence; SAPS, SSA and SANDF should intensify intelligence-driven operations in affected areas through the utilization of sources living in and knowing these areas; thus providing opportunities for early warning on new risk areas. Instead of arresting and prosecuting the instigators and perpetrators, Minson and Misago (2009) saw the police being reluctant to protect the victims (immigrants) but rather assisted in the looting of goods.

The security cluster members regarded the claims made in the popular print media that there were no consequences for the instigators, perpetrators and those who were involved in looting as false. However, the NPA reported to the Coordinating Committee that 40 matters were placed on the court roll and 128 cases had been reported and recorded by April 17, 2015 while the Chief Coordinator of NATJOINT indicated that SAPS arrested 20 people in the first 6 days for 35 cases involving murder, attempted murder, public violence, housebreaking, attempted theft, burglary, assault and robbery in the Umlazi Cluster and theft, intimidation, public violence, assault, murder attempted murder, and malicious damage to property in the Chatsworth Cluster.

The SAPS officials commended the other government departments' efforts in combating the xenophobic violence stating that everything possible had been done by the government and SAPS to fight and defeat xenophobia at all levels and everywhere. These initiatives and actions were planned by task teams that coordinated all the actions of SAPS and all other state institutions daily.

On the other hand, a member of the security cluster indicated that there were questions about SAPS visibility in a number of affected and emerging flashpoints. Consequently, there was an urgent need for special attention for the proliferation of illegal weapons in both foreigner and local communities; the Department of Home Affairs should have checked all existing identity documents and credentials of foreigners for authenticity and thus possibly expedite the deportation of illegal migrants while Home Affairs, eThekwini Municipality, SARS and COGTA should have sharpened the responsibility of profiling and auditing of foreign-owned businesses and ensure compliance with municipal and national regulations.

The SAPS Coordinator declared that while these attacks took place, the promises of the Mayor's Office to regulate the running of businesses in the townships to avoid the mushrooming of tuck-shops could not be followed because of the resistance of the local traders.

## Intelligence Gathering, Consultation and Re-integration

The Home Affairs leader postulated that the state's relevant authorities have the primary duty and responsibility to establish conditions, as well as provide the means, which allow internally displaced persons to return voluntarily, in safety and with dignity to their homes or places of habitual residence, or to resettle voluntarily in another part of the country.

A SAPS coordinator indicated that initially there was very intensive crime intelligence, and those involved had strict instructions to gather all available information about those involved directly and indirectly with the attacks. As a part of this information gathering, there was a meeting between SAPS, municipal officials and disgruntled local shop owners who accused foreigners of selling cheap and expired commodities, selling drugs, engaging in illicit relationships with township women and doing all sorts of illegal things. They also fought against each other. He further said that while things were thought to be calming down the Coordinating Committee that was dominated by the Provincial Government and the Municipality decided to take a number of steps forward to more or less stabilize the situation firstly through the scrutiny of a "case by case" analysis of all legal immigrants and start a process of "community re-integration" through the facilitation of a return to their residences and businesses through a negotiated process. Their other choice was repatriation. In this process, the Department of Home Affairs was obligated to process those without documentation and provide further directives as to the way forward. This was not considered an easy step on the part of COGTA and the eThekwini Municipality leadership which through the Office of the Speaker organized meetings with the Ward Committees of all the affected areas and convinced them to stress to their community constituencies the urgency and importance of the foreign nationals' integration back into their community. These steps started promisingly, but they faded in the process. There were efforts to continue the engagement of all political leaderships in the province and the municipality, which were easy targets, and urge the youth leagues of all the existing parties, religious groups and churches and other organized community formations to quell the attacks and counter-attacks.

Several initiatives and projects were put in place during and in the aftermath of the xenophobic attacks. For instance, the NATJOINT and the SAPS were in the process of intensifying operation FIELA, a widening series of raids on illegal immigrants and undocumented people throughout the country and KZN. It is true that in a number of occasions SAPS representatives were absent from meetings called for and organized by NATJOINT, and to update them as a vital component of the provincial team PROVJOINT was absent. NATJOINT's key position throughout the whole period was that the re-integration process should inform the shelter closing date and that they should be aware of all operational plans for the re-integration process and also the number of people who will need training on the re-integration process (SAPS Officer).

A member of the NATJOINTS observed a host of security challenges in the shelters which was exacerbated by free movement of people into and out of the shelters, increased number of the immigrants in the shelters on days when Operation Fiela was conducted, the presence of firearms and alcohol, illegal structures and electrical connections, theft and illegal businesses.

The above basis was confirmed by one of the Shelter's supervisors who indicated that there was direct interaction between the UN, the displaced and the

Community Safety and Liaison that identified the beneficiaries in the shelters. There was a fear, however, that this distribution would attract more displaced people in specific shelters although there was over-crowding.

## Humanitarianism at Local Government Level

A senior SAPS member who was responsible for the coordination of the shelters at the inception of the xenophobic attacks posited that the Premier tasked the Former UN Commissioner for Human Rights to investigate the underlying causes of the attacks. The police officer further indicated that the eThekwini City Mayor offered humanitarian services to the affected and displaced immigrants, consequently 100 shelters opened in Chatsworth, 276 in Isipingo and 196 in Greenwood Park respectively with the provision of 24-hour police protection.

A number of the informants consistently confirmed that they were flexible on the civil society groups' access to the shelters as they have rendered services and provided the displaced people with necessities. A provincial government expert who was in charge of communication indicated that besides basic shelter and housing there was always an effort to provide eatable food and clothing and fulfill the basic needs such as sanitary pads for women, and viable contacts and connections with national and international humanitarian organizations and CBOs, and religious organizations, which offered their services. Those organizations and individuals had free passage to the shelters because of their efforts to provide humanitarian assistance.

The research participants unequivocally observed that the majority of the displaced people were children, women and those living with disabilities, and government officials were flexible in allowing them to move to other shelters.

An eThekwini Municipality official who was responsible for finance and mobilization indicated that all these services were intact as they were obligated by international laws to pay serious attention to children of all ages, mothers with small children, unaccompanied minors, expectant mothers, female heads of households, persons with disabilities and elderly persons. There was no expectation of gratitude because these were their duties and responsibilities. Hence, it was the official's duty to ensure that these duties were fulfilled according to the circumstances and to facilitate the movement to other settlements if a displaced immigrant wished to do so. This was one of the problems faced because given the different groups in one of them dictated the conditions and the terms of other settlements. Most of the displaced immigrants had the most expensive cell phones and access to data, so communications were perpetual. So, they communicated with and made decisions for their families, connections and compatriots.

## Community Involvement in Fighting the Scourge of the Attacks

The senior coordinating member of all police stations explained strategic plans that were in place and their successes. She said that SAPS was immediately involved in extensive mobilization at least during the first week, and their priority was to communicate with communities and their leaders to could win their support.

There was community involvement and cooperation between SAPS and other role-players because they were severely affected by the situation. This cooperation was everywhere and had different results because in most cases there was a decrease in the incidents of attacks against foreign nationals in the affected areas as the result of thousands of foreigners moving to the shelters. Following the instructions of the Coordinating Committee, all police stations ought to record and profile all spazas and other shops owned by foreign nationals in their areas and patrol these shops for fear of further attacks. Public Order Policing (POP) deployments in most areas continued with on-going visits to shops owned by foreign nationals and it was reported that following this intervention, there was some stability in the situation.

The eThekwini municipal strategic committee member further pointed out that xenophobia and violence against foreigners could only be successfully addressed with the involvement of the host communities as well as the migrant communities, in order to understand the root causes of the violence and the intolerance. However, SAPS did not get involved in planning or educating the local communities. They just got involved with the displaced foreigners in the camps. Such a connection with communities has been a success as shown in different case studies which showed that in various areas, such as in Khutsong, xenophobia can be prevented by communities and CBOs (Kirshner, 2012); De Doorns (Kerr, 2017) and Abahlali base Mjondolo in Durban (Clark, 2018) which mobilized communities to act against xenophobia and discouraged xenophobic and divisive tactics.

## Conclusion

This chapter contributes to the discourse regarding the government's processes, structures and operations, as well as the functions of multiple departments and sectors, challenges encountered and initiatives in the shelters for displaced victims. It demonstrates that the government has learnt from the 2008 xenophobic attacks and improved their response strategies in the 2015 violence as they were processes in place for screening, profiling and verification for the victims to avoid opportunistic tendencies.

Furthermore, SAPS and the Department of Home Affairs were considered to have played a pivotal role in the possible integration and repatriation of the immigrants through consultation with the immigrants recognized leadership. Meanwhile, various departments such as the Department of Health and Education played important functions in providing trauma response, health services to the victims and assisting students. Ironically, SAPS and the intelligence operatives commenced intelligence gathering and analysis post the xenophobic attacks. This chapter consequently argues that the government alone could not have been successful in responding to such complex humanitarian crisis without the assistance of the civil society groups which provided their expertise in solving the humanitarian crisis during and post the attacks.

The chapter concludes that the xenophobic attacks impacted directly on municipalities although they had been ignoring the calls to declare such attacks as a local disaster. The municipalities' failure to manage the crisis with its resources necessitates seeking assistance from the provincial and the national government.

The lack of communication and engagement by government officials and the eThekwini Municipality failure to enforce the by-laws on the proliferation of the illegal small businesses (tuck-shops) due to being intimidated and failure to prosecute instigators and perpetrators suggest that they were complicit in these attacks.

Similarly, the reluctance of the community leaders, including councilors, SAPS, interested groups and the host communities further suggest that they were complicit in these attacks. What is noteworthy in this study is the government departments and agencies focus on protecting the indigent groups including the aged, children, women and those living with disabilities during these attacks.

Whilst there were indigent groups in the shelters; however, the black petit bourgeoisie was also noticed with their unrealistic demands and expectations.

Finally, the study concludes that the 2015 xenophobic attacks were unique because the attacks were also directed against the South African home-owners who were renting their premises to immigrants.

The chapter recommends that the long-term planning by all government departments, agencies, as well the civil society with the involvement of communities that are susceptible to such as attacks is essential.

Both the locals and the immigrants should be involved in such long-term plans as these attacks are sporadic and multi-dimensional.

The SAPS intelligence unit should be empowered in order to prevent the reoccurrence of such a disaster through community participation and engagement. The limitation of the study was methodological as researchers primarily targeted government officials which necessitates future researchers to target house owners who were also the victims of the 2015 xenophobic attacks.

## References

Cabane, L. 2015. Protecting the "Most Vulnerable"? The management of a disaster and the making/unmaking of victims after the 2008 xenophobic violence in South Africa, *International Journal of Conflict and Violence (IJCV)*, (9), 56–71.

Charman, A. and Piper, L. 2012. Xenophobia, criminality and violent entrepreneurship: violence against Somali shopkeepers in Delft South, Cape Town, South Africa, *South African Review of Sociology*, *43*(3), 81–105.

Clark, C. 2018. Why is there so much conflict between Abahlali and the state? *GroundUp*, September 20.

Crush, J. and Ramachandran, S. 2017. Migrant entrepreneurship collective violence and xenophobia in South Africa (No. 67). *Southern African Migration Programme*.

Desai, A. 2008. Xenophobia and the of the refugee in the rainbow nation of human rights, *African Sociological Review/Revue Africaine de Sociologie*, *12*(2), 1–12.

Desai, A. and Vahed, G. 2013. Non-governmental organisations and xenophobia in South Africa: a case study of the Gift of the Givers (GOTG), *Love thy Neighbours*: 241. Farish, 2009.

Displaced Person Shelter Rules VII dated 08-05-2015.

Gordon, S. 2019. A violent minority? A quantitative analysis of those engaged in anti-immigrant violence in South Africa. *South African Geographical Journal*, *101*(2), 269–283.

Kamwimbi, T., Banaszak, K., Khan, S., Morgan, J., Nadori, A. and Ives, A. 2010. Violation of human rights of disadvantaged and vulnerable refugees–victims of xenophobic attacks in South Africa, *OIDA International Journal of Sustainable Development*, *1*(05), 67–83.

Kerr, P.L. 2017. Xenophobia, social change and social continuity: changing configurations of intergroup allegiance and division among farm workers and farmers in De Doorns, 2009-2013 (Doctoral dissertation).

Kerr, P., Durrheim, K. and Dixon, J. 2019. Xenophobic violence and struggle discourse in South Africa, *Journal of Asian and African Studies*, *54*(7), 995–1011.

Kirshner, J.D. 2012. "We are Gauteng people": challenging the politics of xenophobia in Khutsong, South Africa, *Antipode*, *44*(4), 1307–1328.

Médecins Sans Frontières – 30 April 2015; Minutes from the Civil Society Coalition on Xenophobia – 05 May 2015.

Minson, T. and Misago, J.P. 2009. Why history has repeated itself the security risks of structural xenophobia, *SA Crime Quarterly*, *2009*(29), 25-34..

Minutes from the Civil Society Coalition on Xenophobia – 05 May 2015.

Monson, T. and Misago, J.-P. 2009. Why history has repeated itself the security risks of structural xenophobia, *SA Crime Quarterly*, *2009*(29), 25–34.

Murray, M.J. 2003. Alien strangers in our midst: the dreaded foreign invasion and "Fortress South Africa", *Canadian Journal of African Studies/La Revue Canadienne des études Africaines*, *37*(2–3), 440–466.

Ngcamu, B.S. and Mantzaris, E. 2019a. Xenophobic violence and criminality in the KwaZulu-Natal townships, *The Journal for Transdisciplinary Research in Southern Africa*, *15*(1), 8.

Ngcamu, B.S. and Mantzaris, E. 2019b. Media reporting, xenophobic violence, and the "Forgotten Dimensions": a case of selected areas in the KwaZulu-Natal Province, *International Journal of African Renaissance Studies-Multi-, Inter-and Transdisciplinarity*, *14*(1), 131–146.

Ogunnoiki, A.O. and Adeyemi, A.A. 2019. The impact of xenophobic attacks on Nigeria-South Africa relations, *African Journal of Social Sciences and Humanities Research (AJSSHR)*, *2*(2), 1–18.

Palmary, I. 2002. *Refugees, Safety and Xenophobia in South African Cities: The Role of Local Government*, Johannesburg, Centre for the Study of Violence and Reconciliation.

Peberdy, S. and Jara, M.K. 2011. Humanitarian and social mobilization in Cape Town: civil society and the May 2008 xenophobic violence, *Politikon*, *38*(1), 37–57.

Robins, S. 2009. Humanitarian aid beyond "bare survival": Social movement responses to xenophobic violence in South Africa, *American Ethnologist*, *36*(4), 637–650.

Ruedin, D. 2017. *Not Everyone Is Xenophobic in South Africa*.

Saleh, I. 2015. Is it really xenophobia in South Africa or an intentional act of prejudice? *Global Media Journal-African Edition*, *9*(2), 298–313.

Special Reference Group (RSG) on Migration and Community Integration in KwaZulu-Natal. 2015. Report of the SRG on Migration and Community Integration in KwaZulu-Natal, 31 October.

Tevera, D. 2013. *African Migrants, Xenophobia and Urban Violence in Post-Apartheid South Africa*.

# Chapter Eight

# Managing Shelters for the Displaced

This chapter shows that the psychological and legal support offered to the displaced immigrants was the first step in a long and occasionally painful process for all concerned. The situation would have been even worse without the support and major contributions of civil society such as Non-Profit Organization (NPOs), Community Based Organisations (CBOs) and faith-based organizations, which came to the assistance of the displaced in order to support them. The management of a shelter, its challenges and the role of the state and international institutions responsible for its operations are dissected. The relationships of those in charge and the recipients of the services went through a wide variety of emotions, feelings, relationships and misunderstandings on a number of levels. The psychological and legal support provided to the immigrants is examination, in addition to their historical and material roots, as well as the material and spiritual support from NPOs and CBOs. Through their energy and moral and material support, the state's efforts were supplemented. The key interventions in the effort to stabilize the establishments from the resistance of stakeholders has been connected to the legal rules and regulations and their importance for functionality. This process was complicated by the policy and politics of the vouchers of the UN. The serious financial implications of the xenophobic violence conclude the chapter.

This chapter deals with the circumstances in which the displaced immigrants and refugees found themselves, following the xenophobic attacks in Durban that began in Isipingo and spread widely throughout the city and surrounding areas. The terrain of this chapter includes an examination of the displacement and shelter conditions, human and social struggles, power relationships, tattered dreams and challenges on all sides. We discuss the social, psychological, economic, financial, anthropological, political and religious challenges – an attempted dissection of a cultural and human Daedalic reality. We begin with the first and initial assistance of the state to the displaced at the few established centers in KwaZulu-Natal close to the locations where the attacks took place. Psychological and legal support was offered to the victims, helping them on a multi-dimensional journey to a "new unknown." This was a thoughtful beginning that was supplemented by the immediate and generous material and spiritual contributions from civil society organizations, which offered food, clothing, furniture and other items.

**Addressing Xenophobia in South Africa:**
**Drivers, Responses and Lessons from the Durban Untold Stories, 165–185**
Copyright © 2022 by Bethuel Sibongiseni Ngcamu and Evangelos Mantzaris
Published under exclusive licence by Emerald Publishing Limited
doi:10.1108/978-1-80262-479-320211009

These steps were planned to welcome the residents to the shelters during a period of challenges, deep thinking and acting, and building or destroying new and already existing relationships. The instruments of a state with responsibilities are rooted both in its own legislation and in international legal dimensions and conventions. It would be foolish to believe that the state functionaries and immigrants at shelters were the only participants in existing relations within the space. Relationships among the residents were also dictated by outside interventions, new and old relationships, the existing conditions of the establishment, the levels of agreements and disagreements as well the resistance among stakeholders and the existing material realities facing them, including water, electricity, cleanness, behavior, policies, ideologies, money and politics.

## Displaced Refugee Shelters Globally: A Brief View

It is now generally accepted by all people that the coronavirus has had a major and devastating impact on humanity as a whole. In some ways it has been a widespread war against humanity, a powerful and destructive virus that knows no nationality, religion, ideology, belief, color or social status. It is a different kind of war to the ones being waged in Syria, Yemen, Palestine and parts of Africa. These wars are fueled by hatred, ambition, greed, political opportunism or ideological fanaticism and lead to extensive human destruction. One option to escape is the possibility of refuge in another country – escaping to a different land with the hope of a better life. These "escapees" are known internationally as refugees. There is no doubt that when the coronavirus pandemic abates, the already massive international waves of refugees will continue to spread globally like no other. Within this parameter, the present study and lessons learnt from the 2015 xenophobic attacks in Durban could perhaps be useful.

The political refugees are but one massive group of people escaping human-made destruction, but in our particular endeavor, political (or war) refugees is only one of the groups that have faced xenophobia in South Africa for years. The second category is the significant economic or poverty refugees – migrants who, throughout Africa, Asia and Europe, leave their home state and find their way to countries like South Africa to "survive," "get a job" and "make a living."

Of course, South Africa is only one of the countries in the world that face such a reality: poverty, unemployment, discrimination, hatred and war have forced millions to seek refuge elsewhere. Accordingly, a brief comparison of South Africa's migration situation with those of other countries, in terms of numbers, could be useful.

Greece has been hit over the years with masses of migrants and asylum seekers, mainly through Turkey. These refuges hold onto the hope of finding their way to another, more prosperous country in Europe. The majority are genuine refugees and asylum seekers. By the end of 2019, 121,200 of them benefited from direct cash support from the United Nations High Commissioner for Refugees (UNHCR's) Emergency Support to Integration and Accommodation (ESTIA) program. A total of 32,500 people were accommodated through this shelter program. United Nations International Children's Emergency Fund (UNICEF) (2020) has revealed the following about unaccompanied asylum-seeking children:

In 2020, 49,000 households received cash grants; 25,000 places of accommodation established by UNHCR during the 2016–2018 have been handed over to the Greek Government and 5,000 people have benefitted from legal assistance (UNHCR, 2020). In addition, an estimated 42,500 children were present in Greece as of 31 December 2019, up from 27,000 in December 2018. Of all children present in Greece, 48% were living in urban areas (such as apartments, hotels, shelters for UASC, self-settled, etc.); 25% were in accommodation sites and 1% were in safe zones for UASC.

The latest reports on the conditions in the country's multiple refugee camps and shelters painted a depressing picture of the establishments. On two Greek islands that were inspected by the Council of Europe Commissioner for Human Rights, it was reported that people had to queue for more than three hours for food or to use the bathroom. It was stated that the overcrowding was "unbearable," that there was a serious lack of shelter, that hygiene conditions were poor and that access to medical care was substandard. Children with skin diseases were not being treated and there was a complete lack of medications or drugs. Such realities were described by EU officials as "really quite shocking for the European continent in the 21st century." Greece, because of its proximity to Turkey, has been struggling since 2015 to deal with masses of refugees and asylum seekers. At present, it faces undoubtedly the biggest resurgence in arrivals since the beginning of the invasion five years ago when more than a million people crossed into Europe from Turkey via Greece. The official number of asylum seekers and refugees at present stands at 34,000, who are being held in camps and shelters situated on the Aegean Islands close to Turkey. The present right wing government in the country has begun to move more and more refugees and asylum seekers to the mainland, but the continuous surge of new arrivals means that this is difficult. It is not impossible for it to be halted, at least for now.

In order to face the "problems head on," the present government, after blaming the previous "left leaning" administration for the overcrowded conditions, has decided to move more than 20,000 refugees and asylum seekers to the mainland. In addition, in 2019 the country's parliament rubberstamped legislation aimed at amending the asylum process. The bill was condemned by civil rights groups as it sought to restrict protection for asylum seekers. The government has defended the new bill, saying that it seeks to clarify and codify a "disparate set of rules into one rulebook," meaning that those whose applications have been rejected will be deported immediately. The UNHCR and a number of Non-Governmental Organisations (NGOs) have expressed misgivings about the legislation, saying it weakens the protection of refugees (Papadimas, 2019).

## Psychological and Legal Support for Displaced Immigrants

There have been a host of shortcomings and challenges experienced by immigrants in shelters for the displaced after the 2015 xenophobic attacks occurred in South Africa. These include inadequacies in the provision of basic needs and necessities by respective municipalities and other government agencies. During the spate of the xenophobic attacks against foreign nationals in Durban, Womersley et al. (2016) indicated that there was a disproportionately high percentage (85%) of people living in displaced shelters who showed symptoms of post-traumatic stress disorder. The authors argued that the topic of trauma among refugees across the globe has received increasing interest from scholars. According to Womersley et al. (2016), during this period a total of 7,500 (estimated) people, mainly refugees and asylum seekers from the DRC and Burundi, were assisted with medical care and psychological support by Doctors Without Borders. The authors posit that the immigrants in the shelters in KwaZulu-Natal feared both returning to their war-torn countries and to South African communities where they experienced violent attacks and destruction of property.

The xenophobic attacks that occurred in 2008 also saw a large number of organizations, groups and individuals volunteering by providing professional expertise to assist the displaced immigrants. This was noticed by the University of Cape Town (UCT) which at the time was home to 2,308 students from the Horn of Africa. These individuals responded to the crisis by providing humanitarian assistance to the victims of xenophobia (Favish, 2009). The strategic humanitarian response of the university to the xenophobic attacks was aimed at mitigating the impacts of the people displaced in the shelters. Favish (2009) mentioned that a diversity of activities were coordinated and led by a community development organization – the Students' Health and Welfare Centres Organisation (SHAWCO) – which for many years has been managed by UCT students, medical personnel and the Law Faculty Refugee Rights Project. The organization responded decisively during the incidences of human rights abuses.

## Non-profit Organizations' Proactive Response

A wide variety of NGOs have been prominent in responding proactively to xenophobic attacks by assisting vulnerable groups, mostly those displaced in shelters. In 2008, during the scourge of attacks against foreign nationals, Desai and Vahed (2013, p. 241) examined the role of the Gift of the Givers in responding to the xenophobic violence. The organization's response to the disastrous xenophobic attacks was considered to have transcended that of the Government of South Africa in many ways. This was due to the sophistication needed in dealing with donors, governments and the public as well as the perpetrators. Desai and Vahed (2013) argued that the Gift of the Givers played a pivotal role in providing material assistance to the victims of the attacks, although the response was considered to be short, strategic planning. The authors concluded that NGOs can perform a significant role in raising awareness of xenophobia, mobilizing civil society to prevent such attacks and implementing healthy policies in dealing with xenophobia (Desai and Vahed, 2013).

The Treatment Action Campaign is another organization that played a leading role in providing relief to immigrants who had been displaced during attacks against foreign nationals. The latter NPO provided assistance to the displaced in the form of basic needs including food, clothes and blankets and, further, offering legal aid (Robins, 2009).

There have been many organizations such as CBOs that have provided accommodation for some of the displaced migrants. During the 2008 period, a total of 3,000 displaced immigrants were accommodated in churches, a fact that created conflict and controversy at both a local and national government level, due to excessive overcrowding (Bompani, 2013). Nyar (2011), meanwhile, assessed the contribution of the private sector during the 2008 xenophobic attacks, highlighting the unique civil society–business engagement. An interesting study by Peberdy and Jara (2011) on civil society groups in Cape Town in 2008 and how they responded to the xenophobic attacks that occurred there had an interesting conclusion: that the impacts of the xenophobic attacks would have been severe had civil society groups not provided humanitarian assistance.

The sparsely reviewed literature above reflects the serious gaps in empirical research in terms of the significant role played by civil society groups in responding to the emergencies brought about by violent acts against immigrants. The literature clearly shows that the government could not have proactively responded in providing the humanitarian support needed without the support of the civil society groups, including NGOs and NPOs.

### Government Officials' Visits

The South African Police (SAPS) who was occasionally in charge of a number of areas after the attacks commenced stationed in Greenwood Park recalled the following:

> The attacked fled to the Greenwood Park Police Station for safety and they were kept there … I was called to speak to them and what they told me frightened me although I had experience from previous situations such as this.

**Verification and Stakeholders' Assistance.** Civil society groups raised a pertinent issue regarding some of the causes of the xenophobic attacks. A member of a civil society group who has lived in the Bottlebrush informal settlement in Chatsworth for a number of years since 2007, when the informal settlement residents invaded the empty space between Bottlebrush Crescent and Crossmoor Drive, provided this information:

> The rent-a-shack problem is very important both in Bottlebrush and Ekhupoleni because the "landlords" who occupy shacks prefer foreigners as tenants because they can afford the rent on most occasions, unlike locals who cannot. Landlords in these settlements take full advantage of the shortage of housing and increase rentals while at the same time [they] use xenophobic arguments to put pressure on tenants to pay higher rentals.

## Safety in the Shelters

There was an outcry from different stakeholders regarding the level of safety and security for residents living in shelters for the displaced. This point of view was disputed a senior executive in eThekwini municipality agencies who was present at the shelters, who said this:

> I was there for days [going] in and out of the shelters and what I know about these temporary shelters is that all the people who stayed there were safe from outsiders and safety for them was crucial, because they had this attitude that they will be attacked and the police is in cahoots with looters and gangsters. They knew that their move [to] the shelters was for their own protection and safety, but they did not seem to appreciate it; they were agitated most of the time. They were paranoid about new attacks [even though] they saw that the place was safe, with armed guards.

Over the next two days and after the massive demonstration on April 18, 2015, the numbers in the temporary shelters skyrocketed – significant numbers of other victims of the attacks joined them, meaning that the Phoenix temporary shelter had about 3,000 displaced migrants, Chatsworth had about 1,900 migrants and the Isipingo shelter had 300.

## Movement of People to Other Provinces

The government officials were flexible in terms of the movement of people within the country, provided the resources permitted this. The officials opined that the majority of the shelter dwellers preferred to be integrated into their local communities, which was confirmed by a Provincial Joint Operational and Intelligence Structure (PROVJOINTS) official:

> After all, they had freedom of movement in the province and the country and there were plans to move displaced people to other provinces when circumstances arose and it was felt that there were other provinces that were safer than KZN. This was also discussed amongst the various national groups and their leaderships, because every group has a leader or leaders who were the people who had the authority to communicate with the South African departments and their leaders. The displaced were very aware that if they wished, they could be transferred to any other part of the country; they were free to be repatriated immediately (very many have left since then), or to apply for refugee status [in] any other country. This never happened to a large extent because most of the people in the shelters knew the circumstance of most countries in the world [which was] not very friendly to[wards] displaced people or refugees.

A senior official from the Department of Home Affairs, who was based at the Umgeni office, had this to say regarding the reintegration and repatriation of displaced immigrants:

The displaced immigrants have a legal right to relocate to other provinces [or to a different] country and [to] protection for [their] return in areas where their lives can be [at] high risk.

## Site Management

The government officials and agencies who were based at the shelters for the displaced were clear on the roles and responsibilities of the shelter managers. This was confirmed by a Disaster Management Centre (DMC) official who was directly involved at the shelters:

> The site manager is the person who is responsible for the whole situation in the shelter including the security, the safety of everyone, their health, sanitation, food, hygiene, etc. It is a very responsible position because all serious and decisive decisions are up to the manager, and this on many occasions puts the person [in] precarious positions because he/she is also responsible [for] discharging persons. This means that the site manager, despite the fact that he/she has to communicate, debate and follow or make [their] own decisions, [has the] responsibility to make a final decision for discharging. There have been a number of serious situations that create tensions amongst the displaced when they disagree with such decisions, because they believe that they are not safe to return to their homes or places of habitual residence when the site manager or [their] line managers in the public service believe they are safe.

The government officials were fully equipped with the legal knowledge on the rights of refugees in shelters, including illegal immigrants. The executive manager in eThekwini Municipality gave this opinion:

> The issue that has been debated for many hours is the situation of those displaced who are illegally in the country, and there are many of them. The international laws say that, depending on the circumstances of violence, there are no persons facing it who can be refused admission to the shelter. However, the illegals can only be accepted in[to] the shelter after they sign documents accepting conditions that lead to deportation or repatriation as soon as reasonably possible. The state authorities, led by the SAPS throughout the years, operating the safety issue in the shelters have a difficult task because they operate under strict instruction by the legal and political leadership of the country and the province ... [they] must ensure the safety of the displaced and the surrounding communities [and] work [on] the reintegration process with the community and help the site manager in all aspects of the smooth running of the shelter: security, maintenance, hygienic conditions, intelligence, incitement to conflict or violence, possession or use of firearms and other dangerous weapons, etc.

## Conflict in the Shelters

The shelter manager had this to say regarding conflict:

> All these responsibilities on many occasions put the SAPS and private security guards in conflict with both the displaced and the surrounding communities for a number of reasons. The site manager and the police also kept [an] eye on possible conflict [relating to] people following different religions because all religious activities took place in the shelters at specified times and places. NGOs, CBOs, individuals, journalists, etc. could only visit after securing appointments with the site manager.

## Management of the Shelters

The site managers stationed at the shelters for the displaced were appointed by government, with overall responsibility for the management and control of the shelter. Site managers were assisted by other government representatives who had different roles and responsibilities relating to the rendering of various services required at the shelters. Directives, instructions and determinations issued by the site manager or any other government representative were adhered to by the displaced immigrants. Concerns were raised with government representatives or site managers. If a resolution could not be reached, more senior representatives of government (not on-site) were contacted.

## Shelter Challenges and Action Plans

There was a multiplicity of overt and covert security breaches that were seen and experienced in the shelters for displaced immigrants. The site managers felt unsafe, having been exposed to victimization, insults and intimidation by a number of militariszd foreign nationals. Numerous immigrants in these shelters openly displayed firearms and other weapons such as machetes (broad, heavy knives that can also be used as weapons). Furthermore, the majority of the shelter immigrants displayed skilfull military histories and extensive training. Some of them displayed openly aggressive behavior that was against the rules, and in broad daylight. When confronted by the police, these residents would use their military training. The majority of them were influenced by alcohol which disrupted the shelter operations. One of the SAPS members who was stationed at one of the shelters said:

The Department of Home Affairs dealt with the immigrants' re-registration and verification of status, in addition to implementing immigration laws, engaging foreign embassies for voluntary repatriation and reissuing lost documents. The KwaZulu-Natal Department of Community Safety and Liaison developed a reintegration plan, supported operations at the shelters and supervised the time for implementing the reintegration plan. Meanwhile, SAPS was obliged to enforce the laws; its members also ensured safety and security at shelters, assessed and managed illegal firearms, conducted visible policing in high-risk areas and shelters, assisted with crowd management and public order policing, and supported the reintegration process.

The police and security personnel were constantly called to assist to enforce the shelter rules, which were welcomed because of the sometimes brutal behavior of armed immigrants. An eThekwini Municipality official dealing with finances of the shelters mentioned that

> there were 36 visible policing members employed at the shelters/ safety camps at Isipingo, Greenwood Park and Chatsworth in a permanent reporting and visibility capacity at these establishments, who had overtime pay of R74,563.20 per day and R1,714,953.60 for the period between the 8th [and] the 30th April 2015.

The SAPS coordinator confirmed it was evident that residents in the shelters from the DRC citizens were preparing themselves and associates to attack SAPS at some stage. This was especially relevant at the shelter in Isipingo, which for days was the most populous of the three in the region.

Another significant challenge in the shelters was the absence of control measures as both unregistered locals and foreign nationals were moving freely in and out of shelters, which posed a major risk. The irregular movement of people was caused by uncontrolled visits from foreign nationals' spouses, who were mostly South African. It was observed that proper access control was absent and foreign nationals were also vandalizing and removing the fencing that surrounded the shelters. The eThekwini Municipality requested the help of the service provider to fix and secure the vandalized fence, which was totally destroyed within a few days of installation. There was an attempt to remove criminal elements from the shelters, but without much success – SAPS was notified by immigrants' representatives that they were not allowed to forcefully remove unwanted people from the shelters.

## Interventions to Stabilize the Shelters

The eThekwini Municipality's DMC had to intervene and conducted a workshop on the rules of the displaced shelters. The workshop focused on the misconduct of residents in shelters, theft, prohibited business conducted and the legal implications. The workshop was convened in the eThekwini Municipality DMC and targeted the government officials who were stationed at shelters, shelter managers and representatives of the displaced immigrants. The workshops were planned by the UN group in conjunction with the South African authorities, mainly disaster management, in order to provide capacity to the disaster management staff, helping them to be alert to the realities on the ground. The workshops were to be facilitated by the National DMC. The workshops were funded by the UN and were expanded to other provinces such as Gauteng and the Eastern Cape before they were rolled out nationally. In this process South African authorities came to the decision that the Department of Home Affairs should be assisting to provide documentation on-site (National Joint Operational and Intelligence Structure (NATJOINTS) official).

## Resistance from Stakeholders

There was strong evidence of poor coordination between different stakeholders in the processes, functions, structures, aims and objectives of the shelters for the displaced. For instance, there was poor attendance by key stakeholders – including councilors – in community meetings, which were aimed at curbing the scourge of xenophobia. This was exacerbated by negative reporting by the media of the conditions in the shelters. This reality was followed by a number of communication interventions by the eThekwini Municipality after they saw the media articles regarding the status, services and conditions at the shelters, as provided by government departments. An executive member from the eThekwini Municipality shared the following regarding the conduct of the press and their reporting on the shelters. The municipal official indicated that

> they [media reporters] were called [to] the meeting ... because there were problems [in the camps] and they themselves had a role [to play] in these problems; but [they] never came to [the] meetings – only when they did wrong things, they felt they should defend their actions. These were the directives they had from the head office, they said.

There were temporary services including ablution facilities that were installed and serviced by professionals in all the shelters. At one of the shelters there were eight container toilets, eight showers and two mobile toilets (specifically for officials). In the Chatsworth shelter, there were 6 container toilets, 12 showers and 2 toilets for officials. At the shelter located in the north, there were four container toilets and nine mobile toilets, with two for officials. The waste removal activities at all shelters took place daily under the auspices of Durban Solid Waste, which did the collections. There were a total of three bins at Isipingo and eight bins at both Chatsworth and Phoenix. One water tap was connected at the Isipingo shelter, seven taps and a JoJo tank (with a water capacity of 1,000 liters) and four taps in Phoenix. Electricity was also temporarily connected in all the shelters within the eThekwini Municipality.

## The Legal Rules and Shelter Management

There were stringent rules that were put in place by the KwaZulu-Natal Provincial Government, which the displaced shelter dwellers needed to adhere to. The rules of the provincial government for the temporary shelters were informed by the UN Guidelines on Internal Displacement. These guiding principles protect and provide assistance to people who are forcefully displaced as well as when they are reintegrated into communities. The guidelines resonate and are consistent with international human rights law and international law that guide recommend and dictate the functions, structures and priorities faced in the shelters for the displaced. These recommendations guide other interested groups and persons as well as intergovernmental organizations and NGOs (Office for the Coordination of Humanitarian Affairs (OCHA), 2004). The UN representative in the shelter maintained that there are strict rules about the ways the displaced people are treated and have been treated in the shelters because there are always monitors of international organisations such as the UN that keep an eye on the operations and hold the government responsible [regarding] possible violations of the rights of the displaced.

There is a crisis which has been noticed by the humanitarian community regarding the 20+ million people worldwide who are internally displaced persons (IDPs). In 2001, the Secretary-General for Humanitarian Affairs asserted that the IDPs are local and national governments' responsibility, which must ensure that IDPs are protected in conflict and crisis situations. Conversely, in internal crises such as xenophobic attacks, humanitarian organizations (coordinated by the UN) have been accused of prejudice and labeled as biased in their operations, favoring a particular narrative and ideology that is anti-government. An official from the eThekwini Municipality DMC did mention that the UN refused to work with government officials on certain functions:

Their position regarding the role of civil society is also interesting because, besides those which offered real services like food clothing, cleaning material, etc., most of the others really refused to work with the state authorities that were planning all [the] activities to stabilise the situation; [to] repatriate, reintegrate them in[to] the communities etc. Our position in dealing with them [the UN officials] was that they and their moral support were highly appreciated, as were the vouchers to a number of displaced people, but the bottom line was that there was a need for them to work together with the country's leadership that aspired to do its best to solve a situation that was bad. Meanwhile, the immigrants and their leaders as well as the NGOs and the CBOs were requested to report violent acts which [were] directed [at] the foreign nationals and the planned attacks. The security agencies believed that the immigrants were in cahoots with some of these NGOs ... [which was] a hurdle in our efforts to solve the problems.

In 2004, the IDPs were observed by the Secretary-General for Humanitarian Affairs and Emergency Relief Coordinator to be mostly forgotten, neglected and marginalized in many emergency situations across the globe. He further accentuated the fact that IDPs are the most vulnerable members of the human family. The Guiding Principles on Internal Displacement, with a total of 26 principles, was developed by OCHA in 2001 under the umbrella of the UN. These principles have been central in a humane treatment as it is supporting full equality, legal status and without discrimination of the displaced in the shelters. In fact, such principles promote the respect of international law including human rights and humanitarian law, and prohibit apartheid policies and ethnic cleansing against displaced groups. One of the UN representatives in the shelter for the displaced in Durban provided the following view on shelters in Greece that has faced such problems for a number of years:

The Greek Government set up these shelters based on the dictates of international conventions and laws that Greece has signed that deal with displaced people, refugees and other victims of violence who are forced to leave their places of residence or countries. The majority of the displaced immigrants in Greece left their countries due to the myriad of conflicts including human rights violations by their governments, [which may be] natural or man-made disasters [and] organised and coordinated violence. International and South African laws dictate that displaced people deserve to have the same rights, freedom and equality [as] every other person, [and to] live without discrimination and the RSA authorities are legally obligated and responsible to provide humanitarian assistance.

The Guiding Principles on Internal Displacement (OCHA, 2004) indicate that the competent authorities are to provide for the displaced, including proper accommodation, protection from murder, liberty of movement and the right to be integrated into other parts of the country, leave the country and/or seek asylum. Moreover, family members of the displaced are encouraged to live as a family. The guiding principles also promote a standard of living that includes essential food and potable water. Within this internationally accepted legal framework, a senior member of the Provincial DMC provided the following bleak picture regarding the shelters:

There is a catch 22 situation, a very difficult and complicated situation with the humanitarian shelters for the displaced persons. [Regarding] these displaced camps, we start them as a humanitarian service according to our own humanity and values and the United Nations Charter which guides us on [how] to set up a shelter and what is needed on [a] daily basis. The major challenge we are facing is when we start to provide services in which [the refugees] … are not accustomed to and they end up getting [into] a comfort zone. When the government officials start to become pressurised from the locals, who are the instigators … they start to complain in many ways telling us that you are giving the services to the foreigners [at] our expense, using our resources … what about us? These things have happened in Durban and we attempted to manage such complaints as the vast majority of the foreigners [come] from the shack settlements where there are no basic needs including water, proper sanitation, electricity. It starts to cause another tension and there is no one way of dealing with this matter.

The Provincial Government in KwaZulu-Natal developed rules governing the shelters for the displaced after xenophobic attacks occur, as well as the criteria for accepting people into shelters. The criterion that was utilized to accommodate those who had been displaced was explicitly documented; foreign nationals who sought to reside in shelters did so voluntarily and after having agreed to the terms and conditions of the shelter rules. Consequently, the admission procedures for shelters were made clear. Victims of xenophobic attacks were advised to lay a complaint at the police station that was closest to where the attacks took place and to obtain a case number. The police station would then determine the need for the displaced to be accommodated in a shelter; those persons who were vulnerable would then be referred to a shelter.

The senior SAPS officer who was present in most meetings of the coordinating committee provided a bleak picture on the challenges brought about by the distribution of the UN vouchers. This is what the officer had to say:

> From the first day of the Isipingo attacks, NATJOINTS became the coordinator of the efforts and after the first deliberations, met with the UN team in the country in order to coordinate efforts and play a role in sorting out short-, medium- and long-term solutions with the assistance of all layers of government and the key institutions, NGOs, CBOs, churches, refugee groups and the like. Following the opening of the shelters, the negotiations between NATJOINTS, the UN and the rest of the RSA coordinating team members concentrated on the issue of the vouchers on the part of the UN, the recipients and the role of the South African participants. There were a number of disagreements on the proposed processes suggested by the UN and the distribution that was already happening. After negotiations regarding the share of the South Africans in respect of the vouchers, an agreement was reached followed by NATJOINTS indicat[ing] clearly that government would not be involved in moving people to other provinces.

The official from the eThekwini Municipality DMC who was based at a shelter for the displaced provided this background:

> The first thing the [Department of] Home Affairs and SAPS had to establish was that those in the shelters were really displaced after [the] attacks, because there were a few cases where people who had not faced attacks [but] found the opportunity for free food, shelter, clothing and occasional coffee and extra food vouchers. The steps to find a place and be accepted in[to] the shelters are known to foreigners because throughout the years there have been sporadic attacks on them by criminals, youths, etc. and they know they have to go to the police station first to [lay] a complaint and [to obtain] a case number. If there are shelters already operating, the person is accompanied by the police, and after there is [the] verification of particulars; there is the formal registration and signing of papers that set the conditions and rules that are followed by the inhabitants of the shelter. These processes are compulsory and must be followed by all who live in the shelter; it is the duty and responsibility of both parties to ensure that all legal requirements are followed, because this is the first step for the good governance of the situation.

An interview conducted with one of the eThekwini Municipality managers and member of the strategic committee dealing with xenophobic attacks provided an illustration of the relationship with other stakeholders and concerns regarding the shelter operations. The senior municipal member provided this information:

> In this there was a direct interaction between the UN, the displaced and the Department of Department of Community Safety and Liaison that identified the beneficiaries in the shelters. There was a fear, however, that this distribution would attract more displaced people in specific shelters although there was overcrowding. The system of vouchers allowed the displaced to buy groceries from selected supermarkets that were paid directly. This means that no direct payments were made to the displaced.

## The Politics of the UN Vouchers in the Shelters

There were a host of allegations leveled against the UN representatives in the shelters for the displaced. This was confirmed by a member of SAPS who was stationed at one of the shelters:

> The UN leadership was criticised openly by the South African state representatives [due to] the fact that, while they supplied vouchers to the displaced, they never did the same for South African citizens who rented property to foreigners, both in terms of residence and business premises, a number of which were destroyed in the attacks. In this the UN was requested to offer 20% of the available funds to South Africans, otherwise, if this did not happen, bigger problems could be caused. It never happened.

The voucher dispute became a significant issue in the shelters; the vouchers were regarded **by** government officials and other stakeholders as being biased. A senior municipal official gave the following information:

> To this request the UN indicated that they [were having] a challenge in identifying locals that qualify for the 20% fund[ing] available [from] the UN, as these locals are located within the community. However, the Department of Community Safety and Liaison leaders, together with the municipal organs, the Business Support Unit and other relevant departments, were prepared to assist in this effort ... the Department of Economic Development could also assist in identifying these people. In the voucher case, the vouchers were supplied for food in the camps/shelters ... [but the UN] refused [the] 20% [funding for] the South African people who provided their homes to foreigners [for them] to live and trade. In this the UN [members] were advised by NGOs dealing with legal issues, human rights, etc. [and] who got paid for the advice.

In the shelters, the displaced immigrants would be registered in the shelter register and would be required to sign an acceptance of the existing rules. A reference number for administration purposes would then be allocated. The shelter managers played a pivotal role in admitting the displaced people, and used their knowledge and discretion in the process of admission when all legal details needed to be satisfactory and complete. The shelter manager or their delegate provided accommodation to the displaced after seriously studying and considering safety, security, hygiene, health and any other relevant conditions in the establishment. There were also clear conditions relating to the processes of discharging displaced persons from shelters, making it possible for a person or group of persons to safely return to their homes or places of habitual residence. This situation occurred when a person or group of persons voluntarily elected to no longer stay in the shelter or when the government took the decision to close a shelter.

No one was refused admission to a shelter. The rules were clear: no one would be turned away except in the case of the violence ceasing and there no longer being a threat to refugees' safety. In addition, the shelter rules for the displaced admitted immigrants without legal documents, although they were accepted on condition that repatriation or deportation procedures would be initiated as soon as reasonably possible. The residents of shelters were frequently requested to adhere to the existing code of conduct as well as to the laws of South Africa, reasonable instructions issued by government representatives at shelters and lawful processes initiated by government (aimed at reintegration). This was confirmed by the shelter managers, who said:

> There was always a process of profiling those in the shelters, their paper documentation, whether they were legal or illegal, refugees, etc. This was helped by representatives/leaders from the different countries who acted as recognised leaders/spokesmen. The code of conduct also promoted privacy, dignity of all inhabitants and reasonable precautions for safeguarding their own property. The occupants in the shelter were also instructed to take care of their children and other members of their family within the means available to them and [to] live in the shelter with emphasis on cleanliness and hygiene. The immigrants in the shelter were also requested to notify the government representatives of any factor which may adversely affect the safety or well-being of any person in the shelter, refrain from engaging in any activity which may adversely affect the safety or well-being of any person ... and refrain from engaging in any activity which may incite conflict or violence.

The SAPS coordinator who was providing specialized liaison services with different stakeholders gave the following account:

> This is precisely what we did in these shelters when we were asked to provide these legal dictates and assistance to all people in the places. We were obligated to turn the shelters into well-run places

of peace in accordance with the country's laws the dictates of the United Nations and all other international organisations. It was our duties to look after all those in the shelters and this why we paid the most attention to children of all ages, mothers with small children, unaccompanied minors, expectant mothers, female heads of household, persons with disabilities and elderly persons, who were not many. These were difficult services because were not many and while we really did our best we never expected gratitude because these were our duties and responsibilities needed to be completed. All the time there was a great effort for us to ensure that we did our best according to the circumstances ... [we] never denied the request of displaced people to move to other settlements if they so wished. This was one of the problems we faced because, given the differences and diversity in the groups, if one of them dictated the conditions and the terms of other settlements, they communicated and made decisions for their families, connections and compatriots. Most of them had the most expensive cell phones and massive bundles of data so communications were perpetual.

In all the shelters for displaced immigrants, firearms and dangerous weapons were not allowed; such weapons were confiscated by law enforcement in cases where they were found. There were instances where dangerous weapons were confiscated and kept in a secure facility by government officials to return to the owner upon discharge from the shelter. In addition, businesses were not allowed in shelters or within a 1-km radius of the camp. Moreover, occupants of shelters could engage in religious activities with due consideration to persons of other beliefs, and government representatives were responsible for designating spaces within shelters to accommodate religious practices. There were a number of civil society groups in the shelters working collaboratively with different stakeholders. The community development practitioner who was continuously in contact and coordination with NGO and civil society organizations throughout the period shared an experience in relation to the basic necessities provided. This is what the NGO coordinator said:

> This is why, besides basic shelter and housing, there was always an effort to provide eatable food and clothing as well as fulfilling their basic needs such as sanitary pads for women; these initiatives and services were achieved because we had good contacts and connections with national and international humanitarian organisations and CBOs, religious organisations, churches offered their services. Those organisations and individuals had free passage to the shelters because of their efforts to provide humanitarian assistance.

Sports, recreation and cultural activities were allowed in shelters, with due consideration to other persons. Government representatives designated spaces within shelters to accommodate sports, recreation and cultural activities. The displaced immigrants and other persons or organizations in shelters had freedom to enter and leave shelters at their will. In some cases, the government representatives were requested to provide shelter managers or their delegate with an occupation reference number for administrative purposes. There were also cases where a certain visitor or group of visitors could be asked to leave the shelter, where their behavior or actions might negatively affect the safety, security, privacy, dignity or health of any occupant of the shelter.

## Incurred Expenses Because of the Xenophobic Attacks Against the Foreign Nationals

There were very few respondents who had reliable knowledge on the costs associated with the mobilization of funds, shelters, extra personnel and overtime. A coordinator who was responsible for finance and mobilization argued that:

> it is difficult to calculate the exact amounts spent For what? because the whole exercise from day one the whole situation was complicated due to the differences in the existing budgets and contingencies that made things extremely difficult to calculate. For example, the South African Police Services needed extra financial resources available in order to offer the necessary policing numbers, strategies and capacity to address and respond to prevailing threats that kept on becoming more expansive and complicated. These emanated from the attacks on foreigners within the greater eThekwini area as extra services and priorities were important while on the other hand, there was a serious impact on a normal day to day policing. This means, it was said, that there was a wide variety of added SAPS responsibilities and additional personnel had to be mobilised and deployed.

The coordinator for finance and mobilization attempted to provide a picture on the nature of costs that were not planned due to the xenophobic attacks. The coordinator revealed that:

> there were efforts to achieve economy, subsistence and success in basically utilising three ways to utilise existing personnel. The first was to utilise the Municipal Police in a wider space and capacity as their duties and responsibilities were different from those of SAPS. There was a direct and indirect deployment of personnel from outside Durban and the KwaZulu-Natal Province into the eThekwini area and the areas thought to be vulnerable because there was a history of the xenophobic attacks there. Then there was the idea that was supported because of the situation that there should be deployment of off-duty personnel against overtime to supplement duty capacities.

The Finance and Mobilization coordinator, responsible for finance and mobilization cost of all activities, as well as the personnel costs, said that:

> in the sphere of Public Order Policing, which has been described unfairly as a weak link of SAPS by a number of people, the mission was to cover areas of conflict and conflict areas that could emerge in the process of new possible attacks. There were a number of 135 members of the force transported from outside the municipality and their detached duty concentrated on crowd management. Their daily accommodation stood at R500per day, and the subsistence allowances that did not include meals was R110 per day, while for meals they were given R 180per day with a total cost per day at R 113 250. From the 8 to the 30 of April 2017 the total expenditure for this group was R2 603 550, which was considered substantial under the circumstances.

In terms of the costs for personnel in a variety of specializations and special activities, the coordinator who was responsible for finance and mobilization indicated that:

> there was also another group of 33 SAPS members specialising in public order policing in specified areas of potential impending conflict in emerging conflict areas, who were deployed as a support unit to existing similar groups with significant capacities on priority/high-risk days for crowd management. Their overtime pay was calculated at R68 349.60 per day and R410.097.60 for six days. There were 36 visible policing members employed at the shelters/safety camps at the Isipingo, Greenwood Park and Chatsworth shelters in a permanent reporting and visibility capacity at these establishments. They received overtime pay of R74563.20 per day and R1 714 953.60 for the period between the 8 to the 30 April 2015. There were 72 visible policing and Tactical Response Team SAPS members in the Inanda Umlazi, and Chatsworth Clusters busy with patrolling in risk areas and acting as first responders to incidents. This was from the 8 to the 30 of April and cost R149 126.40 per day and R3 429 907.20 overall. The total was R405 236.70 per day and R8 158 500.90 for 23 days.

The deployment and mobilization of personnel were achieved through two means, namely, deploying personnel from outside Durban and KwaZulu-Natal Province into the eThekwini area and deploying off-duty personnel against overtime to supplement on duty capacities. There were cost implications between April 8 and April 30, 2015 (23 days) of R8 158 500.90 for Public Order Policing accommodation and overtime, Visible Policing and Tactical Response Teams (TRT) (overtime) (Report to the Security Cluster Ministers 2015).

The government reported on the financial implications of the different departments that were directly involved during the 2015 xenophobic attacks as well as having a presence in the shelters. The following figures were given (Report to the Security Cluster, 2015):

> The budget of the Department of Home Affairs was basically for the accommodation for deployed specialist 35 officials (R400,000), the transport made available for repatriation to neighbouring states consisting of 10 (65-seat) buses that cost R800,000 and flights to Malawi and [the] Democratic Republic of Congo that cost R1,000,000. The overall cost was R2,200,000. The eThekwini Municipality faced a once-off cost for four ablution facilities with showers that cost R400,000 each (R1,600,000 altogether); fencing that cost R312,000, installation and use and maintenance of electricity and water that cost R6,000,000; six marquees (R150,000); human resources costing R1,000,000 and transport for the march (R309,000). The total cost was R9,371,000.

The following challenges were experienced in all the emergency shelter:

- Some donors pulled out (including the Red Cross), therefore volunteers from the Expanded Public Works Programme (EPWP) assisted with preparing meals.
- There was a request for donations so that the necessary ingredients could be purchased in order to prepare meals for the displaced refugees.
- There was a need to refill gas cylinders that were used to prepare meals.
- There were 1,165 Malawians from Mariannhill who wanted to be repatriated to Malawi. Due to limited space in the shelter, the local leadership was asked to assist with security and for SAPS to be on the look-out for any possible danger that might affect the displaced Malawians.
- There was a shortage of children's food on-site.
- The shelter manager raised the concern that the shelter would need a tent to accommodate the excessive number of people from Isipingo.
- Among the displaced people who arrived at the Chatsworth shelter, there were approximately 100 who were not on the database and had to be registered and accommodated.
- The shelters required more mattresses and blankets.
- Illegal electrical connections in some tents were reported which appeared to be likely since the kitchen lights had been tripping and consumption being utilized simultaneously.
- Daily reports needed to be conducted by various stakeholders in order to obtain a clear understanding of the type of services being rendered in the shelter and the number of people involved.
- The electricity department was needed to advise on possible solutions to avoid illegal connections and to prevent the electricity from tripping.
- Some of the donated perishable items in the fridge became spoiled and had to be discarded. This was due to the kitchen plugs being disconnected by the electricity department as the plug point had been illegally connected.

## Challenges at the Emergency Shelter

On 24 April, there was a commotion at the shelter between SAPS and foreign nationals (who were mainly from the DRC). The commotion was caused by the suggestion that immigrants might be moved from one marquee to another in order to save on hiring costs. One person was injured during the turmoil and the immigrants boycotted breakfast the next morning (25 April). The various services present at the shelter were requested to conduct their operations outside the fenced area for safety purposes.

### *Chatsworth Shelter*

The following problems were encountered in the Chatsworth shelter:

- There was no cold room to store meat and beverages that had been donated.
- A total of 40 foreign nationals were Muslim, who requested Halaal food.
- As people were repatriated, the tents were becoming empty; some residents moved into tents as couples and families. This required intervention from SAPS or Metro Police.
- Expired food discovered on-site made it necessary for environment health to intervene and do testing for all meals provided for residents.
- The speed fencing was easily removable, which required the service provider who installed it to return to the site for repairs.

It is clear that in comparison with shelters for refugees and displaced migrants throughout the world, the situation in the shelters in South Africa can be classified as "civilised," despite the challenges and problems experienced on a number of levels. If one considers similar shelters in Greece, for example, there is hardly a comparison, so great are the differences. This is because of the significant differences in numbers and the presence and support of international organizations looking after refugees and migrants throughout the world. The realities of the life of displaced immigrants and refugees in shelters in South Africa were negatively affected during the xenophobic attacks. The new realities they faced after days shaped by trauma and uncertainty left many of them questioning their existence and continued survival. The shelter residents had to decide on their and their family's future – should they be repatriated or would being reintegrated into their old neighborhood be better? What conditions awaited them: what struggles, relationships, situations and challenges? Their thoughts on their present situation must have been mixed, especially within the shelters' environment and having to contend with the existing conditions, the ways the UN vouchers would be spent and the struggles ahead, mixed with the past, present and future realities.

There is no doubt that the state departments and institutions performed their duties to the best of their abilities, while following the existing national and international legislation, conventions, rules and regulations. When difficulties occurred, the personnel at the shelters defended both the displaced and the locals' rights to compensation in response to the UN's position and actions. The government was significantly assisted by civil society and both interviewees and the existing primary evidence indicates that the thoughtful beginning of an otherwise very difficult and challenging process moved forward despite the difficulties faced, as identified above. The reality of the shelters was a tough situation for all concerned. This included the organs of state, which had to face serious financial and resource difficulties related to the social turbulence caused by the xenophobic attacks.

# References

Bompani, B. 2013. It is not a shelter, it is a church! Religious organisations, the public sphere and xenophobia in South Africa. In Hopskins, Kong, Olson (Eds.), *Religion and Place*, pp. 131–147, Dordrecht, Springer.

Desai, A. and Vahed, G. 2013. The May 2008 xenophobic violence in South Africa: antecedents and aftermath, *Alternation*, 7, 14.

Favish, J. 2009. The role of public universities: examining one university's response to xenophobia, *Gateways: International Journal of Community Research and Engagement*, 2, 160.

Nyar, A. 2011. "Business as usual": the response of the corporate sector to the May 2008 xenophobic violence, *Politikon*, *38*(1), 149–167.

Office for the Coordination of Humanitarian Affairs (OCHA). 2004. *Guiding Principles on Internal Displacement*, Location, United Nations Publications, OCHA/IDP/2004/01.

Papadimas, L. 2019. Migrants in Greece living in "horrible" conditions, says Europe rights watchdog, *Reuters*. Available at: https://www.reuters.com/article/us-europe-migrants-greece-asylum-idUSKBN1XA1O0 [Accessed 22 July 2020].

Peberdy, S. and Jara, M.K. 2011. Humanitarian and social mobilization in Cape Town: civil society and the May 2008 xenophobic violence, *Politikon*, *38*(1), 37–57.

Robins, S. 2009. Humanitarian aid beyond "bare survival": social movement responses to xenophobic violence in South Africa, *American Ethnologist*, *36*(4), 637–650.

United Nations International Children's Emergency Fund (UNICEF). 2020. *Emergencies: Latest Statistics and Graphics, Refugee and Migrant Children*. Available at: https://www.unicef.org/eca/emergencies/latest-statistics-and-graphics-refugee-and-migrant-children [Accessed 22 July 2020].

Womersley, G., Shroufi, A., Severy, N. and Van Cutsem, G. 2016. Post-traumatic stress responses among refugees following xenophobic attacks in Durban, South Africa, *Brief Contents*, *60*, p–p.

Chapter Nine

# Social Cohesion and Social Justice: Can They Solve Xenophobic Attacks?

International literature has described social cohesion as the key to a society that is dominated by a strong sense of community and good social relations despite the existence of racial, linguistic and class differences. A peaceful society is one that is blessed by cooperation and tolerance among all social groups. Such a population has rich social capital and focuses on mutual benefits. This description is the antithesis of the developments taking place in South Africa, even after more than 25 years of democracy. One of the most debated and researched elements that is at odds with justice and social cohesion in the country is xenophobia. *Localized Xenophobia in South Africa* has outlined and gone into a deep analysis and understanding of a wide array of hidden realities, causes and repercussions of xenophobia. This has caused deep hurt to the vast majority of South Africans, despite the fact that, since 1994, we have aspired to become a "real Rainbow Nation" of dreams steeped in honesty, African and human solidarity, tolerance, justice and human rights. These are the aims and objectives clearly identified in the country's Constitution, the Bill of Rights and many other laws, rules and regulations of the country. The state's efforts to build, plan and implement processes to improve social cohesion and social justice begin with the brief exploration of ubuntu and its meaning. We also need to dissect the political, ideological and social context associated with xenophobic attacks. Through peaceful community integration and reintegration of foreigners into neighborhoods affected by xenophobia, we can begin to mend the conflict in society. This is followed by a brief exploration of the meaning of social cohesion, its foundations and material and societal characteristics that make it a foundation of an integrated, peaceful and flourishing community.

A periodization of the policy measures and state initiatives undertaken include the influential National Development Plan, the Integrated Social Crime Prevention Strategy of the Department of Social Development, the National Strategy on Social Cohesion and Nation-Building released by the Department of Arts and Culture, and the Integrated Urban Development Framework from the Department of Cooperative Governance and Traditional Affairs. These policies highlight the importance that the government has placed on the planning

**Addressing Xenophobia in South Africa:**
**Drivers, Responses and Lessons from the Durban Untold Stories, 187–199**
Copyright © 2022 by Bethuel Sibongiseni Ngcamu and Evangelos Mantzaris
**Published under exclusive licence by Emerald Publishing Limited**
**doi:10.1108/978-1-80262-479-320211010**

and implementation of social cohesion, unfortunately without much success. We briefly discuss the seminal National Action Plan (NAP) to Combat Racism et al. (2019) and consider its shortcomings and gaps.

The final section in this chapter is dedicated to future plans that have been mentioned in this study as well as national and international research that has been done. This body of evidence can be described as the fundamental elements of the revitalization of social cohesion and social justice in an integrated and/or reintegrated community. This involves key state departments, Non-Governmental Organisations (NGOs), Community Based Organisations (CBOs), every single member of the country's civil service, the political community, the business community and leaders of immigrant/refugee groups. The possible amendments of existing legislation, the fundamental role of the local and national police and the future role of the Community Work Programmes (CWPs) would also be of importance.

*Anguish Longer than Sorrow*

If destroying all the maps known

would erase all the boundaries

from the face of this earth

I would say let us

make a bonfire

to reclaim and sing

the human person

Refugee is an ominous load

even for a child to carry

for some children

words like home

could not carry any possible meaning

but

displaced

border

refugee

must carry dimensions of brutality and terror

past the most hideous nightmare

anyone could experience or imagine

– Keorapetse Kgositsile

Africa's history has its roots in the deep meaning and practice of "Umuntu ngumuntu ngabantu," loosely translated as "to be human is based on the recognition of humanity of fellow human beings." The philosophy of ubuntu is founded on the principles of common humanity and brotherhood, dignity, tolerance, solidarity, inclusivity, mutual respect, human rights and tolerance toward outsiders.

Humanist philosophies based on such principles are vital in cementing solid human relationships in any society where people are respected. This is especially so in Africa, a continent with a complicated history and which faces multiple and complex challenges including economic, financial, political and social issues.

In one of his life's many poetic moments, in 1998, Thabo Mbeki, the country's deputy president, offered an emotional plea for African unity based on common historical foundations (Mbeki, 1998):

> I owe my being to the Khoi and the San whose desolate souls haunt the great expanses of the beautiful Cape. I am formed of the migrants who left Europe to find a new home on our native land. Whatever their actions, they remain, still, part of me. In my veins course the blood of the Malay slaves who came from the East. I am the grandchild of the warrior men and women that Hintsa and Sekhukhune led, the patriots that Cetshwayo and Mphephu took to battle, the soldiers Moshoeshoe and Ngunyane taught never to dishonour the cause of freedom. I am the grandchild who sees in the mind's eye and suffers the suffering of a simple peasant folk … I come of those who were transported from India and China. Being part of all these people, and in the knowledge that none dare contest that assertion, I shall claim that I am an African!

Mbeki's plea was a call to real unity, ubuntu and common struggles for developmental steps forward, based on brotherhood, common plans, peace, mutual tolerance and cooperation at all levels. Above all it appealed for peace among all Africans. When these wishes became a reality, he believed that the African Renaissance would have been achieved.

What has really occurred in South Africa over the last two decades is that violence has led to the death of fellow Africans, South Africans and others; tens if not hundreds of shops belonging to fellow Africans have been looted or destroyed, and thousands of people have been displaced, requiring them to live in makeshift camps after the attacks. These have been a devastating series of attacks that have devalued the historical achievements of the democratic government. Inevitably, both organized and unorganized "spontaneous" attacks on foreigners by small groups have had serious negative repercussions, not only among African governments but also internationally. This is especially so, given the dire economic, financial and social realities facing South Africa in the midst of the coronavirus pandemic (BBC, 2019; Bremmer, 2019).

The attacks and their aftermath inevitably caused serious breakdowns in relations between the South African Government, the Southern African Development

Community (SADC) and the African Union, and led to series of attacks on South African embassies and businesses (Made for Minds, 2019; Unah, 2019; Quartz Africa, 2019).

Inevitably there have been serious attempts by many academics and researchers of all ideological, political and educational backgrounds offering prepositions and proposals of "ideal solutions," plans and initiatives that would solve the problem. This has led to a wide variety of debates and multiple proposals. It is hoped that the present book has added to existing knowledge and understanding of the origins, dynamics, realities and "untouched, forgotten dimensions of xenophobia."

However, without well-thought-out initiatives leading the way forward in the effort to defeat xenophobia, our very painful history will remain a perpetual threat and the vision of a united Africa will remain a pipe dream. In order pursue an African Renaissance, we need a secure a foundation of human harmony and common respect for diversity. Initiatives to combat xenophobia must first and foremost be based on our historical roots and the heroic struggle to combat crimes against humanity, as epitomized by the leadership of people like Mandela, Sisulu, Tambo, Hani, Sobukwe and Biko. Their ideas, thoughts and actions were instrumental in defeating the apartheid regime and setting in motion the foundations of a new society. They all fought against the existing inequality, injustice and inhumanity, dreaming of a peaceful, democratic, non-sexist, non-racial and all-inclusive society built on the idea and practice of ubuntu. Such a society would have two foundations: social justice and social cohesion. This foundation was set, but sadly has not lasted.

Following the continuation of the xenophobic attacks, there was national and international outcry and the government took a number of practical steps to update and introduce policies and legislation. This led to the launching of the NAP to combat xenophobia and various actions that have brought the country into disrepute.

## Initial Actions and the Introduction of a NAP Against Xenophobia, Race and Discrimination

Social cohesion, a fundamental element of social justice, has been a popular theme in a wide variety of disciplines such as anthropology, psychology, political science, public administration, sociology, even law. It was the French sociologist Émile Durkheim whose epistemological realism created theories for phenomena as diverse as suicide, the division of labor, modernity, coherence, integrity, religious life, deviance, social stratification and social cohesion. The main difference between Durkheim and a number of his contemporary social scientists was that his created theories were based on serious empirical research led by his own creation and positivism that was based on Auguste Comte and structural functionalism. Durkheim's research resulted in him describing societies that viewed social cohesion as possessing the characteristics of collective moral support. These characteristics are instrumental in guiding individuals to share resources with their fellow human beings, thereby creating and maintaining a collective energy and life (the "ubuntu" of an earlier century and under different circumstances) (Fonseca et al., 2019, p. 233).

The subsequent analysis and definition essentially indicate that a community with social cohesion is peaceful and has a high degree of social capital characterized by good human and community relations, cooperation, coordination between groups, social organization and networks aiming at mutual benefits (Reitz et al., 2009).

Social cohesion has been the focus of an abundance of theoretical and empirical work in numerous human sciences disciplines. Nonetheless, the complexities of the post-industrial world – even before the coronavirus pandemic – have resulted in contests, unresolved controversies and endless contradictions, as Friedkin (2004, p. 410) has shown. Even social cohesion has been transformed into a contested terrain in the humanities.

Despite this fact, the most serious theorists and researchers have described the key characteristics of social cohesion in communities to be solidarity, trust, connectivity, common participation during social occasions and initiatives that encourage mutual help among diverse social groups (Larsen, 2013). In fact, the Organisation for Economic Co-operation and Development (OECD) describes the "appropriate" definition of a society founded on social cohesion as one that fights social marginalization and exclusion across the board through the creation of a deep sense of belonging, elevating trust and providing its members with opportunities to achieve upward social mobility because of existing opportunities (OECD, 2011).

For many years, the South African Government's policy documents, including the National Development Plan (National Planning Commission, 2012), have described social cohesion as the foundation of peace and social justice. These are very important elements in the efforts to combat violence and crime that have been evident throughout the country for many years. In fact, the National Development Plan describes the lack of safety in communities as a repercussion of the absence of social cohesion (National Planning Commission, 2012, p. 357).

A year before the official publication of the National Development Plan, the Integrated Social Crime Prevention Strategy (Department of Social Development, 2011) indicated that the building, strengthening, maintaining and prioritizing of social cohesion was a guarantee of peace and stability for families and society at large.

The National Strategy on Social Cohesion and Nation-Building, released in 2012 by the Department of Arts and Culture, defines social cohesion as the level of social integration, solidarity and inclusion in a community and society, and the existence and spreading of mutual solidarity among all communities and people. The strategy promoted the building of volunteerism and social capital as crucial elements of the processes strengthening social cohesion. It was a comprehensive and detailed strategy but without the provision of a number of empirically based, tested suggestions and recommendations on the way forward. This would lead to the effective planning and implementation of tactics resulting in the building of social cohesion and community social integration (Department of Arts and Culture, 2012, pp. 31–32).

The Integrated Urban Development Framework, released in 2016, espoused investments in people and the country's economy coordinated by the state, which would ultimately lead to good governance, social cohesion and inclusive growth (Department of Cooperative Governance and Traditional Affairs, 2016, pp. 27–28).

The question arises of whether the term and especially the planning and implementation of social cohesion could be used throughout the years as the practical activation of ubuntu, as envisaged in the official documents. This means that a person's or a community's behavior is rooted in the principle that humanity is founded on a person's social and individual behavior and that social/community interactions are characterized by tolerance, unity in diversity and considerate behavior at all levels.

In many ways, and in relation to xenophobia, this has not been the case, a fact acknowledged directly and indirectly by government. After a long consultative process, the state introduced a NAP aimed at combating racism, discrimination and xenophobia. It was an initiative that sought to address the perpetual abuses of fundamental human rights that have arisen from xenophobic and gender-based discrimination and violence.

The NAP to Combat Racism, Racial Discrimination, Xenophobia and Related Intolerance (RSA, 2019) was described by the Presidency as the outcome of the collective conviction of South Africans who are united and possess the means to eradicate these ills completely. The document was based on a comprehensive process of consultation that included government, civil society and all Chapter 9 institutions. It is founded on inclusion and participation, the fundamentals of universality, accountability, indivisibility and the interdependence of human rights, progressive realization, non-discrimination and equality.

The plan is based on the belief that the successful implementation of its aims and objectives relies on the commitment of society as a whole in a collective effort to promote and protect human rights. This can be achieved through efforts to raise awareness of anti-discrimination, anti-racism and equality, and a close collaboration between relevant government departments and Chapter 9 entities in order to implement the planned educational priorities.

Research on these key issues was planned as a key intervention, which is instrumental in psychological and social support for the victims of xenophobia and the prosecution of offenders. One of the most interesting initiatives was identifying existing legislation that requires amendment or adaptation, which would aim at improving victims' protection. This in turn would lead to the strengthening of a more equitable society at large.

The NAP was described as a clarion call for all South Africans to commit to a high moral compass and behavior for growth and renewal, which is needed in all spheres of society: in the home, in the classroom, in restaurants, at stadiums, in workplaces and in supermarket queues, among others.

NAP was a detailed, well-structured and researched document that was supplemented by the NAP and set for the period 2019/2020 to 2023/2024, to be finalized post the 2019 elections.

Undertaking research, holding debates and launching the plan was mostly correct in its intentions, but there is evidence that the realities "on the ground" pinpoint a number of gaps, beginning with the documents' continuous emphasis on historical truths (i.e., the emphasis on apartheid's legacy and the thin emphasis on concrete actions, to be found in 10 out of the 67 pages of the document). A deeper analysis of a subject of such importance should concentrate on social issues such as the recent increasing levels of social and economic inequality, their causes and repercussions, the measurements of accountability in all spheres of government, and existing oversight mechanisms on public education, the police, budgets and the existing realities and challenges at all state levels. The conditions at rural schools and clinics in the country are well known. Blaming the continuation of such harsh realities on the apartheid past no longer stands as being believable.

On the issue of xenophobia, the question still remains whether this reality and its social, economic and political repercussions have been tackled with the seriousness and commitment that it deserves. It is true that it is mentioned, albeit peripherally, with the document pinpointing a number of realities of life researched and outlined. Serious research needs to be conducted on issues such as economic competition, xenophobic attacks and the existing levels of inequality. However, there have been serious aspects that have been researched, such as criminality, youth unemployment, local politics and politicians (Misago, 2017) that have not tackled these important and ground-breaking aspects.

## What is to Be Done?

Having outlined the basic political, policy and conceptual significance of social cohesion as a fundamental reality that can help to combat xenophobia, a number of steps are outlined that we believe can play a significant role for future peace in communities throughout South Africa. The planning and implementation of initiatives can be instrumental in the process of achieving social cohesion.

The continuous and relentless attacks on immigrants and refugees call for the implementation of both holistic and immediate steps that will guarantee societal peace in the most challenging era in the history of South Africa's democracy. The devastation of the virus pandemic and its consequences are of great importance. However, if a careful examination, analysis and dissection of the recent xenophobic attacks and deaths is taken seriously, it becomes a historical necessity to proactively (and no longer reactively) implement social cohesion interventions and existing integration policies. The responsibilities of the Department of Home Affairs, the Department of Cooperative Governance and Traditional Affairs, the police and all other relevant departments in the South African Government have increased, and all state entities should take advantage of the existing policies that outline key initiatives to be undertaken. These aim to build the way forward on the path of social cohesion and social justice that can and should last. A careful and committed reading and study of the White Paper on International Migration (Department of Home Affairs, 2017) will open up opportunities for all to collectively understand the dynamics, circumstances and historical lessons leading to the development of a well-researched and comprehensive integration policy that is based on South African and international best practice and high standards. There cannot be success in such efforts without a combined action and collaboration among different state departments as outlined in the Department of

Home Affairs' Strategic Plan 2015–2020 (Department of Home Affairs, 2015). It appeared before strategies dealing with integration, repatriation and the resettlement of refugees and immigrants advocated appropriate partnerships with state departments. The strategies to be undertaken through a collaborative partnership include the Department of Cooperative Governance and Traditional Affairs, the Department of Arts and Culture and the Department of Justice and Constitutional Development in a collective effort to plan, create, implement and develop short training interventions for refugees and all foreigners at large. Such a programme would deal with key aspects and realities of South African history, culture, customs and traditions, social etiquette, civil rights and laws and responsibilities as outlined in the Green Paper on International Migration. The most successful plan for such an initiative can be achieved through the direct collaboration between the elected leadership of communities. This would include the municipal councilors, ward committees, recognized and accepted community leaders, as well as the leadership of refugee and immigrant groups, NGOs, CBOs, mediators and service providers who are acceptable from both sides. The contribution of civil society organizations has played a key role throughout the periods of xenophobia and there is a belief that they can be trusted by all parties, at least in most cases, hence their importance in such a process to build and develop common trust and belief in the process of building social cohesion and the integration of immigrants. This is a process based on inclusion and on planning and implementing a genuine multi-stakeholder approach that includes communities, society, foreigners, refugees and government. In fact, it is up to the leaders of such initiatives to identify, after thorough negotiations, the physical locations where such social cohesion-building campaigns, educational programs and other useful initiatives could be conducted for both local communities as well as immigrants and refugees.

It is important for all sections and every single member of the South African public services to be educated on the key fundamentals of the country's democratic and humanistic beliefs which are clear that all human beings in the country, irrespective of official documentation and regardless of their immigration status, are protected by the Bill of Rights, as found in Chapter 2 of the country's Constitution. These rights are the sole foundation of a democratic, just and free society and apply to every person in the Republic irrespective of their legal status (with the exception of the right to vote). In the seminal judgment of the Supreme Court of Appeal Case *Minister of Home Affairs and Others* v. *Watchenuka and Another* it was stated clearly that human dignity has no nationality because it is inherent in citizens and non-citizens. This is because of a very simple reason: both are human beings. The judgment stated that a person who happens to be in South Africa must be respected and has the protection of section 10 of the country's Bill of Rights (South African Court of Appeals, 2004).

Relevant authorities, including the political leadership of the ruling party, need to control the acts of local political leaders and their relationships with community groups who, as research has shown, need to be alert to existing political vacuums in their communities that ultimately lead to attacks on foreigners. Cases where either local business-people, entrepreneurs or groups masquerading as "concerned residents," "local business groups" and the like need attention as they may lead to xenophobic attacks. Local police need to monitor and control the movements and actions of community leaders and business-people who are known to harbor anti-foreigner sentiments.

Statements such as those of the deputy police minister in 2017 need to be rigorously and decisively opposed. He said:

> The question of [the] dominance of foreign nationals in illegal trading and also businesses that are here in Hillbrow is an economic sabotage that is taking place against our people. We are supposed to be those who are running those particular businesses. (Lekabe, 2017)

A thorough investigation needs to be conducted in selected branches of the Department of Home Affairs, mainly front-line officials and their behavior toward refugees, drug dealers, syndicates and entrepreneurs. This is regarded as an urgent necessity.

The Refugees Amendment Act, 2017 (Act 11 of 2017) needs to be amended in order to safeguard South Africa's pioneering position in the African Union and the SADC as well as to be instrumental in the effort to restrict new arrivals of large numbers of undocumented refugees. These restrictions lead to exclusion, meaning that in practice it is the very antithesis of social cohesion.

The passing of the Hate Crimes Bill means that a path has opened for the prosecution of crimes committed against South African citizens and foreigners. This reality is instrumental in allowing serious hate crimes to be investigated and prosecuted. The legislation needs to be the foundation of the future awareness of South African Police (SAPS) as they respond to cases involving xenophobic hate crimes.

The possibility of local community leadership and the equivalent of foreigners' groups coming together and working alongside one another can become a reality that needs to be emphasized and pursued at all levels. When this is achieved, common problems can be debated and their solutions found in a collective manner. Throughout South Africa there has been strong evidence that despite a wide array of differences between leaders and community members, communities have created alliances and "united fronts." Through collective planning and mobilization initiatives, there can be successes in solving problems such as crime and poor service delivery. A number of peaceful delivery protests that have been organized by local community leaders and/or politically aligned leaders have nonetheless been instrumental in fueling xenophobic attacks. The possibility or reality of community leadership, especially the activation of ward committees, municipal councilors is crucial to ensure success and create an alliance and understanding with the leaders of immigrants' groups. In most cases that have been researched, community leaders on both sides have been the key elements in mobilizing a community's collective actions because of their alliance and domination over local organizations in existence, including street committees (Freedom House, 2017, p. 25).

In many ways, community leadership alliances (including political, civil, councilors ward committees, religious organizations and trade unions) having common agreements and plans are almost a guarantee in dealing with common challenges including the possibility of xenophobic attacks. Such a grouping and alliance can lead to opportunities to improve social cohesion. Differences in plans and actions can be solved through connectivity and continuity as community members express the common platform of unity through solving problems and seeking solutions. Such social alliances may provide the only path to social cohesion in communities, which would include the social inclusion of immigrants and refugees. A collective approach such as this would create the material basis of unity, self-respect, tolerance, peaceful coexistence, and the defense and protection of each and every community member, resulting in a cohesive and strong community environment.

There is a strong view among many serious researchers and students of xenophobic violence over the years that one of the key requirements for the better utilization of police officers would be understanding – in terms of interactions with foreigners. Such a view is correct for a number of reasons. First, because police stations are the initial point of contact for victims in every criminal case, but also because they are the key agents in preventing criminal acts against people. Second, the training of police personnel would be beneficial as it would give them an understanding of the dynamics and circumstances under which xenophobic and other community-based attacks and violence take place. This could be instrumental in building a solid consciousness related to the relationship between thorough investigation and the protection of victims of intolerance and prejudice, which could lead to the culprits' prosecution. Such initiatives undertaken to uplift the skills and consciousness of law enforcement officials need to be rooted in specific and crystal clear guidelines that outline the most appropriate, law-based and effective way to respond to xenophobic attacks and all crimes motivated by bias. If this necessary training were to take place, the possibility for direct and honest interaction between police and victims can lead to deep and continuous social cohesion.

The CWP is a Department of Cooperative Governance and Traditional Affairs initiative (Department of Cooperative Governance and Traditional Affairs, 2016) that provides participants (mainly unemployed people) with a stipend for two days of work per week. The initiative was established primarily to provide unemployed people with an employment safety net. The latest statistics available in 2017 showed that there were 216 CWP sites in 203 municipalities, costing R1.7 billion (Government of South Africa, 2017). Empirical research has shown that the CWP, which has been operating throughout the country for many years, has had both successes and failures. The successes have revealed that the role of the programme in the community in strengthening the fight against crime and violence can lead to the elevation of social cohesion (Bruce, 2015). The programme includes youth work utilizing sports and mentorship activities, developing early childhood programs, conducting community patrols and joining forces with the police to assist victims of domestic violence. In serious empirical research, it has been shown that such community initiatives could become important in facilitating a spirit of unity, togetherness and solidarity among community members. This is due to the fact that its functions and activities are the basic ingredients needed to strengthen community bonds. These bonds are founded on the common roots and experiences of care, assistance and a conscious understanding of community solidarity and support for the less privileged (Langa et al., 2016). Despite the recent expose of corruption on the part of public servants in the Department of Cooperative Governance and Traditional Affairs and the challenges ahead (Comrie, 2020), recent history has shown that such community initiatives, when led by socially conscious NGOs, can be useful in cementing all aspects of social cohesion, something that includes immigrants and refugees.

On Sunday August 23, 2020, on the first page of the *Sunday Independent* there appeared an article entitled *SA UNDER FOREIGN CONTROL*, subtitled *Bleak future on job front for many after lockdown as companies turn to exploiting foreign migrants* (Ngoebe and Wa Africa, 2020). Such despicable headlines fuel negative sentiments and feelings on social media of people like Twitter phantom *@ uLerato_pillay*, leading the well supported *#PutSouthAfricaFirst* campaign.

*Localized Xenophobia in South African* may be the first among equals that deals with the role of journalists, newspapers and social media in supporting and spreading xenophobia. This situation will continue because it is evidently orchestrated with serious interests behind it: those that are ideological, political, economic and social. They will continue unless they are stopped immediately and forever.

This becomes more evident by the day as there have been recent attacks against foreigners over the past years, some of which pass by without serious publicity in the mainstream media, with the exception of the attacks on foreign truck drivers by locals who demanded 100% employment in the sector.

One of the key issues that needs more debate and action is the real, or sometimes perceived, knowledge of the general public as well as that of the victims and their families as it related to the punishment of those arrested for attacking foreigners, looting their shops and causing injuries or even death. The questions only appear to come from the victims or their families regarding the fate of those who were arrested. They also need to be given an answer on compensation for damage, serious injury, hospitalization or the loss of a loved one, but no answers appear to be forthcoming or action taken against those found guilty. Nothing or very little has been done in terms of the serious investigation of crimes and perpetrators, with few exceptions. Politicians' xenophobic outbursts pave the way to increasing hatred, discrimination and violence.

The Refugees Amendment Act of 2017 contains the clause declaring that asylum seekers remain in "processing centres." It is argued that this arrangement would remove their need to work or study. During the period of regulations and restrictions related to the coronavirus pandemic, asylum seekers and refugees were excluded from having access to relief packages that could help them, yet they were not allowed to engage actively in the country's economy after the lockdown. The question then remains: How do the communities in which these vulnerable groups reside feel about such treatment? Do state actions mean directly or indirectly that these groups are foreign to the country? And in the long-term, aren't such acts and messages a direct or indirect contribution to the rise of xenophobic attacks? Has the dream and aspiration for a united Africa been thrown into the dustbin of history?

The inevitability of preventing future ongoing xenophobic attacks is non-negotiable, but the mobilization of those who really care, love and respect South Africa and the vast majority of her people must have as their ultimate objective the realization of social cohesion and social justice. This should be underpinned by a genuine character and behavioral, radical, humanistic, ubuntu-rooted change toward refugees and asylum seekers who see South Africa as their last hope for a better life and future.

# References

BBC. 2019. *South Africa's Xenophobic Attacks: Why Migrants Won't Be Deterred*, September 26. Available at: https://www.bbc.com/news/uk-wales-49797720 [Accessed 15 August 2020].

Bremmer, I. 2019. What the xenophobic violence gripping South Africa means for future of country, *Time*, September. Available at: https://time.com/5671003/what-the-xeno-phobic-violence-gripping-south-africa-means-for-future-of-country/

Bruce, D. 2015. Preventing crime through work and wages: the impact of the Community Work Programme, *South African Crime Quarterly*, *52*, 25–37.

Comrie. 2020. Who's eating Cogta's R13bn Community Work Programme? *Amabhungane*, January 19. Available at: https://amabhungane.org/stories/whos-eating-cogtas-r13bn-community-works-programme/ [Accessed 15 August 2020].

Department of Arts and Culture. 2012. *Creating a Caring and Proud Society: A National Strategy for Developing an Inclusive and a Cohesive South African Society.* Available at: http://www.dac.gov.za/sites/default/files/NATIONAL-STRATEGY-SOCIAL-COHESION-2012.pdf [Accessed 15 August 2020].

Department of Cooperative Governance and Traditional Affairs. 2016. *Integrated Urban Development Strategy*, Pretoria, Department of Cooperative Governance and Traditional Affairs.

Department of Home Affairs. 2015. *Strategic Plan 2015–2020.* Available at: http://www.dha.gov.za/files/Strategic_Plan_2015-2020.pdf [Accessed 28 August 2020].

Department of Home Affairs. 2017. *White Paper on International Migration.* Available at: http://www.dha.gov.za/WhitePaperonInternationalMigration-20170602.pdf [Accessed 15 August 2020].

Department of Social Development. 2011. *Integrated Social Crime Prevention Strategy*, Pretoria, Department of Social Development.

Fonseca, X., Lukosh, S. and Brazier, F. 2019. Social cohesion revisited: a new definition and how to characterize it, *Innovation: The European Journal of Social Science Research*, *32*(2), 231–253.

Freedom House. 2017. *Social Cohesion: South Africa Community Social Cohesion: A Synthesis Report.*

Friedkin, N.E. 2004. Social cohesion, *Annual Review of Sociology*, *30*, 409–425. doi:10.2307/29737700

Government of South Africa. 2017. *Community Work Programme 2017.* Available at: www.gov.za/speeches/com [Accessed 15 August 2020].

Langa, M., Masuku, T., Bruce, D. and Van der Merwe, H. 2016. Facilitating or hindering social cohesion? The impact of the Community Work Programme in selected South African townships, *SA Crime Quarterly*, *55*, p–p.

Larsen, C.A. 2013. *The Rise and Fall of Social Cohesion: The Construction and De-construction of Social Trust in the US, UK, Sweden and Denmark*, Oxford, Oxford University Press.

Lekabe, T. 2017. Mbalula's deputy accuses foreign nationals in Hillbrow of economic sabotage, *The Citizen*, July 14. Available at: https://citizen.co.za/news/south-africa/1574446/ mbalulas-deputyaccuses-foreign-nationals-of-economic-sabotage-spouts-alternative-facts/ [Accessed 16 July 2020].

Made for Minds. 2019. *Xenophobia in South Africa Strains International Relations.* Available at: https://www.dw.com/en/xenophobia-in-south-africa-strains-international-relations/a-50275526 [Accessed 20 May 2020].

Mbeki, T. 1998. The African Renaissance, South Africa and the world. Speech delivered at the United Nations University, April 9. Available at: http://archive.unu.edu/unu-press/mbeki.html [Accessed 6 May 2019].

Misago, J.P. 2017. Politics by other means? The political economy of xenophobic violence in post-apartheid South Africa, *The Black Scholar*, *47*(2), 40–53. doi:10.1080/0006 4246.2017.1295352

National Planning Commission. 2012. *National Development Plan 2030. Our Future – Make It Work*, Pretoria, The Presidency.

Ngoebe, B. and Wa Africa, M. 2020. South Africa under foreign control, *Independent on Sunday*, August 20.

Organisation for Economic Co-operation and Development (OECD). 2011. *Perspectives on Global Development 2012: Social Cohesion in a Shifting World*, Paris, OECD Publishing.

Quartz Africa. 2019. *Nigerians Aren't Targeted More Than Other Africans in South Africa's Xenophobic Attacks but the Damage Is Done*, September 11. Available at: https://qz.com/africa/1708146/nigerians-not-hit-more-than-other-africans-in-xenophobic-attacks [Accessed 2 March 2020].

Republic of South Africa, 2019. *The National Action Plan to Combat Racism, Racial Discrimination, Xenophobia and Related Intolerance.* Available at: https://www.gov.za/sites/default/ files/gcis_document/201903/ national-action-plan.pdf [Accessed 09 August 2021].

Reitz, J.G., Breton, R., Dion, K.K. and Dion, K.L., 2009. Multiculturalism and social cohesion: Potentials and challenges of diversity. Springer Science & Business Media.

RSA. 2019. *The National Action Plan to Combat Racism, Racial Discrimination, Xenophobia and Related Intolerance.* Available at: https://www.gov.za/sites/default/files/gcis_document/201903/national-action-plan.pdf

South African Court of Appeals. 2004. *Minister of Home Affairs and Others* v *Watchenuka and Another* 2004 (4) SA 326 (SCA). Available at: http://www.refugeerights.uct.ac.za/usr/refugee/Case_Law_Reader/Minister_of_Home_Affairs_v_Watchenuka.pdf [Accessed 2 March 2021].

Unah, L. 2019. Xenophobic attacks in South Africa spur reprisals across Africa, *TR World*, September 11. Available at: https://www.trtworld.com/magazine/xenophobic-attacks-in-south-africa-spur-reprisals-across-africa-2968875 [Accessed 11 November 2020].